TH[illegible] WAY F[illegible]ZZA

ON FOOT FROM ROME TO ENGLAND

Brian Mooney

THOROGOOD

Thorogood Publishing Ltd
10-12 Rivington Street, London EC2A 3DU
Telephone: 020 7749 4748 • Fax: 020 7729 6110
Email: info@thorogoodpublishing.co.uk
Web: www.thorogoodpublishing.co.uk

A CIP catalogue record for this book is available from the British Library.

ISBN: 1 85418 816 X • 978 1854188168

Book designed and typeset in the UK by Driftdesign

Printed in the UK by Marston Digital

For Gail, Ros and Jon – who each played their part

Contents

map 1: Rome – Lausanne 7

map 2: Lausanne – Canterbury and Coggeshall 8

FOREWORD
Future Perfect 9

ONE
Quo Vadis? 11

TWO
Tuscan Idyll 31

THREE
Plain Sailing 53

FOUR
Aiming High 75

FIVE
Alpine Diversion 91

SIX
Swiss Roll 107

SEVEN
French Nots 131

EIGHT
Water Course 151

NINE
Spaced Out 177

TEN
Home Run 203

Appendix 221

Map 1:
FROM ROME TO LAUSANNE
1079 Km. on foot, 35 stages.
JURA
L. de Neuchâtel
VAUD
L. de Joux
LAUSANNE
SWITZERLAND
AUSTRIA
Lac Léman
FERRY
GENEVA
R. RHÔNE
Villeneuve
Eiger
Martigny
VALAIS
Mont Blanc
RHÔNE
Sion
Visp
FRANCE
COL du THÉODULE
R.B.T.
ZERMATT
Matterhorn
COL du GRAND ST BERNARD
Monte Rosa
Breuil-Cervinia
AOSTA
Châtillon
R. DORA BALTEA
Hône
IVREA
ITALY
L. Maggiore
L. di Como
TICINO
Caviglia
Vercelli
L. di Garda
Mortara
PAVIA
VENICE
PO
Belgioioso
FERRY
Piacenza
LIGURIA
Adriatic Sea
GENOA
Fidenza
MONACO
Bagni San Andrea
Apennines
R. AULLA
Berceto
LA SPEZIA
EMILIA
Pontremoli
Ligurian Sea
Ponzano Superiore
ROMAGNA
Marina di Pietrasanta
LUCCA
PISA
Fucecchio
FLORENCE
MEDITERRANEAN SEA
R. ARNO
H.B.
Gambassi Terme
San Gimignano
Colle di Val d'Elsa
TOSCANA
SIENA
G.V.T.
San Fabiano
VIA CASSIA
R. ORCIA
L. di Elba
R. OMBRONE
Gallina
Monte Amiata
Radicofani
Proceno
CORSICA
Tyrrhenian Sea
L. di Bolsena
Bolsena
LAZIO
VITERBO
L. di Vico
Capranica
L. di Bracciano
Campagnano di Roma
VEIO
Isola Farnese
TEVERE
R.
ROME
SARDINIA
N
DRAWN TO NO RELIABLE SCALE! J.H. 2013.

1038 km. on foot, 28 stages.
Map 2:
FROM LAUSANNE TO CANTERBURY and COGGESHALL
COGGESHALL
COLCHESTER
LONDON
Gravesend
FERRY
Basildon
R. BLACKWATER
ROCHESTER
R. THAMES
ESSEX
R. MED.
WAY
NORTH SEA
ENGLAND
Charing
J.H.
CANTERBURY
KENT
Dover
FERRY
CALAIS
THE ENGLISH CHANNEL
- LA MANCHE -
Desyres
PAS DE CALAIS
Montreuil-sur-Mer
VIA
FLANDRE
BELGIUM
ABBEVILLE
R.
LE HAVRE
AMIENS
SOMME
ROUEN
Poix-en-Picardie
CAEN
R101
PICARDIE
BEAUVAIS
R. OISE
Auvers-sur-Oise
PARIS
ORLY
ÎLE DE FRANCE
Draveil
R. MARNE
SEINE ET MARNE
R.
La Mée-sur-Seine
Forest of Fontainebleau
LOING
SEINE
FRANCIGENA
Montereau-fault-Yonne
R. YONNE
SENS
R.
Migennes
CANAL DE BOURGOGNE
Flogny-la-Chapelle
CHABLIS
Chassignelles
BOURGOGNE
Pouillenay
R.
DIJON
SALON
Pouilly-en-Auxois
Brazey-en-Plaine
R. DOUBS
Chaussin
FRANCHE-COMTÉ
ARBOIS
Andelot-en-Montagne
JURA
Mouthe
VAUD
L. de Joux
L'Isle
L. de Neuchâtel
CÉLIGNY
T.N.
LAUSANNE
FERNEY-VOLTAIRE
Lac Léman
SWITZERLAND
R. RHÔNE
GENEVA
Eiger
FRANCE
N
DRAWN TO NO RELIABLE SCALE by J.H., June 2013

FOREWORD
FUTURE PERFECT

I SAT BY THE TIDAL BASIN AT BEELEIGH FALLS with my yellow rucksack on the grass beside me, and my feet resting on the balance beam of the familiar lock gate through which the Chelmer Navigation meets the River Blackwater. With only ten miles to go, and by my reckoning 1,313 miles behind me, I was finishing my last ration of nuts and chocolate. I savoured the moment: all those long, parched days; the hill climbs; the country roads; waymarked tracks and canal towpaths; all the diverse human habitations from hamlets to metropolis; the churches and cathedrals; all the people I had encountered – I had enjoyed it all so much that I would have done it again. The adventure (about which I had been so doubtful, at least at the start) had worked, but like all good things was coming to an end. Getting up for the last time, I shouldered my bag to follow well-rehearsed paths by the old railway cutting and the banks of the River Blackwater to Braxted and Kelvedon.

Three hours later, as I came to the southern gateway of Coggeshall by the white clapboard cottage at Pointwell Mill, I spotted someone ahead playing hide-and-seek behind one of the big willows, a figure in red and white that I pretended not to see, and I walked on until Gail sprang out to meet me. Reunited, we continued along the flood plain, across the old Abbey fields and up the recreation ground towards the churchyard trees and the tower of St Peter ad Vincula, the starting point of my walk to Rome two years ago. Now I was home, having – like any pilgrim from this part of Essex over many centuries – covered the ground on foot in both directions. It was time to light a candle; we went in.

Back outside, we walked down the path to the lych gate, and there a little way along Church Street was the house, unseen by me for ten summer weeks; now that autumn was approaching, its shape was subtly changed by Gail's new studio and the completion of a west wing. Invisible, behind the old sashes, was Gail's expanded and revamped kitchen, and I wondered what it would be like taking a chair in the transformed room. Gail must have been reading my mind.

"I've prepared the most delicious dinner to welcome you home," she declared.

"Oh, great," I replied. "As long as it's not a pizza."

ONE
QUO VADIS?

WITH HINDSIGHT, I BLAME VRON.

"In the Middle Ages," she had said, "pilgrims walked home. They didn't have the luxury of Ryanair."

Leaving aside the bizarre suggestion that the low-cost Irish airline had anything to do with luxury, Vron's throwaway remark had sown a seed. Two years before, I had just flown back from Rome after 76 days on the road, walking 2,100 kilometres – 1,300 miles – to St Peter's from my home in Coggeshall in north Essex. We were sitting around the supper table in our warm kitchen, and once again I could enjoy the glow of good company in my own hearth and revel in the thought that the following day I would not have to roll out of bed and boot up to walk 32 kilometres.

Vron is a good Catholic, which is more than I can say for myself, and she takes her religion very seriously. She has a commanding presence, with a look that is as serene and alluring as a Sienese Madonna, and in the months that followed I could never quite let go of her innocent injunction. Most likely, I did not want to. This unintended challenge was an excuse to get on the road again; besides, I am a sucker for a long-distance walk.

And so, two years on, I found myself at Stansted Airport at 5.00 am on an overcast English summer dawn, lining up at the Ryanair check-in to fly back to Rome. It was 14th July – Bastille Day. I was setting out to walk up Italy, over the Alps and across France in the hot

European summer; that at least was the plan.

I had to despatch my yellow rucksack at a special desk – the belts and buckles are too obtrusive for the standard baggage conveyor. Parting with it was not easy. The bag itself, checking in at 12 kilos, held everything I would need for the next ten weeks – boots, socks, a few extra shirts and a spare pair of trousers, pills for this and that, water flask, camera and mobile phone charger, compass and maps. The bag itself was vital. I thought I had worn it out on previous long walks, including my journey to Rome in 2010; however, when I laid its successor alongside it at Coggeshall I knew which one was coming with me. Though it was more than 15 years old, and patched and repaired in several places, nothing quite matched this stiff-framed Lowe Alpine Crossbow Contour for strength and comfort; besides, its distinctive (if faded) colour gave me a degree of security while walking on continental highways: when needs must, it made me highly visible.

"Will I see it again?" I asked the lad manning the outsize luggage carousel, watching my old friend, and the entire trajectory of my next ten weeks, swallowed into the bowels of the airport on its own conveyor belt. My walk depended upon its safe and timely transit from Stansted to Ciampino.

"Well, put it this way," he said, "you have more chance of picking it up in Rome if you send it through here."

It was unsettling to start a long walk strapped into a plane seat. After my walk to Rome in 2010, I had flown home, and ten years earlier, at the end of a similar long trek, I had jetted back from Santiago de Compostela. Neither experience was good. On both occasions I had felt almost insulted by the speed of the flights, belted into a cramped seat and transported as if on a magic carpet at 500 miles per hour over ground on which I had laboured for many days and weeks at three miles an hour. Now, however, as I looked down on the empty expanse of France and as we crossed the Jura Mountains and the Alps and gradually descended over the wooded slopes and hilltop towns of central Italy, I was able to see it all wind out in reverse: the immensity of the distance that lay ahead. I also noticed that there wasn't a cloud in the sky.

Italy was in the grip of one of its scorching African summers and, when the crew opened the door of the now landed and parked plane, the heat blasted back into the cabin. Having booked a priority seat by the forward door, so as to be first off the plane and first through passport control, and therefore first to the baggage carousel, I found myself asking why. What point was there in this anxious haste, when I had more than 2,000 kilometres of walking ahead of me? It was time to slow down, and, to be sure, the baggage handlers at Ciampino saw to that. Long after most of my fellow passengers had departed with their suitcases, I was finally reunited with my yellow rucksack.

A taxi was waiting for me at the exit to the Arrivals Terminal, my name on a printed sheet between the raised hands of the driver. He was to be my last link with executive life – a final indulgence before I took to the road and became once more, in the eyes of many who would pass me, a tramp and a mendicant.

The transition was more than symbolic. We walked out together into the dazzling Mediterranean sun, and he waited inside the air-conditioned limousine while I sat on the dry grassy bank and changed and booted up. I packed my fleece for the last time for many weeks, and I swapped my Merrell slip-on trainers – from now on for evening-wear only – for a new pair of 1,000 mile socks and a just worn-in pair of Meindl boots. Lastly, with sunhat on my head, I applied professional lashings of sun cream to my face and arms.

I had booked the car for St Peter's Square in the Vatican City, and we slipped off the highway, turning up into the Via Appia Antica, and sped towards central Rome. It was just at the moment we were passing the Church of Domine Quo Vadis that the driver asked me where exactly I wanted to be dropped. What a place, I pondered, for such a question. The church marks the spot where – so the legend goes – the Apostle Peter, renouncing his mission to the City of Rome in the face of persecution, ran into Christ heading in the opposite direction.

"*Domine, quo vadis*? Where are you going, Lord?" Peter asked.

"I am going to Rome to be crucified again," the Lord replied, and at that rebuke Peter turned and confronted his destiny.

Peter, I reflected, may never have even set foot in Rome, and Jesus may not have been everything that he is made out to be in the Gospels and Christian teaching, but these challenging thoughts had in no way diminished my enthusiasm for following in the footsteps of those who had journeyed to Rome from over the Alps to pay homage to Peter, or for undertaking its necessary sequel. And so I told my driver, "Drop me anywhere by St Peter's. It really doesn't matter. I am setting out from there, on foot, for London."

In the rear mirror, I watched his expression go from disbelief to stupefaction.

"*Un po' pazzo*," I said, "a bit mad."

"*Al contrario, è molto avventuroso.*"

I liked that. The Italians have a delightful way of using language to soften and embellish harsh reality. No one in England would dream of saying that slogging it on foot from Rome to London was adventurous, but I was back in Italy, and, as the driver embraced the empty streets of a Roman Saturday morning, and stepped on it through the Porta Ardeatina and past the Circo Massimo towards the River Tiber, he got into the spirit of my adventure.

"Will you be living off berries?" He had conjured an image of me scavenging in forests, and had no clearer notion than a typical London cabbie of the practicalities of long-distance walking. "There are lots of wild berries and fruits in Italy."

"I'll need more than wild berries to get me to London," I replied.

We crossed the Ponte Vittorio Emanuele and turned up Via Conciliazione. At its far end, St Peter's was glowing in the mid-morning sun. The last time I had set eyes on the Basilica was from Monte Mario, the day I arrived in Rome in August 2010. Then it was with a sense of pure elation, now it was with a certain foreboding. St Peter's Square was haunted with the wrong sort of memories: I wanted to nod quickly and be on my way.

I entered the *Ufficio del Pellegrino* on the south-eastern corner of the piazza and took out my pilgrim passport – the slim booklet supplied by the Confraternity of Pilgrims to Rome as a *bona fide*.

"I am doing it backwards," I said, to explain why the passport was completely blank. "I am following St Augustine, starting in Rome and walking to Canterbury."

The girl didn't appear to take in a word. She duly stamped the passport with the *Opera Romana Pellegrini* seal and automatically reached into the drawer to take out a Pilgrim Testimonial – the certificate given to those who have completed the pilgrim journey to St Peter's tomb by following the Via Francigena, as the way from Canterbury to Rome is known.

"No, no," I told her. "I don't need a Testimonial; I am walking back to Canterbury."

She looked puzzled. The Vatican Pilgrim Office was evidently not accustomed to people departing. This was an arrivals' office. I am not sure that she had even heard of Canterbury, and I wasn't about to lecture her on St Augustine, the Benedictine abbot of noble birth despatched by Pope Gregory in 596 with 40 Italian monks in his charge, to re-establish the Christian Church in England. By all accounts, Augustine and his party were so reluctant to carry their mission to the uncouth islanders that they had to be coaxed on their way. Indeed, Augustine himself, on reaching Aix-en-Provence, turned back to Rome, and Gregory had to stiffen his resolve before sending him off once again.

In any case, I had my Pilgrim Testimonial, well earned in 2010, hanging on a wall back in Coggeshall, so once more declining her offer I stepped into St Peter's Square and approached a Chinese tourist. I asked him to take a photograph of me next to the fountain where I had stood for a similar pose after arriving from England. He was a student, studying engineering at Nottingham, in Rome with his parents. They spoke no English, but when he explained that I was walking all the way to London they insisted on joining in the photo-shoot. Their son snapped shots of them, both smiling and clasping my shoulders – the new Orient embracing the eccentric West.

The hands on St Peter's clock reached 10:30am, the thermometer on my sports wrist-watch registering 39 degrees; it was time to go. I tightened the straps of my rucksack and walked through Bernini's arches into the Via Porta Angelica, and as I left the square I reached for my mobile phone and called a friend whose footsteps were now closing with mine from far to my north.

I had dined with Harry Bucknall in his London club before he set out to walk to Rome, and we had agreed that our next dinner would be in Tuscany. He had served as an officer in the Coldstream Guards in the Bosnian War, and he was now a writer, brimming with humour and good cheer. I had followed his progress from London, down through France and across the Alps, sending him a series of encouraging SMS texts, and he had just reached northern Italy. I could think of no one better to talk to as I set out on my backwards journey; now it was Harry's turn to encourage me.

Breakfast at Stansted Airport had long since faded, and by the time I reached the Piazza del Risorgimento, just a few hundred metres into my journey, I was assailed with hunger and thirst. So I hurried up Via Leone, passing the restaurants and bars that cater for tourists visiting the Vatican, and after crossing into Via Trionfale I found a likely place for lunch: a pizza bar. *A Long Way for a Pizza* is what I had called my account of the 2010 journey to Rome, though very rarely did I eat a pizza; I don't actually like them. But I fell on a plate of *pizza al pomodoro* with the relish of discovering a new food, and for several days out of Rome a slice of pizza was my lunchtime staple.

I was finding myself haunted by my outward journey. I felt melancholic and sad, missing the friendships I had formed during the final days of the approach to Rome; I suppose I was craving the sense of fulfilment and untold joy of my arrival. It was as if I were trespassing on my own past. Walking the 'wrong' way, I felt I had no right to be here; I was an impostor. I tried to work out why I was doing this thing;

what was this crazy compunction that had driven me to undertake such a long journey, backwards, and all over again?

Via Trionfale led uphill, snaking round the park of Monte Mario, Rome's highest hill, from where two years before, after 76 days, I had finally seen the dome of St Peter's. I didn't look back now, concentrating on steadying my stride with my laden rucksack. Hot work: all I could think of was getting out of Rome as quickly as possible, so as to convince myself that my new journey had really begun. A side road named Via Cervinia gave me a fillip. It was from Cervinia that I intended to cross the Alps over the Théodule Pass into Zermatt.

The exit from Rome around the busy intersections by the *Gran Raccordo* ring road was as perilous as my entry – uncomfortable stretches of fast road without the benefit of a pavement. But I was soon on the relative safety of the old Via Cassia, which in the suburbs has retained its pavements, striding towards La Storta – another staging post on my approach to Rome. I had stayed there in a modern box hotel the night before arriving at St Peter's. This time, though, I wanted to be clear of the suburbs and properly into the country, and so for my first night I had chosen the antithesis of La Storta, Isola Farnese, a hamlet on a promontory of tufa rock a bit further on.

Isola is explained by the topography, while the rather martial palazzo on its crown was once owned by the Farnese family. Everything urban was left behind where the lane turned off the Via Cassia, and, a mere 18 kilometres from the centre of Rome, I was instantly in the country surrounded by growing crops and budding fruit. Arriving at Isola Farnese, I watched an old man intently watering the tomatoes on his garden plot overlooking the wooded valley.

"No rain?" I asked him.

"None since May, and we won't be getting any until September."

The Hotel Tempio di Apollo has an ambitious and rather pretentious name. It is really just a converted brick farmhouse in the centre of the village, set around an inner courtyard, and with a terrace that gives a finely framed view of the distant Alban Hills. I was the only guest, and the restaurant was closed. But I found a watering hole for my evening meal close by, and celebrated my first night with a *spaghetti carbonara* and a bottle of local fizzy white wine, which helped to chase away the misgivings of the morning in Rome.

The following day, turning down a lane at the foot of the castle, I was soon picking my way through the ruins of the ancient Etruscan city of Veii to find the footpath that would lead me back onto the road to Formello. I was now using GPS – albeit a rather primitive version with Google maps on my BlackBerry – and each day, walking north and west, I began to rely on it more and more. The little green dot on the hand-held screen which told me exactly where I was would never entirely replace the look and feel of a map and the certainty of a compass needle, but it was a huge improvement on my navigational methods on my outward walk, and for instant reassurance nothing could beat it.

It was so hot by nine o'clock that I had already larded myself in sun cream and donned my embarrassing flower-pot sun hat. By then I was on the Vicolo Formellese walking towards Formello where I would pick up the Via Francigena again.

Once in Formello, an old stronghold of the Orsini, I made the mistake of dropping into the same bar where I had stopped with Everdiene, a young female school inspector from the Netherlands. Everdiene and I had shared two days together on our approach to Rome, and despite going our own way on the final day from La Storta we had somehow contrived to arrive in St Peter's Square at the same time. We had kept in touch, and had sent strange messages to each other sharing memories of our respective journeys.

"You write of all sorts of questions about reality," Everdiene had said in one exchange. "When is a fact a fact? I asked myself the same question during my pilgrimage. You will probably think I am a lunatic, but I saw a man in white in a forest in France. He was sitting on a hill and he was afraid. I told him not to be, and after a few minutes he was gone." Vanished: a ghost. We had quite a correspondence about ghosts; and now, sitting in that bar in Formello, I seemed to find her ghost and sense her shadow enveloping me.

Out on the road again, I reached the entrance to the Veio Park where, in 2010, Everdiene and I had missed a crucial waymark and made the mistake of walking into a combe which came to a dead end. Now, much to my surprise, I found the entrance to the park, where we had finally exited, barricaded and aggressively fenced off with barbed wire. I took off my rucksack and, using it as a ram, forced a passage through a tiny gap. My path, perfectly distinct, zigzagged down through forest to the valley floor; but from no further than the first bend the cause of the footpath's closure had become all too apparent. The scene of storm damage before me was like the aftermath of an earthquake – huge trees had tumbled down the side of the hill, ripping out the banked earth and laying bare the steep rocky escarpment. The path itself was buried in debris and blocked with trunks and broken branches. Common sense told me to turn back, but the demon in me chose to press on; so, taking out my camera to record this natural chaos, I started to pick my way through the wreckage.

And there at the bottom, of course, when I hacked my way out, was the laughing ghost of Everdiene. The waymark we had missed had been removed, and I could see that diversions and other interruptions to the way would not necessarily be signalled to those walking backwards. No one was being sent up that path.

Picking up the familiar Via Francigena signs following the narrow river that meandered through the park fringed with borders of hawthorn and vivid dogwood, I recalled Everdiene with renewed cheerfulness. She was planning to be in Italy in the coming days, and I hoped that we might meet up. There was even the possibility that she might step out with me for a bit of anti-pilgrimage. But my thoughts were interrupted by the Italian landscape.

The climb out of the valley past the Santuario della Madonna del Sorbo was an abrupt reminder to lungs and legs that the Essex pilgrim was back in a country which is four-fifths hill. I rested by the chapel, from where I could see rising ground ahead, and rehearsed to myself the almost unbroken rule about walking in Italy: if there is a hill ahead, then it is a pretty sure thing that it will have to be climbed. My wristwatch altimeter told me that I was already 200 metres above the tomb of St Peter and this, I knew, would soon be 400 metres, and as I made my way ever upward on rural tracks in the searing heat I found myself stopping frequently, both to admire the view back to Rome and to ease the strain on my unfit legs.

So it was a relief to arrive at my day's destination, Campagnano di Roma, just on midday and to get out of the sun before it scorched the earth and set the crickets off on their screeching noon chorus. I had covered only 24 kilometres, but this was intentional. I needed to pace myself until I was up to walking long distances in the heat.

Once again I had booked into the Hotel Benigni chiefly because I remembered, from last time, the gorgeous cold buffet of Italian vegetables – quite one of the best assortments I had ever eaten. It was over those vegetables cooked in oil and garlic, and accompanied by dishes of pasta and local red wine, that Everdiene and I, along with another pilgrim all the way from Holland, had celebrated before going our separate ways to Rome.

But before I could get at the Benigni vegetables, I all but messed up the entire walk, stubbing my big toe on the sharp flange of the shower basin and opening a bloody gash. Sitting in the shade of the park trees that afternoon, nursing the wound, I worried whether the cut would survive being wrapped up in a sock and chafing for hours on end in a boot. So when Harry called to ask how I was getting on I was far too ashamed to tell the old foot-soldier that I feared it might be game over all because of my big toe! I just let his words of encouragement work on the wound.

The Benigni buffet proved to be one of the few occasions where returning to the same restaurant did not prove to be a disappointment. I had to tell Everdiene.

"Hi Brian – It must be very strange to walk from Rome, so many wonderful memories; and now you are on your own eating at the Benigni. We had a great dinner there. I can well imagine that every step brings memories back. By the way, how do you find your way? Reading the Lightfoot guide backwards?"

Everdiene raised a very pertinent question. As in 2010 on the outgoing journey, I was indeed equipped with the Lightfoot Guide: just two volumes this time because for the last third of my return I would be abandoning the Via Francigena. But just the two were anything but light and hard enough to follow going in the direction of Rome, which is what they are for. Yet by some strange perversity I found them no more difficult to read backwards, and certainly the last of the three volumes, which would take me back as far as Vercelli in northern Italy, proved its worth in finding hotels and, on several occasions, suggesting helpful short cuts. I knew the way, or at least remembered big chunks of it, and I confidently began devising my own special routes, at times out-trumping both Lightfoot and the official Via Francigena. The latter, too, proved more dependable than two years previously with much improved waymarking – even for someone going north. In any case, for much of the time I steered with my compass and cross checked my position with the GPS on my BlackBerry.

I went spectacularly wrong on only one occasion. This was on the third day, and it prompted one of my final despatches to Everdiene.

"Hi. What a day! I left your shadow at Sutri and walked on rather circuitously because I lost my way to Capranica where I am staying at La Locanda Monticelli with a French couple who are travelling in a cart pulled by a donkey with three infant daughters. The Via Francigena is casting strange spells. The Cassia was just short of suicidal – Monday rush hour – but I eventually found the safe ground of the lateral road and stopped in Monterosi to dust off the vehicular shrapnel."

"Yeah, we pilgrims are a bit nuts," came her reply. "We get lost, do suicidal things, get pains in shoulders, feet and legs, we wear the same clothes for a few months and smell. Why? Hmm... not easy to explain to others. I hope the Via Cassia, where we met, was not too dangerous today. And what about the weather? I hope it is not too warm. Here in the Netherlands it is cold and wet, like autumn. It is unbelievable, horrible."

The day had started with a short-cut up the Via Cassia which was by far the busiest road I walked on. You do not play Russian roulette with Italian rush-hour traffic. For a few kilometres I headed face-on into two lanes of fast traffic. Although not recklessly dangerous, it was uncomfortable enough to set me hacking through the brambles inside the crash barrier. This was the same short-cut on which I had led Everdiene on the day that we had met, although on the south side there was a lateral road for much of the way, and it somehow seemed safer and less insane. Eventually, I managed to cross over to that lateral road and made my way gratefully into Monterosi, a hilltop town that had been emerging slowly in the distance.

Secure at last, I bypassed the café in Monterosi where Everdiene and I had stopped and instead entered a strangely sparse store in the town centre, Chinese-run and with no recognizable brands on the shelves. But the one thing I needed they had: my energy staple of dried fruit and nuts.

I spent much of the remainder of the day on farm tracks and country lanes, including a section of old Roman road, and started to meet pilgrims coming the other way. First was Tim Clifford, a freshly retired Mergers & Acquisitions specialist, hiking to Rome to draw a line under his 30-years in the City of London. I commented on the lightness of his pack.

"Just about the only thing in there is a litre of water," he said.

Soon afterwards, I missed a waymark by the Italian Golf Academy, in much the same way that I miss simple putts, but I extricated myself in time to encounter two more Englishmen, the brothers Philip and Tom Singleton, who were proud to inform me that they had navigated all the way from Canterbury with GPS.

But my troubles weren't over for the day. To be sure, alongside the Roman amphitheatre at Sutri, I was able to wave farewell to Everdiene's ghost – it was here, negotiating a stretch of the busy Via Cassia, that

I had first encountered her. Going north now, there would be no more twists in the road to comment on, no more shared views down stony tracks to remind me of her cheery presence.

At the far end of the hilltop town, buoyed up with thoughts of the afternoon and evening ahead at the old Etruscan house where I would be staying in Capranica, I let a Via Francigena sign lure me down a *strada bianca*, one of the myriad unmetalled byways in the Italian countryside whose white chalky granules throw up a cloud of dust every time a vehicle passes. But this one was utterly deserted; there were no cars or tractors to give me directions, and five kilometres later my readings confirmed what I had already begun to suspect: that I had gone badly wrong.

Nearing the railway station at Capranica, I was way to the south of where I had meant to be, and the dog-leg back to north and east would bring my day's total to 34 kilometres, more than I wanted at this early stage. I could have pressed on and taken pot luck, but my stay in 2010 at La Locanda Monticelli had been one of the highlights of that earlier walk. I cursed the misleading waymark and crunched the extra kilometres.

The locanda, an old house built on top of an Etruscan cave, is owned by Paolo, an architect. Some things had changed since my last visit. The *padrone* had swapped his Italian wife for a new Polish girl from Lublin, Magdalena. His elderly parents were visiting from Rome and seemed to take the new domestic arrangements in their stride. This was the new Europe after all. The place retained all its ancient charms, augmented by its splendid modern swimming pool, and my evening was made all the more memorable by unexpected fellow guests.

The first I knew of their arrival was a commotion at the gate, led by the loud braying of a donkey. The donkey was pulling a four-wheeled wagon not much bigger than a rickshaw; and on board in twin chair seats and a cot were three small children, all girls, under the watchful care of their parents, Matilde and Edouard. They were travelling to Rome from their home in central France, the children aged from six months to three-and-a-half years. Almost at the walls of Rome, they planned to stay here with Paolo and Magdalena for two nights to prepare themselves for the final stages of their unusual journey. The logistics of travelling such a long distance with a four-legged animal that needed feeding, resting and watering every night would have challenged a childless couple; the added responsibility of tending to a babe in arms and two toddlers in the full heat of summer set the exertions of merely walking the Via Francigena on two legs – even both ways – in a very different light.

I spent the evening captivated by the faith and courage that had propelled them this far. They had crossed Alps, braved Italian roads, threaded their way through cities, hauled their cart over high passes and along rough tracks, and each night found somewhere to victual their donkey and rest the children. Having put the little ones to sleep in a large double bed, Matilde and Edouard joined us on the candlelit terrace for a pilgrim dinner that, with their tales of an enchanted journey, stretched far into the night.

Next morning it was the donkey's bray that served for my early alarm call. As in 2010, dawn departures became routine; I was away by 6:15 and had arrived in Viterbo, my 30 kilometres for the day, by 11:30. That way I could hole up in shade during the hot afternoons. I began the day weaving through hazelnut groves on a network of white tracks using Lightfoot upside-down as my guide. Crossing the Via Cassia at Querce d'Orlando, I departed from the Via Francigena, which makes an unnecessary loop through Vetralla, climbing instead into the Cimini Hills. Here lies the Lago di Vico, one of Italy's highest lakes at 500 metres above sea level. The ancients ascribed its scooping out to Hercules, but it is the drowned crater of an extinct volcano. Initially I had views of open countryside, reminiscent of Dorset, but as I turned away from the lake down a lonely track in the direction of Convento S'Angelo the hillsides gradually took on a mantle of un-Dorset-like forest. I have to thank a farmer who pointed me in the right direction. I had dropped into his farmyard to ask if I could refill my water bottle; still unaccustomed to the great heat, I was getting through water at an alarming rate. The farmer told me about a junction ahead with three tracks: "Take the middle one. Otherwise you will get helplessly lost."

The woodlands of beech and chestnut, rich with yellow foxgloves and other bright flowers, were enchanting but without any sign of human life; it was a relief to spot the roof-line of the conventual church. From here the route was unambiguous, a small road descending the forest to San Martino al Cimino. Viterbo was now within easy reach.

San Martino al Cimino is about as far south in Italy as you will find an abbey church – here Cistercian – with its gothic bones intact. It dominates the town that later became a fiefdom of the Pamphili who transformed much of the rest in the language of classicism. Francesco Borromini himself was charged with constructing the monumental main gate, through which I descended with Viterbo, my destination, framed in the arch.

In the two years since I had last walked there, Viterbo had lost none of its charms. The Hotel Tuscia remembered me, even to the extent of putting me in a room on the airy first floor. I took my pilgrim passport to be stamped at the Papal Palace and then thought about a massage. A Thai lady advertised her services in Italian, but she turned out to be more Chinese than Thai, and she hardly spoke a word of any European language. Thinking back to that unexpected Spartan store in Monterosi, I wondered whether the Chinese were not insidiously taking over the wreckage of post-Berlusconi Italy. Dinner, however, at the Ristorante Scaletta on Via Marconi was an entirely Italian affair. I gave the starter – a dish of *fagioli e gamberi* – three stars in my diary and slept the sleep of a pilgrim who, for once, hadn't put a foot wrong.

By now I was getting into my stride. The following day, 18th July, I comfortably covered the 36 kilometres to Bolsena in just over seven hours. Leaving Viterbo alongside its great municipal cemetery, my eye was caught – I had missed them coming the other way – by the admonishments attached to the impressive gates. This house of the dead was a school for being more considerate, said one of them. Early as it was, in England it was about time for Thought for the Day.

I stopped at the nearby thermal springs to bathe my feet, and felt once again that this is surely one of the most rewarding stretches of the Via Francigena. From Viterbo north, it follows long sections of intact old Roman road, and you can keep your head up to observe the vast dome of the basilica at Montefiascone emerging gradually through woods on the hill by the southern shores of Lago di Bolsena. There is more Roman road after Montefiascone, paved in hexagons of black basalt, and giving fine views across vineyards, sloping gently to the lake below. For the last stage into Bolsena, the path descended steeply to a wooded stream-bottom before emerging into fields.

I had booked myself some modest luxury, partly because the Holiday Hotel in Bolsena has four stars, but chiefly because it is right on the lakeside, and my bones and skin were aching for a good swim. I negotiated the stony foreshore with some gingerness – to avoid banging my still sore toe – and dipped into it, but I later forsook the cool water of the lake for the hotel's pool where it was more comfortable to lie out on a sunbed. My fellow sunbathers included some English tourists, one reading the *Financial Times*, but I wasn't letting on.

In the late afternoon, I strolled back into the centre of town to inspect the Church of Santa Cristina, named for a very early Christian martyr, some say from Tyre, some from Persia. But her fame had been totally eclipsed by a miraculous occurrence in this church, one which gave rise to centuries of misunderstanding about transubstantiation: the consecrated bread at a mass in 1263 had spontaneously sweated blood. I came in to find the high altar where the miracle occurred, surmounted by a fine 9th century canopy on four Doric pillars, surrounded by people in silent prayer. For earthier fare, I returned to the lakeside and ordered a supper of fish from the lake, with pasta and clams washed down with a bottle of Est! Est!! Est!!! wine from the Mazziotti vineyards that I had walked through earlier in the day. You couldn't do better.

A four-star hotel means round-the-clock service, seldom available elsewhere, and the night porter happily fixed me up with a breakfast of yoghurt, fruit and tea at 5:30. It was still dark when I left the hotel, and mercifully cool. I followed the road beside the lake and then turned up the same lane I had descended two years previously – this time stopping to admire a succession of Etruscan caves carved into the tufa cliffs above the road. Some still had remnants of timber gates and doors; they had been inhabited within living memory.

I stopped for *tè freddo* in the principal piazza at Acquapendente, one of my staging posts on the way south, and it was enough to fortify me for the hills above the Paglia Valley. Soon, without too great discomfort, I was in sight of Proceno, the last town of the old Papal States before they merge into the borders of the Grand Duchy of Tuscany. The town is dominated by a medieval fortified castle, complete with tower and a hanging garden; and in this very special apartment hotel – as it now is – I was booked as a guest of Giovanni and Cecilia Cecchini Bosini. My room, at battlement level, had a terrace from which my eye could sweep over an undulating carpet of sunflowers and ochre cornfields ripe for harvest, to the east to Umbria, and to the north to the twin Tuscan redoubts of Radicofani and Monte Amiata, which I would be ascending tomorrow. I had covered my 28 kilometres from Bolsena by eleven o'clock, which gave me ample time to laze in the castle swimming pool below the ramparts and to relax and cool down before what I well knew would be some hard days ahead. In the early evening under the closing light of another brilliant day, dinner was served by the pool – fried vegetables with pasta and ham, all the more nourishing for being paired with the castle's own estate red wine. It was so delicious that I could easily have been tempted to stay on another night.

It was barely light when I breakfasted on the contents of a hamper kindly left outside my door: a cornucopia of fruit, bread and cereals, more suited to an opera *aficionado* picnicking at Glyndebourne than a Via Francigena pilgrim. I left the castle as day was breaking and headed down country lanes tucked against the sides of valleys whose chestnut and beech woods opened out to momentary views of Proceno on its commanding hilltop.

By the time I reached the stone farmhouse of Podere San Vincenzo, with its fields and olive groves straddling the invisible border between Lazio and Tuscany, the sun was high and the day uncomfortably hot. Time and place for early elevenses: a good swig of the apple juice saved from breakfast readied me for the long slow ascent of Monte Amiata. The start of my climb was up a white track between a succession of broad-roofed farmsteads whose names all seemed to honour saints or archangels – Santa Lucia, San Rafaelle, San Gennaro and San Isidro. When they ran out, my track joined a by-road climbing straight up to Piancastagnaio and, above it, to the abbey of San Salvatore.

Majestic views of southern Tuscany now spread out before me – to the east the great sentinel of Radicofani on the far side of the Paglia Valley, which I had climbed on my way to Rome, and where, as I came down, I had encountered a lone wolf. The twin sentinels of Radicofani and Monte Amiata are like Pillars of Hercules guarding the almost mystical land of southern Tuscany, and as I gained height the broad vale below me unfolded in splashes of light and shade – corn fields newly harvested into rounded bales laid out along clean cut lines, and other wide swathes, billowing still with their crops, waiting for the blades of the new mega-harvesters and their extended cutters.

But my mind was fixed more firmly on my feet. Not that toe; it had kept up well. But Piancastagnaio lies at just over 800 metres above sea level, and its tiled rooftops and vast Bourbon palace were proving an elusive target. The higher I climbed in the growing heat of the morning, the further away they seemed to get. With all the big climbs ahead, this – my first major test since Rome – was proving to be almost too much. I was struggling, and once or twice had to stop and sit down. At last I dragged myself into the town and collapsed at a bar close to the palace, and rested there a good 15 minutes before, refuelled and revived on tea and lemon cake, I set off on the much gentler climb through chestnut woods towards the Abbey of San Salvatore.

The Benedictine abbey of San Salvatore is one of Tuscany's oldest monasteries, once holding sway over large tracts of the Grand Duchy.

It had acquired its fine Romanesque interior and exterior in 1035 under the unforgettably named Abbot Winizzo. The crudely shaped volcanic stones of the west front, the triple arched colonnaded Norman windows and the irregular towers adjoining the monastery, which I had seen in photographs, give the building a noble simplicity, and I was expecting to see it proudly crowning the hill I had worked so hard to surmount. Imagine my surprise, therefore, when I turned down a back street and came into a down-at-heel square to find this majestic building hemmed in by a modern suburb. Close inspection, however, did not disappoint; the light stone walls of the interior gave way to a striking succession of rounded and deeply carved arches spanning an upper choir and altar approached on a sweeping flight of stone steps, and when I went down into the crypt it had breathtaking spaciousness.

I was now entering the Val d'Orcia, the rolling savannah of southern Tuscany, but for much of the early afternoon I remained on the spurs of Monte Amiata from where I could measure my progress against the hilltop castle of Radicofani, receding steadily to the south. A soft breeze took the edge off the heat, and in Campiglia d'Orcia, which also sits on its own high crag, I took off my boots and socks and plunged my feet into a fountain while I downed another *tè freddo*. This set me up for the weary descent to the valley floor where I joined the Via Cassia and found a refuge for the night after 45 hard and hot kilometres.

The inn at Gallina was just what was needed. It was no more than a bar and restaurant attached to an old fashioned *affitacamere* with plain rooms and a shared shower and loo at the end of the corridor. The Capitani was reassuringly anonymous; its one notable feature, announced at the roadside, was that it stood on the 43rd Parallel. My room was dark and fusty, and so, opening the shutters onto a courtyard that was covered in ripening vines, I dropped in on an earnest discussion between local farmers on the effects of the drought, but all too soon, with the zephyrs of that refreshing breeze entering the room and the sun toasting my sore feet, I fell into a blissful sleep.

If you had asked me what €18 could buy, I wouldn't have reckoned on the quality of the food the inn served when, later, I made my way downstairs. It was one of the tastiest and best value meals I have had in Italy – *bruschetta al pomodoro, pasta al aglio*, and *meringue*, washed down with a jug each of red and white wine. It was all the better for a call from Harry. We had communicated most evenings, making what we jokingly called 'radio contact', comparing our progress. The old soldier was now practically within range; he had just dropped down from his toughest day so far, a rugged climb over the Apennines to the Tyrrhenian shore, and if all went to plan, we would be docking in less than a week. Meanwhile, I had another reunion to look forward to: Gail was joining me for a few days.

TWO
Tuscan Idyll

The following morning, Saturday 21st July, a week out of Rome and starting my first full day in Tuscany, I was on the road before dawn. I had decided to walk the old Via Cassia as far as Castiglione d'Orcia, cutting off another Francigena loop and saving precious time. For the first time, I was in a hurry because I had a rendez-vous. Gail was flying in from London, and we would be meeting at Castel San Fabiano, my destination for the night and a good 40 kilometres distant. This would be the start of a hectic round of social engagements; Gail will travel a long way for a dinner party, and we had several planned over the next few days, including the one with Harry. But unlike most people's social rounds in Tuscany, ours would be encompassed on foot. I had told our art dealer friend Jonathan that I would be at his house on Castel San Fabiano estate by lunchtime.

Typically for an Italian Saturday, there was virtually no traffic at that early hour. I had southern Tuscany to myself and I could pace myself along a road on which men and women have trodden to and from Rome for centuries, watching the arrows of first light expand in the east into a bright red aurora. With dawn came picture-postcard views of neat cypress-lined avenues leading up to hilltop farmhouses; and all around them wondrous landscapes of sunflowers and rolling fields.

Just before the small town of Bagno Vignoni, I crossed the River Orcia, in late summer no more than an apprentice stream. But here it had cut itself a deep gorge, and the scoured water marks told me that in full flood it would more than earn the right to give its name to this most beautiful quarter of Italy. For breakfast I stopped in the hilltop town of San Quirico d'Orcia. I had stayed here on my way to Rome and I paused again to admire the south portal of the Romanesque *Collegiata*, its doorway flanked by lions and caryatids.

The waymarked Via Francigena led me on towards the town of Torrenieri down farm tracks and through fields, and from there to make up time I braved the Via Cassia again through Buonconvento to Ponte d'Arbia. Once more, I regained the Via Francigena as it climbed away from Ponte d'Arbia on the western slopes of the river valley, and here it was time to embrace another friendly ghost from 2010, the Dutchman, Kees. We had fallen in together along this section and struck up a friendship that had lasted during intermittent and casual reunions until, within an hour of one another, we had arrived in St Peter's Square. Kees had tipped me off about Everdiene, and I owed that special encounter to him; I was glad to savour again the spirit of our first walk together.

But such memories were doomed to evaporate under the blast of the sun. Without any trees to shade me, Tuscany danced before my eyes in a shimmering haze. It was nearing midday and when I put my hand to the latch of a crossing-gate of an old branch-line to continue up the track on the other side, it recoiled, scalded. I sweated on up the ridge, and the views opened – to the distant village of Vescovado in the north, and to the band of hills that rise between the Arbia and Ombrone rivers, dotted with isolated farmsteads. All the land around me was scorched yellow, and even the flies were lying low.

The Via Cassia rises on concrete stilts at Monteroni d'Arbia as it steps across the western corner of the San Fabiano estate, for which I was bound, and I took the slip road under it to join the long driveway that leads to Jonathan and Elisabetta's house and, after it, up to the castle. The lunch table was laid when I arrived; Gail, having landed at Pisa airport, was exploring the Duomo and would be joining us later. Soon the washing machine was whirling with my dusty clothes;

the pool beckoned, and for the first time since I had left England a week earlier I came to a blissful halt.

Gail and I spent two nights at San Fabiano. There were changes to be expected. Since my last visit, the old Count had died and Andrea, Elisabetta's elder brother, had moved into the castle. He was slowly making the place his own, and it had lost some of its treasures, notably the table on which Benito Mussolini had hammered out the Lateran Treaty with the Vatican. But the castle had lost none of its charm and style, and I wondered what Harry would make of it. He would be staying there as a guest of Andrea.

Our friends in the lower house had not changed: Jonathan talking with Gail late into that first evening about his art world and the intrigues of Italian politicians, and Elisabetta recounting stories of an extraordinary upbringing in Roman *dolce vita* high society. On the last night, they drove us into the hills up past the Benedictine Abbey of Monte Oliveto Maggiore to the town of Asciano to dine at La Locanda Il Paradiso, a restaurant famed for its homemade pasta and *ribollita* soup, and with a wine list that confines itself to local vintages. I still feel a little naughty about keeping quiet to Gail about the abbey cloister as we drove back down in the dark. If I had mentioned those near-perfect Signorelli frescoes of the life of Saint Benedict we would have needed another day before leaving.

Or perhaps not: on the day we were to leave, poor thing, she dropped her varifocal glasses on the floor tiles of our guest room, and, made of the real stuff – glass – they shattered into tiny fragments. We carefully gathered the pieces and talked rather optimistically about finding an optician to reunite them. Jonathan, insisting that the world's best opticians were in Siena and that his was the best of all, offered to run in later in the day on his Ducati motorbike to deliver the pieces in person to his own optician; and he did, but to no avail. Like Humpty Dumpty, broken spectacles cannot be put back together again. Gail would have to get by with her contact lenses – not so easy at night – and it remained to be seen how her eyes would cope with the intense light of the Tuscan countryside. Undaunted, nevertheless, as befits a soldier's daughter, by both this serious mishap and the early alarm-call, on July 23rd Gail booted up and stepped out with me to walk from San Fabiano to Siena.

We set out northward over the estate land, passing the castle, to the boundary formed by the Arbia. However, rather than negotiate the ford, which might have invited further calamity, we crossed the metal foot bridge over the river and took an underpass to the other side of the Via Cassia to rejoin the Via Francigena at Cuna. We were soon on the crest of hills above the valley walking into a high wind which blew up clouds of dust and tiny particles that by some mysterious means of navigation found their way behind Gail's contacts. Then her sunglasses snapped, and she had to proceed through the gusts of wind with half-closed eyes. The last time she had joined me on such a walk was during the final days of a pilgrimage to Santiago, we were at cross purposes from the start, and it had been a disaster. We had come together on different *caminos* – myself charged up and racing for the end, Gail all for a few days of gentle ambling through Galicia. This new joint enterprise in pilgrim walking wasn't getting off to a good start either, but a few pilgrims coming our way, who had left Siena that morning, helped to cheer her. Their freshness and friendliness, notably the alacrity of a smart young Frenchman called Marc, seemed to reassure Gail that Siena was not so far off.

Gail, the art historian, was as puzzled as I was by the single anomalous structure that confronted us before we left the hillside. Somewhere between a giant tin can and an airport control tower, it stood in our way swathed in rusted scaffolding. What was a derelict soup factory doing plonked in the midst of golden cornfields? Dropping down into Isola d'Arbia, I realised that I had lost the Via Francigena. Concentrating on dodging the gusts of wind and gazing at the abandoned soup factory, I had failed to follow or read the marks. We got back on track, but only by hacking over stubble fields and through barbed wire to cross a section of unfinished road, route finding that was not designed to raise my new companion's confidence. But when, from the chapel of San Pietro a Paterno, Siena came into full view, my map-reading reputation was sufficiently restored for Gail to relax and enjoy the walk. Two valleys away, the city presented itself as an inviting skyline of low rooftops and towers embowered among gentle green hills.

We entered the city up the steps by the Porta Romana and made our way directly to the Piazza del Campo, and, after settling into our hotel, Gail revived and was back in her element. She escorted me to the Duomo and showed me all the things I had missed two years before, above all the beautifully inlaid marble floors, the play of the black and white stone of the nave piers, and the Baptistery with its early Quattrocento sculptures. As arranged, we met up with Jonathan; although his optician had been able to do nothing with Gail's broken glasses, Jonathan had at least enjoyed an outing on his Ducati, and we shared a final drink before returning to the Piazza del Campo to follow his recommendation and dine al fresco at the Ristorante al Mangia, where I momentarily lost Gail in her *soufflé di porcini*.

"More of this and less walking would be nice," she said.

Early next morning, so as to keep the day's walk as short as possible, we took a direct route out of Siena via San Martino. The Piazza del Campo, which we crossed as the clock tower marked 6.45 am, was again deserted; this time there were not even the street cleaners who had sent me on my way to Rome. Byroads led us down the valley and due north to rejoin the Via Francigena as it worked its way through a dense forest of holm oaks. I began to appreciate new stone markers that had been dug in at the side of the track every few hundred metres. Much had changed in Tuscany in the two years since I wandered down the tracks through these same woods, as if blindfolded, with no waymarks to guide me.

Monteriggioni's girdle of 13th century stone walls retains its defensive turrets, standing erect like watchmen. When they were still new, the Tuscan poet Dante Alighieri used them as an image to describe the "horrible giants" guarding his *Inferno*. There are 14 of them, and

Dante's "horrible" seems not quite fair on today's charmed and peaceful hilltop borgo. It was characteristically quiet when we entered the car-free piazza through the south gate. Following our stiff climb up to the ramparts, I was aware that Gail was beginning to wilt under the combined effects of heat and hill: time to rest, so we stopped at the bar for a cooling drink and to look around the little church a century or more older than the walls. It also seemed opportune to put my head into the tourist office. Two years ago, I had been there to complain about the scrappy waymarking along the Via Francigena, which they were promoting with a special exhibition. Now it was gratifying to register my praise.

For Gail, though, there was no such satisfaction. The rest of the day would be a struggle, not even the sight and sound of a *zampogna*, a rustic Italian bagpipe, being played outside the castle at Strove for a wedding party, could lift her spirits. It was just too hot and far too hilly. A snake slithering across the path in front of her – under my feet in fact – did not help, and by the time we arrived in Graciano d'Elsa I was a pilgrim with a silent mutiny on my hands. The only fair option, I decided, was for Gail to take a taxi or bus-ride on into Colle di Val d'Elsa, where another expat friend, the Australian artist and photographer Stephen Roach, was due to meet us in the main square.

"Why are you so keen to walk every inch of the way?" Gail kept asking. I didn't know how to reply. I had no good answer.

First things first: a sit down, another glass of iced Fanta. How about taxis? I asked at the bar. None in town. Buses? Timetable on the wall outside. There were just two a day, one early in the morning and the other late in the afternoon, which would be coming along in about five hours – pretty good for a country where some local services run only once a week, but not much good for Gail.

I coaxed my wife: "Five hours – take you less time to walk."

"Not with your map reading," she muttered.

But she gave in, and I even surprised Gail by steering us into the piazza in under an hour. We arrived just after two, some 28 kilometres from Siena, and by the time Stephen had hooted his horn at us we had enjoyed a much-earned *gelato*, and were almost speaking to each other again.

The car took in a supermarket on the way – Gail found new sunglasses while Stephen stocked up on wine for the evening – and then Stephen drove us into the hills above Poggibonsi. We were going to Il Poggiolo, his converted Tuscan farmhouse, and on the way Stephen reminded Gail of its most unique feature. It is one of the few places in this part of Italy from which there is no other building visible – not even a light after dark. That, I remembered as they talked, had been a disorienting factor when I first came to stay here on my way to Rome. I had wondered how I would ever get back from such a remote spot. As we swept up the bump drive, Fabrizia, an alluring Italian Sanskrit Professor, was there to greet us at the great glass door of the former barn at the back of the house.

"You look exactly the same," she told me, "only more strained."

"That's Gail's influence," I replied, half in jest. "She really doesn't like walking!"

The two dark-haired daughters were there. Dione, fresh from art school in London, snatched my pilgrim passport and sketched over a whole page a sinuous mermaid – a complement to the full-page drawing of Il Poggiolo she had done in my passport on my way to Rome. Later, I couldn't resist buying one of her beautiful figure paintings.

Her sister, Iante, a graduate from Oxford and recently returned from working in Lebanon, had very continental European insights into the British.

"In my three years at Oxford, I never met a normal public school boy. They didn't know how to be friends; they just wanted to get their leg over. It isn't like that in Italy."

We were dining on the terrace, the only light from stars and a sliver of new moon. At our side were friends from our Oxford days, Mark and Heather, now living in Florence. Fabrizia had prepared a game stew. It was a scented Tuscan evening.

"Are you sure you want to leave us?" Fabrizia asked Gail in the morning.

"No," she replied. "But I have another dinner date this evening."

It was the promise of dinner with Harry that kept Gail going all day; and even that nearly proved not enough. At least Stephen gave us a bit of a start, putting us back to within striking distance of the Via Francigena more or less where he had scooped us up. He dropped us in Colle di Val d'Elsa at the mouth of the track that led up the valley to La Collina. Going on from there, he assured us, to the hamlet of Bibbiano, we would find the road to take us to the towers of San Gimignano.

"I did a lot of trekking in the Australian outback," he said as we parted. "And things always look a bit different from what you expect."

We set off up the track like twin doubting Thomases, with Stephen's warnings ringing in our ears and Gail voicing her concern that a wrong turning would add kilometres to an already long day. At the first farmhouse we saw an old man tending his garden, just the person to ask about the way. He said he was called Hugo and was proud to tell us that he was 95 years old and, although somewhat bent and doubtless shorter than he had been in his youth, still active; and to prove it, he skipped back to his garden shed to produce a tray of newly dug potatoes.

We stopped to talk. I told him we were from England. This seemingly insignificant snippet of information triggered a gleeful admission. Hugo had been a prisoner of the British during World War II.

"We were captured in North Africa and they shipped us to Pretoria in South Africa. In a way, we were lucky," he said.

He would have been 21 when conscripted into Mussolini's army. As a P.O.W., he spent almost four years behind barbed wire at Zonderwater, a sprawling complex that came to be regarded as the Hilton of World War II prison camps. How strange and accidental are our lives. I asked Hugo whether he had ever been back to South Africa, or visited his 'host' country, England.

"Good heavens, no! After four years drinking English tea in South Africa, I couldn't wait to get back to Tuscan olives and fruit."

And so to our problem: were we on the right path? Of course we were, and with Hugo's reassurance we climbed steadily on up the valley through terraced vineyards and hillside farmsteads and came eventually, as we had been told, to the road junction at Bibbiano. It was obvious from here which road to take: it looped agreeably down to the valley of the River Ferribbie, which we followed to the turn up to Monte Oliveto, from where San Gimignano came immediately into view. I had noted, on leaving the town two years ago, that the vistas over my shoulders were the best of all; but nothing quite equalled encountering them front on, and watching the eight principal towers gradually take shape above the rooftops, sloping olive groves and vineyards that make their setting.

The last time Gail and I had been there was by car; she had raced up from the car park to see what painted mugs were on sale. Now I tried to refuel her from my own experience. "This," I tried to persuade her, "is definitely the best way to see San Gimignano." But I could see that she had already lost all interest in the views around her. The day was growing remorselessly hotter, and now Gail's single focus was on climbing the steep hill to the city's gates.

We paused in San Gimignano for refreshment and wonder: long enough, too, for Gail to buy one new mug and a miniature Della Robbia roundel of the Infant Jesus for our brand-new Spanglish grand-daughter. Then, locating the Porta San Matteo, we thrust ourselves back into the cauldron of the Tuscan summer. By the time we reached the Sanctuary of the Madonna of Pancole, a chapel built on an arch over the road where devout pilgrims are rewarded with a plenary indulgence, it was obvious that Gail's walking legs were beyond salvation. She kept asking to stop, a request I firmly refused.

"It's still early, we have plenty of time," Gail pleaded.

"Not in this heat. We must get through it as quickly as we can, and that means pressing on."

"This is worse than the pains of childbirth," Gail insisted. "I feel as if I am on one of the circles of Dante's *Inferno*".

We did press on, but the final climb into Gambassi Terme, an ascent of more than 200 metres up a long farm track, was the last straw. Thirty kilometres over hilly country in seven and a half hours, with a total altitude gain of 843 metres, was not Gail's idea of easy going, nor, to be truthful, mine.

We checked into the Albergo Pinchiorba, cooling off with a prolonged shower in a minute bathroom and, later, sitting on the village's warm stone ramparts with a big ice cream, looking back southward and taking in practically the entire rugged terrain of our day's journey.

Harry turned up just before six o'clock. His appearance took me by surprise. When I had first met him in London he was altogether what you would expect of a Guards officer, dapper and trim in well pressed trousers and polished shoes. The beaky nose and post-box grin were still there, but he was thin and worn from many weeks on the road, and, with a bag slung over his shoulder, a bulky rucksack on his back, face unshaven and crop-headed, shorts showing off bare knees, and staff in hand, Harry looked more ready for combat.

"All that weight," I exclaimed.

"Oh, it's nothing, the rucksack just slips onto the back and away I go," he replied. "It only weighs 17 kilos."

That is indeed true; after many weeks on the road, long-distance walkers forget the weight they carry on their back. Ten days in, I was just beginning to get used to my more modest 11 kilos.

"But what's that you are carrying in the shoulder-bag? Looks like a machine-gun."

"That's my laptop."

The ex-soldier was indeed still armed, not with ordnance but with a keyboard on which to tap out the blog on his journey and take notes for the book he would write, which he had provisionally titled *Like a Tramp Like a Pilgrim*.

At supper, I teased Harry over the appropriateness of the title, a phrase with many sources, but chiefly a line in Paddy Leigh Fermor's *A Time of Gifts* where he characterises his younger self walking from the Hook of Holland to Constantinople as "like a tramp, a pilgrim, or a wandering scholar".

"A tramp you aren't, at least you don't look like one," I said. "You buff up too well. As for being a pilgrim, that, of course, isn't for me to judge."

"You should see some of the places I have stayed in. I think that qualifies for living both down and out."

Leaving London and Paris out of the equation, Harry had certainly taken heed of Leigh Fermor's advice that there is much to recommend moving from straw to four-poster. He had checked into our hotel, and soon he was due at the castle of San Fabiano; and now the three of us sat on the terrace and tucked into a three-course meal, and the litres of wine we enriched it with meant that long into the night we were swapping tales of the road, every episode shot through with Harry's infectious enthusiasm for people and Gail's searching comments about the oddity of it all.

I see Harry as a professional people-watcher. His observations of human foibles had landed him in deep trouble not long after he left the army; he had swapped sword for pen, and ended up writing a book about the inhabitants of the Greek islands. Harry has a jocular way with people; he likes giving them nicknames, and he generously bestowed two on me. I became Tom Jones because my top shirt buttons were invariably open, and also the Papal Nuncio because I stayed in posh hotels, which made Gail the Papal Nunciata.

"You've got to fictionalise people and play around with their names, it helps stir them into life," said Harry.

"I would have thought that most of the characters you meet on this walk are real enough," I suggested, instancing pilgrims we had both met, including Marc, the sprightly young Frenchman from Briançon whose path we had both just crossed among the cornfields south of Siena.

"Ah, that was the fellow I met outside Vercelli," said Harry. "His kit was all over the shop; he had spent the night sleeping in the woods and looked like a cherry surprise after the mossies had had their way with him. I helped smarten him up."

"You must have made a big impact on him," said Gail. "He was very neat, rather frightening in fact. He looked so professional that I wondered how amateurs like me could ever hope to survive the Via Francigena."

At that, Harry's face became one big smile; and I couldn't help wondering whether Gail's observation would change the way Marc would turn out for parade in *Like a Tramp Like a Pilgrim*.

"Of course, some of the people you meet on the Via Francigena aren't real at all," Harry continued. "Every so often you meet an angel."

Gail and I exchanged a wary glance. Angels, we were thinking, what in heaven was Harry going to say next? It was getting late and there was no time left that evening to pursue these supposed apparitions, but in the coming weeks I was to find out more about Harry's angels on the Via Francigena.

Next morning, the three of us regrouped for breakfast with our neatly buckled-down packs at the one bar in Gambassi Terme that was open at seven, the Caffè Pontormo opposite the main church. The *padrone* was just packing his wife and children off to the seaside for the annual holiday, and we detected a certain lightness in his step. In fact he was so relaxed that he took time out to photograph us three pilgrims before we set out – Harry waving as he descended the hill that had tested us yesterday, and Gail and myself turning our faces due north towards Castelfiorentino.

I had hatched a plan to make the day easier for Gail. I had gone through my maps and swapped the arduous hill-hike that lay ahead for a gentler route along the valley of the River Maremmana. But Gail had already devised her own plan, and, as we reached the outskirts of Castelfiorentino and came level with the sign to the station, she sprung it on me.

"I am going to leave you here. I am taking the train to Lucca."

I was at first disappointed, perhaps even angry that Gail had stayed the course as long as there were 'parties'; and now, our social engagements over, she was doing a runner. To take the strain off her, and by re-routing our exit from Gambassi Terme, I had done myself out of the chance to walk the hills and was now committed to the less scenic route along the valley floor. But I quickly came to my senses. Gail simply could not face any more route marching.

"Why are you so determined to walk every inch of the way?" she asked again.

"It's a sort of madness, but I cannot imagine any other way."

I called our hotel in Lucca and booked her in for an extra night, and we parted in good spirits and on good terms – Gail to plumb the mysteries of Italy's rural railways and myself to notch up another day under the hot Tuscan sun.

One reason I had set my heart on the upland tracks was that, on the way down, I had missed a vital Via Francigena waymark that would have kept me in the hills. But I found this default route, a continuous lane winding through the village of Dogana and on under the hilltop town of Castelnuovo d'Elsa, which grew on me and offered pleasant walking; and in the end I got my scenic reward after Canneto, where I climbed back into the rolling hills and rejoined the waymarked Via Francigena.

The commune of Calenzano gave me a vista of the country ahead and the opportunity for a rest and a drink. I had already spotted the tower of San Miniato's Rocca castle, and now, looking down the Valdarno, I could see Empoli, where Gail, as it happened, was wrestling with a change of train on her rail journey to Lucca. In the far distance I could make out the faint silhouette of Florence. The bar where I stopped in Calenzano had its own Via Francigena stamp that the *padrone* insisted on applying to my pilgrim passport. It was worth it: as well as the Via Francigena insignia, it had the scallop shell for Santiago de Compostela. The road from Rome was opening out.

After San Miniato I followed farm tracks to the banks of the River Arno, which I crossed at Fucecchio. I could measure my progress, and soon after reaching the north bank I made for the purlieu of the Fucecchio trading estate to check into the brand new Hotel La Campagnola – an unlikely spot for a comfortable stopover. I carpeted the tiled terrace of my ground floor room with freshly washed garments, which were soon roasted dry in the afternoon sun, and that evening I sat by candlelight alone but content on the hotel's outdoor restaurant by the side of the main street contemplating a plate of spaghetti and curried prawns – a subtle and hearty fusion of Tuscany and the Orient.

Ponte a Cappiano is just up the road from Fucecchio, and one of my bad memories of 2010 was the hostel there on the covered bridge where I had been given a cell in what had otherwise been a rough dormitory for Albanian refugees. I nodded at the door in the dawn light; no need to find out what had happened since. That night had come on the heels of a wretched trek through La Sanmartina forest where all waymarks seemed to be missing. To avoid a repeat performance, I opted for the road to Galleno, rejoining the Francigena as it slipped gracefully back into its past, paved with wheel-rutted stones of great antiquity. The stone track leads down through oak and ash woodland to Greppi Bridge and Greppi Hostel – landmarks which pilgrims of the Middle Ages would have noted in their itineraries, as they would have the Romanesque abbey of St Peter in Pozzeveri whose Camadolese Benedictine community dedicated themselves to the care of passing pilgrims. When I came this way in the summer of 2010, the brick and stone shell of the church was derelict; birds nested in the belfry, and from the rickety panels of its locked doors hung this angry placard:

"The abandonment of this historical building, which dates back to the 10th century, is a disgrace. We call upon the community of Badia Pozzeveri to save this church."

Two years on, I was thrilled to see scaffolding embracing the narthex and to spot young people of both sexes at work round the walls of the nave. They were archaeologists, or – to be exact – bio-archaeology students from Ohio State University, excavating the graves. Their director was the head of Ohio State's Department of Anthropology, Clark Spencer Larsen; bearded and grey as becomes a senior academic, with dark rimmed spectacles, and the top of a blue pen protruding baton-like from the pocket of a neat short-sleeved blue shirt, he looked and talked as if he were the conductor of a symphony orchestra.

"My students are the brightest," he assured me, as if I were an envoy sent from Heaven to inspect his work. "We take only the best, so the dead here are getting first class attention." I noticed afterwards from the card he gave me that he is Distinguished Professor of Social & Behavioral Sciences; and a small Camaldolese devil made me wonder what an 'undistinguished' professor of the same discipline might be.

The Ohio State dig is the first stage of a programme to restore and renovate this ancient building, which is therefore in some way being brought back to life by the skeletons which lie buried in its shade – some of them, no doubt, once pilgrims.

This time, I was allowed inside. My eye travelled directly to an angel floating above a cloud of vibrant blue, the surviving fragments of a fresco which once covered the entire apse and chancel. The body of the church was in a similar state of decay, the loft stripped of its organ; but the stone floor of the nave was a living workshop, with young students examining and testing the bones that they had retrieved from the nearby graves.

Back in the sunlight, I watched two of the students, cross-legged on the sandy ground, intently dusting off a skeleton, its hands joined together in prayer, apparently at peace in the shallow grave, which the 21st century had now disturbed. These Ohio apprentice bio-archaeologists are unfolding a story of medieval burials, children's graves, plague pits and more recent entombments, and at the same time they are uncovering the foundations of the former monastery and its cloister: they are opening a peephole onto the long chronicles of the pilgrimage to Rome, and in so doing breathing new life into the Abbey Church.

The Via Francigena resonates in the Province of Lucca, and the local communes have bedded in freshly gravelled paths on the way to Porcari where I ran into Emily and Claire Macht, Canadian sisters walking to Rome from Lausanne; they simply wouldn't believe that anyone could be mad enough to be doing it all over again in reverse. I approached the next town, Capannori, on tip-toe, concerned that I might run into the pensioner who had lured me into his house on my way south to make me read Dante aloud to him and his grandson.

By the time I had got to Lucca, I had done 32 kilometres. Gail wouldn't have enjoyed the day; it was one of the hottest so far. Before meeting her, I did the formalities – popping into the Duomo of San Martino to obtain my pilgrim stamp and pausing in the shade outside to tackle a triple-toned *gelato*. Now I could make my way to the hotel; Gail was waiting for me outside, her boots firmly left to kick their heels on the floor of our room for the last 48 hours. Relieved and re-born, she had devoted her time to Lucca's Romanesque churches and *Quattrocento* sculptures.

"This is the way to be a pilgrim," she said, taking me by the arm and leading me back to the Duomo to share her wonder at the marble tomb of Ilaria del Carretto. The sculptor was Jacopo della Quercia; here, more than 600 years ago, he succeeded in capturing for all time the beauty of this Lucchese aristocrat, who died at 26 in childbirth. The contemplation of Ilaria's tranquil repose was the prelude to a tender afternoon together.

When I set out from Rome I had only the smallest confidence that I would make it all the way to England in one go. In the back of my mind was the notion that I could complete the return trip in stages; it didn't matter, after all, because I had already done the outward leg. Besides, I had a melancholy let-out clause – the frail health of Prue, my mother-in-law, which might necessitate an instant return to Coggeshall. But in Lucca I was now 400 kilometres into my walk home, and for the first time I began to imagine that I could actually do it all in a single arc, or, failing that, get over the Alps before packing it in for the season. Pausing north of the Alps would make the logistics of starting again next year that much easier.

My social rounds in Tuscany now over, and with Gail flying home from Pisa, I was free once more to make my own timetable and cover larger distances. I decided on a day by the sea to celebrate the milestone. I slipped out of our hotel on Piazza del Giglio shortly before 6.00 am with the first rays of the sun catching the tall campanile of the church of San Michele, and turned west down the narrow street of San Paolino to the archway of the old city walls and then threaded through the suburbs to the banks of the River Sérchio. The tree-lined path beside the stony river-bed was deserted, and I began to sense myself moving with a new assurance and swiftness. A fortnight out from Rome, I had reached the stage when walking was almost effortless; in time with nature, not against it.

Crossing the river at Ponte San Pietro, I saluted the statue of the saint guarding the central arch of the bridge. Did I imagine it, or did the Apostle, with staff in one hand and keys of Heaven in the other, the first Bishop of Rome, not look distinctly miffed that I was going in the 'wrong' direction? In any case, he caught me out a few kilometres later by making me miss the waymark to a good footpath by the church of San Michele Arcangelo; this meant walking by road to the hamlet of Piazzano. It was a steep climb in densely timbered country through which, once in a while, I could catch glimpses ahead of the hilltop villages of Stabbiano and Fibbialla. They were in the foothills of the Apuan Alps, and I would stay on their forest slopes through Valpromaro and Camaiore until the far side of the hills began to reveal distant views of the Mediterranean towards which I descended to the quarry town of Pietrasanta, just three kilometres from the coast.

I had missed Pietrasanta on my way down to Rome, but now I had a chance to see it in party mood. The town was marking the 80th birthday of its adopted son, the Colombian sculptor Fernando Botero, by throwing open its streets to an outdoor exhibition of his work. The Piazza del Duomo had been taken over by horned-eared horses and exaggeratedly curvaceous houris, while the adjacent streets sprouted similarly striking presences hewn by the sculptor from the marble of the Apuan Alps. In the same way that Michelangelo drew his best marble from nearby Carrara, Botero has set up a second home in Pietrasanta to be close to his quarry, and the town was now honouring him, although the scale of his work, set against the backdrop of the modest Romanesque duomo, looked more like an invasion than an exhibition.

Once again I chose the same watering hole by the sea – the elegant Hotel Coluccini at Marina di Pietrasanta – and although the staff welcomed me back with open arms and furnished me with a room and a terrace overlooking the umbrella-dotted beach and the blue Mediterranean, the place didn't feel so special: even though I had walked 40 kilometres in the day, I was arriving at the sea far too early on my return journey. Walking south to Rome, I had reached here after seven weeks on the road, and the pleasure of wading into the water, letting go and floating away on the wavelets, was unsurpassable. This time, on the road for just two weeks, I felt almost guilty entering the sea; I hadn't done enough to deserve it. But forget that: I set my guilt aside and spent a day dipping in and out of the water and lazing on a sunbed, and wondering what a similar day would be like should I ever reach Calais.

As I set out north along the seafront early the following morning, the succession of private beaches, with their names invitingly blazoned on arched gateways, provided me with a source of delight: *Roma Imperiale*, *Divina Provvidenza*, *Orizzonte*, *Haiti*, *Miami*, *Pirata*, *Maddalena*, and finally, before I left the seafront, *Reality Disco Bar*. The beaches gave out by the port of Marina di Carrara, where huge slabs of marble, some even larger than standard 20-foot-long containers, were stacked on the dockside waiting to be shipped, most to be sawn into bathroom and kitchen tops, but maybe just a few to re-emerge in some faraway land from the blade of a sculptor's chisel. From Luni Mare, at the mouth of the River Maga, I turned inland towards Sarzana where I had stayed on my way down. This pretty town with its loggias, narrow streets and Tuscan liveried black and white stone duomo would now serve me for my lunch – a plate of pizza and three cold bottles of water, which I stashed in my rucksack before an afternoon which promised heat. The path I would be climbing I recalled as both precipitous and ill-waymarked. Harry had assured me that the waymarks were now more plentiful, but he had described the section from Sarzana to Aulla, over the spur of the Apennines, which runs down to the Gulf of La Spezia, as the worst of all the climbs. It was also, I recalled, where I had become hopelessly lost on my way to Rome.

This time, I was heading for a bed & breakfast at Ponzano Superiore, the second part of its name signalling that I would be climbing high. A promising track led up through olive groves to the ruins of the Castello della Brina, where, sitting in the shade of a tumbled round tower, I enjoyed what turned out to be my final panoramic views of the Mediterranean.

The bed & breakfast, La Costa, was a little way beyond the village, on its own ridge above the valley surrounded by its own fields of olives and vines. My stay there was marred by an unfortunate incident. Having checked in and cooled off with a swim in the pool, I returned to my room to write up the log of the day's 40 kilometres – I always tried to do this before heading out – and I had then walked back to Ponzano Superiore to explore the alleyways around its miniature piazza and admire the church of San Michele with its outdoor relief of the saint spearing a dragon on the adjoining wall. By the bastion that commands views of the valley, I sat enjoying a beer at the only bar before returning to La Costa. It was then that I discovered that I had somehow left my pen open on the bed and that ink had oozed out onto the pink bedspread. I owned up and my hostess, Signora Giannoni, took it away to wash, and while it was whirling away in the washing machine she served me a dinner of homemade pasta and pesto, with salad and *rosato* wine from the estate. For taste and freshness, especially the sweet onions and garlic flavoured beans, it eclipsed just about every restaurant I had visited. But this lovely meal ended on a sour note; after dinner I was presented with the calamitous news that the stain had not come out in the wash. I sheepishly offered €10 for dry cleaning. But did that mark ever come out? It haunted me for days, and even now it still disturbs me, because I pride myself on always leaving my rooms spotless and exactly as I find them, even to the extent of restoring electric plugs to their rightful sockets and hanging up wet towels. But I like to think that my hostess forgave me; she thrust two boiled goose eggs into my pockets as I left early the following morning.

Harry's warning that the next section over the Apennine ridge was hard going, combined with my own bad experience of walking the thickly wooded slopes of Monte Grosso without the benefit of a single waymark, filled me with foreboding. I set off at 5.45 am by way of Ponzano Superiore, and beyond its last straggling houses I found the forest track and walked into a veil of mist. Cloud had descended to 350 metres, and the air dripped with moisture. My shirt was soon soaking wet, and for much of the morning it was as if I were paddling through a rain forest. The shrouded atmosphere, punctured by drips, added to the loneliness. The path was a narrow, steep track that spiralled up to 500 metres through canopies of young sweet chestnut and hornbeam. I passed a remote shepherd's hut, fearing as I approached that I might be set upon by a 'friendly' dog. There was no trace of life, but, providentially since my earlier experience, the waymarking had been much improved. Now, every few hundred metres, I would spot a red and white marker, often with the initials VF. I paused in front of one in particular at the top of the ridge; it was the marker I had finally stumbled upon when I had got lost here two years previously. I looked back at the line of tangled hills from which I had emerged, and I wondered how I had ever found my way out. The path continued along the ridge, crossing a succession of supplementary valleys, one with a stream to leap across, and then made a precipitous descent to the village of Verchietto with its copybook church and campanile. As I lowered myself gingerly down, I thought of Harry and the battle-gear with which he had heaved his way up this path.

A handful of red tiled, shallow roofed houses perched above ancient terraces on the edge of the woods, Verchietto was still asleep. Some houses in the centre of the miniature borgo were arcaded over narrow cobbled lanes, whose dark tunnels heightened the sense of an enclosed and secret world. I could have been back in Tibet, until the eerie stillness was broken by a procession of about a dozen French pilgrims, at their head a priest in walking gear with a pressed shirt and dog collar, advancing vociferously towards me up the track from Bibola. They were surprised to learn that I was walking back home, away from Rome.

"Rome is our goal," said the priest. "I am not sure whether meeting you brings it closer or further."

"Don't worry," I said. "You have a nice climb ahead today; then you will be down on the coast, and Rome will feel a good deal closer."

I wished them well and, walking on for a few hundred metres, ran into two stragglers.

"You must be the last of the 12 apostles," I said.

"Not apostles, but penitents," replied a woman in her thirties, giving the distinct impression that she would rather not be there. I could see from the deep furrows around her eyes that she was struggling, and, recalling Gail's recent battles with Tuscan hills, I tried to reassure her.

"It will be easier after tomorrow," I said.

At last the cloud began to lift. The French pilgrims had opened up a new line of thought, and, as the Magra Valley spread out below me in the sun, I began to play with it. Pilgrims who came this way in the Middle Ages were of course almost all penitents, seeking remission and pardon for their sins. Maybe modern pilgrims are, without knowing it, also penitents. Perhaps we, too, are walking to cover our tracks, or to stamp out and obliterate the things that we do not like about our everyday lives.

Aulla, one of the stops on my way to Rome, did not keep me long. I dropped into the abbey church of San Caprasio to salute the 9th century Provençal hermit for whom it is named, and whose relics helped encourage pilgrims to use this route. When I last passed this way, the tomb beside the high altar was under restoration and looked like a gaping wound. Its stone cladding, having suffered major damage from a World War II bomb, was now fully reinstated, and the saint could at last be said to be at rest once more; its completion marked a significant stage in the programme to restore the abbey to its former glory.

Upstream from Aulla, I remained in relatively flat country, and for the rest of the morning I sauntered up the western flanks of the Magra Valley on chestnut-shaded lanes with the traffic of the A15 autostrada humming alongside the river below me. The day took one last bite out of me – a stiff climb up to the borgo of Lusuolo where I had reckoned on finding lunch. Instead, the place was deserted; but I found a fountain by the gateway below the ruined castle, and made do handsomely with its water and the two goose eggs that my hostess had given me as I left La Costa. They would, of course, have been improved with some bread and salt, but, ravenous, in a deserted hamlet in the Lunigiana foothills, I wasn't complaining.

Two things compromised my return to Pontremoli – the onset of cloud and drizzle and, I admit it, my own impatience. Ai Chiosi, the farmhouse bed & breakfast that had been such a delight on my way south, was shuttered, and my hostess, when I called her mobile, wouldn't be back for three hours. Reluctantly, because I was tired and damp, I pushed on into the town, having clocked the signs for the Napoleon Hotel. A brash new box, it would have to do; and it did. I was not ready to spend my last afternoon in Tuscany sitting in the drizzle. Rain or no rain, Pontremoli came to life in the evening; they were gearing up for tango in the main piazza, but long before the dancing began, having wrapped myself round a plate of *spaghetti alle vongole* and finished a bottle of white wine, I was fast asleep.

THREE
Plain Sailing

The night porter at the Hotel Napoleon grudgingly provided an early breakfast for me, and I was back on the road at 5.30 am – a road, indeed, which would last me through the next two days. The SS62 over the ridge of the Apennines dividing Tuscany from Emilia-Romagna is an ancient route, superseded by a more direct autostrada which cuts through the hills, and which is therefore now virtually traffic free. Another glorious day of clear skies and bright, burning sun lit up a rapidly changing landscape of interlocking valleys, among which the old road snakes along natural contours up to the Cisa Pass. To the east, swathes of forest fell away towards the jagged hilltops of the higher Apennines with cut-out fields dotted about their lower slopes, while to the west, far below me, I could make out the thin line of the Magra Valley and its river. The morning's ascent to the Cisa Pass was more than 800 metres, hot work in such sun, and I was grateful for the fountain of pure water I found at the mountain village of Montelungo. As I was filling up, an elderly villager approached and told me in no uncertain terms that I was going the 'wrong' way.

"Rome is to the south," he said. "You are going north."

"I know," I replied. "I like doing things backwards."

He went away shaking his head.

I had another reason for stopping in Montelungo. Walking to Rome, I had visited a roadside bar here which served the most delicious home-made *torta dei frutti di bosco*, and this morning I was intent on proving it wasn't a mirage. In the dimly lit interior of the bar, almost windowless and characteristic of a mountain dwelling, I could just make out a plastic cover with the selfsame round tart inside. The *padrone* cut me a slice and I took it out to a sunlit table. That second slice, its forest fruits glowing on my fork, washed down by a second iced tea, so far exceeded my expectations that my disappointments way back down in Pontremoli were instantly forgotten.

These simple pleasures carried me to the pass itself. Formerly the frontier post between Parma and Piacenza and the Grand Duchy of Tuscany, it is today a single listless street of stone houses, carved into pine forest at over 1,000 metres above sea level; at the far end there is a flight of steps to a modern chapel. I climbed to the top to take in the view back down the valley road and say another goodbye to the Tuscan stage of my journey. Pausing for another *tè freddo*, I pressed on down to Berceto, which sits invitingly in the Manubiola Valley among the lower folds of the Apennines.

The welcoming red-tiled rooftops of the miniature city, banked around the square 12th century campanile of the Duomo, appeared at the first big bend of the SS62 from the pass; and there a Via Francigena sign took me onto forest tracks and out of the full glare of the midday sun. A sudden crashing in the undergrowth announced a sounder of wild boars. As a result of recent restrictions on hunting boar, there are increasing numbers roaming the Italian hills, and they make unpredictable walking companions. They are dangerous when the females are on heat, but none were rutting for mates and they scampered off.

I arrived shortly after midday at Berceto, without a hole in my leg, and satisfied with the day's progress. The Alps and the Jura were still before me, but I had walked 28 kilometres over a high Apennine range in seven hours, and I had eaten the best *torta* in the world and braved – politicians apart – a gang of Italy's most dangerous creatures.

Berceto retains a medieval core of narrow streets encircling the Duomo; its preserved stone façades constitute a tourist Mecca. My early arrival gave me time to buy postcards and send them, an increasingly quaint practice, but still more personal than its successors – SMS, email and Facebook – but once again I found myself up against the old, over-regulated Italy. Vendors of postcards do not usually also sell postage stamps, that being the privilege of the *Tabacchi* through which the state maintains its monopoly on both tobacco and stamps. There are just two outlets in the centre of Berceto with the white-on-brown 'T' sign – a bar and a *Tabaccheria*, and on the day of my arrival they had both contrived to run out of 85 cent stamps. As it was by now afternoon, the *Poste Italiane* was also closed. I raged at the inefficiency of it all. I was only trying to put Berceto on the map for my friends, and my cards of the Romanesque tympanum of the Duomo of San Moderanno had to wait until the next day to be posted.

Before leaving the SS62 on my way down from the Cisa Pass, I had noticed signs warning people not to pick mushrooms. Like the sale of its postage stamps, Italy regulates its mushrooms and decrees a strict mushroom hunting season. In fact, it takes mushrooms so seriously that they are classified into more than a dozen families, among them *funghi, porcini, champignon, gallinaccio*, *prataiolo* and *ovolo*. The restaurant at the Albergo Da Rino, where I was staying, has built its reputation on them, and it would have been churlish not to eat them – a platter of assorted grilled mushrooms in garlic for a starter, followed by *tagliatelle ai funghi,* made for a great repast and for dreams untroubled by boars and bureaucrats.

A full moon hung in the western sky as I climbed away from Berceto at dawn on 2nd August. I was heading for the village of Cassio, over the last high pass of the Apennine foothills before they surrender to the Taro Valley and the gently rolling country beyond which beckoned me down to the plains of northern Italy. With every step north, the horizon ahead of me expanded, and I could gaze into more and more distant valleys. The landscape around me grew lighter as cultivation replaced forest and the hillsides regained their mantle of fields and meadow.

I kept to the SS62, which remained virtually traffic free; just the odd motorbike to disturb the quiet morning. The roadside here is peppered with Via Francigena waymarks – milestones with the icon of the bearded pilgrim with his staff and satchel whom I would meet again in a few days' time in his original sculpted guise at Fidenza. A corkscrew bend where engineers have reinforced the banks with concrete has retained its overlay of anarchist messages. On my way down, I recorded graffiti calling for the abolition of all armies and of all frontiers. The same angry tagger, perhaps also concerned about the supply of postage stamps, had been back since with a new demand: *Ne Dio, Ne Stato* – Neither God, Nor State.

Reaching Fornovo di Taro, I forsook the hotel I had stayed at last time, the Cavalieri, for lunch in the centre of town, where I shared a table outside a bright, glass-fronted modern café with a Polish couple who were walking to Rome. They were puzzled by the direction I was taking, and even more bemused that I had some Polish, picked up when I was Reuters correspondent in Warsaw during the Solidarity Revolution in the early 1980s.

"This is a very cosmopolitan place," I explained, warming to my role as an Anglo-Irishman speaking Polish in an Italian city. "Fornovo di Taro was liberated at the end of World War II by the Brazilians."

I should perhaps have held my tongue. Although they had no choice in the matter, the Polish nation had stuck steadfastly to the fight against Hitler all the way from 1939 to 1945 – they had gone the full distance both at home and abroad, only to be rewarded after the war with four decades of Communist rule. The Brazilians, on the other hand, had jumped in at the last minute to catch the anti-Fascist tide. The Polish couple found this hard to swallow. It didn't seem fair to them that Brazil had even been allowed on board at the tail end of the war.

"It's my belief that history isn't fair," I said. "If it were, there would be no need for historians. In any case, the Italians also came to the party quite late in World War II, and they re-wrote their own history. The Italians talk of the war of liberation from the Fascists, conveniently forgetting the years during which the vast majority of them were enthusiastic devotees of their own home-made dictator, Benito Mussolini, and he held the copyright on Fascism itself."

I am not sure if my speech quite undid the damage; but we parted friends, the Poles heading south in the proper direction, while I continued north. But I can't have been entirely misguided, because a few minutes later I came to a Via Francigena waymark at the bridge over the River Taro which pointed to both Rome and Canterbury – the first signpost to the city of St Augustine on my homeward journey. Less welcome was the digital gauge on the tower of a large cement plant indicating a temperature of 36 Celsius. Once across the bridge, I followed the footpath that skirted the dry riverbed up to the town of Felegara, where I found an *ufficio postale* that was actually open. A sheaf of postcards and all my southern maps despatched to England, I turned up the pretty Dordone Valle towards the thermal springs of Sant' Andrea Bagni, walking besides lush pasture, clearly till recently fed from the river, and now alight with summer flowers.

The town is typical of old-style spas with grandiose buildings and oversized hotels no longer seeming to occupy a place in today's health regimes, which are more geared to medication than cures in thermal baths. The grandeur was gently decaying, but its desertedness may have been deceptive – it was after all August, when most Italians are swimming not in sulphur, but in the salt sea.

I stayed in the Hotel Salus – a place once good enough for Field Marshal Kesselring, the commander-in-chief of Hitler's army in Italy. He had fought a determined and masterful retreat up the Italian peninsula, making the Allies pay dearly for every river crossing, summit and ridge, and for a time he headquartered his military command in a bunker in the hill at the back of the hotel. He was popular, both with his men and his Führer, but also with his opponents in the Allied armies who bestowed on him the nickname 'Smiling Albert'. After the war, Kesselring maintained that the Italians, far from putting him on trial for war crimes, should have built a statue to him for preserving so much of their country's heritage and for saving many lives. This was not a view shared by Italian partisans, who blamed Kesselring for a number of brutal reprisals for which a British military war crimes trial in Venice in 1947 sentenced him to death. The sentence was commuted, and the old Marshal was set free in 1952 to live out his last years in West Germany, where he died in 1960 aged 74. It was perhaps not his fault, but his memory is not much revered in Sant' Andrea Bagni: in a failed attempt to blow up his bunker, the Allies bombed the town on 12th November 1944. It is not clear whether the Field Marshal was even there, since he was at the time recuperating from a battlefield wound.

Be that as it may, the Hotel Salus took a direct hit only to be rebuilt after the war in a style replicating its Mussolini-era swagger. The cavernous entrance is encased with marble and would make a fitting set for the Pharaoh's tomb in the final act of Verdi's *Aida*. The spa's baths were closed, so I made do with some foot cream from the local *farmacia*, and dined on the terrace of the hotel on pasta and fizzy white wine, alone but for the smiling ghost of Albert von Kesselring at my side.

Starting in half darkness, I swapped Apennine summits for the hillocks that step down to the Pò Valley; from Miano, the first village above Sant' Andrea, I could see the flat plains ahead, stretching to infinity. The shallow slopes are scored intermittently with gullies, ridges of scorched bare earth and strips of scrub forest, like the tops of overturned shells, giving the landscape an almost lunar quality, a sense heightened by the moonlight itself radiating in the dawn sky. A start so early would allow me to spend much of the day in Fidenza, a city which, perhaps of all my landfalls on my southward journey, had helped to unlock the meaning of my own pilgrimage.

Crossing the Recchio Valley down a white track descending in a broad arc among tawny-red fields of stubble to a now reduced trickle of a river and then climbing what proved to be one of the last sinewy spurs to an outlying farm of the hamlet of Cella, I was greeted by a fierce-looking Alsatian dog. Unversed in the ways of pilgrims, the unleashed animal did not seem to be expecting me, but I need not have worried; a trim man in his 60s appeared and brought Bonzo quickly to heel. Not an obvious farmer, I thought, noting his shorts and singlet and the sun-hat over bushy grey hair. I thanked him for his courtesy.

"*Non fa niente*," he said. "Think nothing of it. You are in Emilia-Romagna, and we are the very nicest of Italians."

Roberto had worked in Asia most of his adult life as a power station engineer. Retirement had brought him back home to manage a dairy farm supplying milk for the prime local product – *Parmigiano* cheese. It was hard to think of more contrasting lives. He invited me inside his comfortable, modest farmhouse, sat me at his kitchen table and poured fresh lemonade, insisting that I share bread and olives. I could hardly refuse; if I had, in my concern to press on quickly to Fidenza, how else would I have made the connection between cheese-making and earthquakes?

Nearly one million 'wheels' of *Parmigiano*, a third of the region's annual production, had been damaged in the recent quake, Roberto told me. Whole stacks of wheels, weighing 40 kilos and worth over €700 apiece, had come crashing down inside the warehouses where they are stored to mature – they had not been built to withstand seismic shocks of this magnitude. Like much else in Italy, the €1.2bn Parmesan industry was suffering badly in the recession.

Back outside, Roberto pointed to the parched valley I had just traversed.

"We've had no rain for three months. You can see the hills are being sucked dry. Strange things are happening here now."

"But there are always droughts in Italy," I countered, drawing on my three years' experience of the country as a Reuters correspondent based in Rome. "Summers are often bone dry."

"Not as dry as this year. Why, only last night I saw a pack of wolves racing across the hill over there. They were looking for water; they were raging with thirst."

"Perhaps it was the nearly full moon," I said as we shook hands, recalling the glowing hemisphere I had seen in the western sky these last two mornings, and also my threatening encounter with a lone wolf on my way to Rome. I was glad, in any case, that I had run this gauntlet without knowing what could have been waiting for me back there along the dry riverbed. All that had stirred, as I followed the path across, were grazing deer.

Approaching Fidenza, the dairy farms and arable fields gave way to vineyards, and although it was still only mid-morning I could feel the full blast of the sun as I finally came down to the plains. This miniature city is a key staging post on the Via Francigena new and old; the south tower of its Duomo sports a sculpted frieze of pilgrims from the Middle Ages, the perkiest of them brought back to life as the graphic symbol of the modern pilgrim route. Fidenza is in effect mission control of the Via Francigena; it hosts its corporate headquarters, the seat of the *Associazione Europea delle Vie Francigene*. The pilgrim centre beside the Duomo reminded me of my encounter with the charming Flora to whom, on my way to Rome, I had explained the modalities of my journey; she had chosen to question my status as a pilgrim, insisting that the Via Francigena office was there to help poor pilgrims, those who needed to stay in hostels and parish houses; as for pilgrims who lodged in hotels, they didn't count and weren't to be helped. Two summers later, as I walked in shortly after ten o'clock, Flora was still there, but she didn't recognise me, though in the meantime she had lost none of her native charm.

"The waymarks are much improved since I was last here," I told her. "But there are still some bad patches."

Barely looking up from her desk, Flora shrugged her shoulders. "What do you expect? Haven't you noticed that there is a crisis in Italy? The Communes have no money for footpaths."

Yet elsewhere in Fidenza I was welcomed back with open arms – at the *Centro di Benessere* quite literally with four of them. On my way to Rome, a young girl from Romania, Loredana, had worked magic on my sore thighs, and as soon as I had coaxed my pilgrim stamp out of Flora and checked into the Astoria, I called to book a return visit. When I arrived at the brand-new building in the southern residential quarter of Fidenza, I explained to Ernesto, the manager, that I was a returning customer, but with the difference that, this time, I was walking back to England. He parked me in a cane chair on the shaded terrace at the entrance, opened a bottle of mineral water for me, and told me to wait and rest. I had nothing better to do than watch Ernesto's customers arrive for beauty treatments and a workout in the basement gym. Normally, after 20 minutes, my patience would have worn thin, but I had arrived in Fidenza early in the day and there were plenty of hours left. It was, besides, sheer pleasure just to be sitting.

And then I was being overwhelmed with a totally different pleasure: I had been ushered upstairs to one of the treatment rooms – clean, fresh and spacious – where to my surprise stood the same Loredana, smiling shyly, her long auburn hair swept up in a bun. She remembered me well enough to enquire whether my sunburned back had recovered; on the way south it had taken a direct hit from the sunrays and ever since, as a precaution, I had walked, cowboy style, with a handkerchief protecting my neck.

From the moment I lay down on the couch, an even bigger surprise was in store. I began to feel strange sensations all over my body – first a very forceful pressure on my shoulders and almost simultaneously, or so it felt, a gentle rubbing on my bruised thighs. I glided away like a leaf over water and, almost at the point of sleep, I suddenly twigged that Loredana was not alone. She had been joined by a colleague. Fidenza certainly knows how to look after its returning pilgrims; Ernesto had arranged a four-handed massage.

For much of the afternoon I sought out the company of the pilgrims of the 12th century – the carved figures on the southern tower of the Duomo who had so inspired me in 2010. My particular friends are the mounted knight with his hunting leopard, also on horseback, and the cowled pilgrim on foot, staff in hand and satchel over his shoulder. With a few touches of artistic licence, this is the pilgrim who has become the emblem of the modern Via Francigena.

But other figures also caught my eye. A sculpted frieze on the right of the main façade preserves marvellous contemporary vignettes – a lion cub playing with its mother at one end and human lion hunters at the other. In between are two smiling pedlars, a couple who seem to be pulling each other's ears – most probably in anger – and another engaged in something more intimate: the beswoded soldier has one hand slipped inside the lady's dress. He looks pleased with his action and possibly also with the reaction; the lady is demure and startled, one arm clasped over her breasts, the other aloft in surrender or alarm. As night fell on Fidenza, I returned to my sculpted friends to dine within sight of them on the terrace at the Trattoria del Duomo.

Since leaving Rome, I had invariably managed to negotiate some form of sustenance before setting out. The Hotel Salus, for instance, had left me a plate of fruit, juice and yoghurt in the cavernous dining room. But the Astoria in Fidenza failed me. That is how I found myself rattling the platform-side door of Fidenza's station buffet, a stone's throw from the Astoria, a few minutes after 5.00 am, the time it was meant to open.

This was not a good move. When the bar's owner finally got round to opening the glass door and letting me in from the platform entrance, where I had been waiting, it was soon evident that he was both hung over and thoroughly bad tempered. It was Saturday morning.

"What do you want breakfast for at this hour?" he demanded. "There are no trains until six."

"I am not catching a train. I am walking," I said.

"What?" he snapped, "in the middle of summer. What sort of lunacy is this?"

He and I were not going to bond, so I asked for bread; and tea with cold milk as well, *per piacere*.

"Cold milk, my God, what next! Why the devil do you want to put cold milk in tea?"

I had no answer, secretly agreeing with him that squeezing lemon, as they do in Italy, makes a more refreshing tea than adding milk. I had ordered the cold milk out of habit. I meekly took my milk and tea and sat at my table waiting for the bread.

"I have to defrost the loaf first," he said. "It will take a few minutes."

"Well, please be as quick as you can," I replied. "I want to get away as soon as possible."

"Where are you walking?"

"Piacenza."

"But that's just up the road! Are you quite mad? Why do you need to leave so early?"

Our conversation petered out and I ate breakfast in silence. All right, the *padrone* could have been more welcoming, and I could have been more patient. But I privately acknowledged that his comments were not totally out of place.

The city of Piacenza was indeed just up the road – 38 kilometres in a dead straight line on the Via Emilia, the Roman road constructed as a military thoroughfare by Aemilius Lepidus in 187 BC, down which many pilgrims will have passed in the Christian centuries, while the modern Via Francigena meanders along country lanes to the north and south of this direct route. The 17 kilometres these meanderings add to the distance ensure that most walkers following this section of the Via Francigena take two days, breaking the journey halfway at the city of Fiorenzuola d'Arda, a name promoting more than it delivers. I was happy to give a miss to this market-town for a tract of featureless farmland, the birthplace of Giulio Alberoni, the gardener's son who rose to be a cardinal and a minister of Charles III of Spain. I had no wish to stay there. I would walk the Via Emilia, the SS62, and I wanted to gain as much ground as possible before the weekend traffic got going, and that is why I was taking breakfast early on Saturday morning; but I wasn't about to unfold my reasoning to my grumpy host and let him take more pot shots at me. I paid up and walked to the station exit along Platform 1, imagining for one blissful moment that I was about to board a train, and then made my way to the Via Emilia, with a relieved glance up at Fidenza's splendid Lombardo-Gothic town hall, whose crenellated cornices the first rays of sun were coaxing into flame.

The sun, indeed, was a constant of the day, and later I would stab the words Russian roulette into my diary. The Via Emilia has, throughout the length I slogged along it, a consistent margin strip on its left side, and I spent much of the day on it in an unpleasant confrontation with traffic far denser than I had envisaged at the station buffet. Road-walking is not for everyone. There are some purist long-distance walkers who won't ever tread on asphalt and macadam; they will go a long way to avoid both, scouring their maps to find an equivalent footpath. But in covering big distances in crowded Europe, this is not always possible: outside the mountains and other remote regions, there are sometimes no paths and tracks, or none that work. Most walkers, therefore, will happily take to country lanes when there is no alternative. Moving – some would say – into the outer reaches of sanity, there is then also a band of diehards, of whom I am one, who will pit themselves against busy roads such as the Via Emilia.

Walking into a country's native motor-traffic requires determination, and it is a reflective process. At a fundamental level, there is the reassurance that this is a legally permitted activity. Although this will never be an Olympic sport, pedestrians still have the right, astonishingly, to walk on all roads except designated motorways. Until a few years ago, it was quite common to see village folk walking on highways, and, in southern Europe, donkeys and mules as well. Walkers, now, are a rare sight. Cyclists are still there, claiming their rightful space, and motorists on the whole respect them; pedestrians, however, sometimes have to fight for their space, but they do have the one distinct advantage of facing the oncoming traffic, and they can eyeball the 'enemy'. Harry and I had discussed this during one of our evening field calls.

"Actually, they are your friends," he had suggested. "That's the way I like to see passing cars."

To this extent: far from maiming, killing or intimidating his or her prey, every driver that passes, exercising great care, has indeed performed a friendly act. But the reality is that with the concerted speed and concentration of traffic today, drivers don't really see pedestrians most of the time. The walker comes into view at the last second; a touch on the steering wheel and they speed past. Power- driven steering makes avoidance quicker and more effective. The cars to watch, I find, are the old ones, often with elderly drivers and without power steering. They respond more slowly to the wheel and take longer to veer off. Most of the time, I reflect, and I am sure my friend at the station buffet in Fidenza would concur, drivers see people who choose to walk the roadsides as escaped lunatics or down-and-out tramps, or a combination of the two. Walkers are certainly the lowest form of life on the road, vermin almost, and it is easy for them to feel disenfranchised: Mr Toad rules.

And the strip of tarmac between carriageway and ditch, the hard shoulder on bigger roads, provides a lesson in what happens to vermin of all sizes, presenting to eye and nose scenes of carnage, an unbroken trail of dead bodies in various states of decomposition – winged or decapitated birds, ironed-out snakes, squashed rabbits, rotting dogs, crunched badgers and the occasional mangled hedgehog. All around are shards of metal and shreds of rubber tyre that have been washed down the camber by rain and the whoosh of traffic. At foot level, the pilgrim has plenty to see.

Most of these victims have 'bought it' standing or trying to cross, whereas the attentive road walker is ready to take emergency avoidance action, and it should be said that, in many years of walking, I have rarely had to step aside for an oncoming vehicle, let alone jump for my life. The vast majority of drivers are indeed attentive and pretty friendly. That morning, walking up to Piacenza, it may have felt a bit like Russian roulette, but I was never really threatened; there was always a safe distance between me and the polish of passing cars.

Apart from the detritus under foot and the steady stream of traffic on my right side, there wasn't much else to catch my eye. The fields I walked by were ripe with maize and tomatoes, while large wayside hoardings, advertising local brands of Italian dried meats, also told me that I was in salami country. And so, only pausing for *tè freddo* and a slice of lemon cake where the road cut through Fiorenzuola d'Arda,

I covered the 38 kilometres up the Via Emilia in eight hours, just short of five kilometres an hour: the sterling advantage of road-walking is that the smooth surface makes for good speed.

Piacenza is a large city founded by the Romans at the confluence of the two rivers, Pò and the Trebbia; it grew to prominence as a strategic crossroads between Rome and the Alps. The city has several imposing hotels to match its size and continuing status, and once again I had chosen the Grande Albergo Roma, which offered the increasingly rare luxury of a bath, an especially welcome treat at the end of a hard day's walk; for economic reasons, most hotels have torn out their tubs and replaced them with showers. I was in the heart of the city, close to Piazza Cavalli, and I spent the afternoon revisiting city centre sights, including the Lombardo-Romanesque Duomo, whose resplendent colonnaded apse and dome had formed one of my strongest impressions in 2010. That first time, I had missed the marvellous crypt; among its slender columns, I now felt I could easily lose my way, just as in the Great Mosque at Cordoba.

I sat slowly sipping a cool beer at the terrace of a bar in Piazza Cavalli, and returned to the Piazza del Duomo for an al fresco dinner. A party of Macedonians was celebrating a wedding; they had taken over half the tables, and, in between my forkfuls of garlic pasta and mouthfuls of sparkling *Bonarda* red wine, their laughter and song took me back to the wild mountain villages of the Balkans.

Breakfast the following morning was, by comparison, a very quiet affair, served to me at 5.30 am in the fifth-floor dining room, with its panoramic views of the city. The night porter having kindly agreed to look after me so early, I was the sole customer, and, while he laid my place, I stepped outside onto the terrace and watched the sun cast its first rays on the domes and Roman roof tiles of the city below. My bread, cereal and piping hot tea could not have been served in a finer setting, nor more obligingly. Recalling my breakfast in Fidenza, I complimented him on his service.

"We do things in style in Piacenza," he replied. "What else would you expect from a city where Giorgio Armani was born?"

"Good heavens!" I exclaimed. "I had no idea."

"Well, you know, they don't tell you everything in the tourist books."

Nor do they necessarily tell the story of Hannibal, in 218 BC, trouncing the Roman Republic's army either side of the Trebbia, whose riverbed, when dry, affords a shortcut out of the city. But I had taken advice: despite a summer-long absence of serious rain, the braided channels between the shingle were too dangerous to ford. So instead, I crossed by the Via Emilia road bridge and followed its far bank along to the River Pò. Here I had a *rendez-vous* with my old friend Danilo Parisi, ferryman of the river, and recently promoted (in lore and legend) by the redoubtable Harry to the rank and title of Admiral of the Pò.

The Admiral lives in a farmhouse tucked into the lee of the embankment at Soprarivo, a short walk through the maize fields beyond the sleepy hamlet of Calendasco. A terrace, shaded by trees and vines and decked out with tables and chairs, encloses the simple two-storey stone house, and I had expected to see someone there. In fine weather, the patio is the principal living area, indeed the hub of the house, but now there was no sign of life; even this early the ferryman was out plying his trade. I dropped my rucksack by the kitchen door and headed to the riverbank to wait for the throb of his returning launch.

Danilo figures in many accounts of contemporary pilgrim journeys to Rome. A large man, as befits an ex-Rugby player, with a thick nose that obviously took a knock or two, and with wisps of grey on his weathered scalp testifying to a former head of fair hair, Danilo Parisi is like a modern St Christopher. He has been ferrying pilgrims across the River Pò for all of the 15 years since the Via Francigena was formally resurrected in 1998 with a grant from the European Union. He runs his ferry service back and forth from the quay at Corte San Andrea to his home at Soprarivo down the same four kilometre sweep of the river that pilgrims of previous generations crossing from Lombardy to Emilia-Romagna would have taken in a boat propelled by sails and oars. They would have included Sigeric, one of St Augustine's successors as Archbishop of Canterbury, who had the forethought to order a scribe to keep a record of his journey in 990 back from Rome to Canterbury, which is the template for the stages of the modern Via Francigena.

Danilo names his service after Sigeric – *Guado di Sigerico* – but that is the only direct link with the medieval past; pilgrims today have the advantage of being able to book his ferry by mobile phone. He charges only a modest fee, and chiefly plies the river for the love of it. The Via Francigena is his passion. He is not just a ferryman; he is one of the gatekeepers of the modern pilgrim journey to Rome.

Danilo was climbing the bank when I arrived, escorting two more pilgrims. He had expanded around the girth in the two years since we had first met; he was unshaven, and looked drawn. Things had not been easy for him. But this was a special moment for both of us, and we fell into each other's arms. I was one of a handful of returning customers. Most of the people he ferries across the river he never sees again. Their passage, however, is not forgotten. Each one inscribes his or her name in the great leather-bound pilgrim book kept at Soprarivo.

Like almost every honest person in debt-burdened Italy, Danilo is struggling. Recently, his outboard motor had been stolen at night – an expensive piece of kit, because it needs to be powerful enough to punch against the current; after replacing it, and with the small amount he charges each pilgrim, he was barely covering his costs. It is not as if the local authorities give him any help; they had recently installed a new landing stage on the north bank at Corte Sant' Andrea, at a cost, he told me, of €90,000, without even acknowledging his ferry service, let alone contributing towards it.

I spent a few pleasant hours in Danilo's company, accompanying him upstream to pick up two more pilgrims. It was at once apparent that it wasn't just money that was troubling Danilo. The river had silted up and, in high summer, there was so little water by the shore at Soprarivo that he had to moor his boat further up river and, once on board, it was touch and go as the bottom grated over the sand banks until we got into clear water.

"If it carries on like this, people will end up walking across the Pò," I said.

"You may not be joking," Danilo replied.

Our fares were a French girl from Toulouse and her boyfriend from Santander, both uncompromisingly good looking – Laura in a short skirt, yellow tee shirt and colourful bandera holding up her dark hair, and blond, blue-eyed José, dressed in a pair of Nike shorts and a trim grey singlet. They were a Via Francigena couple. Having met the previous year walking a section of the way to Rome, they had joined each other again this summer to complete another stage to Siena, a fair proof of the Spanish saying that the world is a pocket handkerchief: "*el mundo es un pañuelo*."

"My daughter and baby grand daughter live in Santander," I told José as we sped back down the river, the pair of them in the midday heat enjoying that wonderful sensation of the rush of cooling air. I photographed them in a moment of repose and their smiles recalled my own first trip in Danilo's launch. But I could see that José and Laura were grappling with the string of coincidences that had brought them onto a launch on the River Pò with a Spanish and French speaking pilgrim from England who said he was walking to London while palpably travelling south. By the time we had berthed at the embankment close to Danilo's home, however, they had more or less sorted it out.

Back on the terrace, Danilo produced cold drinks, and his official pilgrim stamp and the great pilgrim book – a sort of Domesday record of the Via Francigena. We talked about Harry; he was registered on the 11th July, together with a friend from army days, Jock Davis. Harry had appended a cartoon drawing – a smiley face with eyes and mouth and a quiff of hair, but it was missing its nose. I wondered why, and I was about to learn.

"My God, did they drink!" exclaimed Danilo. "We had to send out for more bottles. It's not often that an Italian house can be drunk dry. But that Bucknall man, it would have been simpler to plunge him headlong into a barrel of wine."

I raised my eyebrows as I slowly drew at my Coca Cola. "I assume you are exaggerating somewhat?"

"Put it this way, the wine went down as fast as one of my fuel tanks," Danilo laughed.

I made a note to call Harry that night and tell him that, out of shame and embarrassment, I had paid his wine bill at Danilo's.

Laura and José signed the book; and now it was my turn. First I leafed through the pages to find my entry in 2010. There it was, and I duly completed the new entry with a note that I had come this way on foot to Rome on 17th July 2010.

The number of pilgrims walking from the Alps or north of the Alps to Rome has grown each year, according to the records that Danilo compiles from his book; in 2012 the annual total exceeded 500 for the first time. This does not take into account the many who walk far shorter distances to Rome, starting for example in Siena, and others, also unaccounted for in his book, who cross into Piacenza by the bridge at Pieve Porto Morone.

When I crossed the River Pò on 5th August 2012, I was the 307th pilgrim of the year, and by the end of 2012 Danilo had ferried a total of 525 pilgrims, compared to 350 in 2011 and 317 in 2010. Of the nationalities crossing on Danilo's launch from the time he began his service to the end of 2012, the overwhelming majority were Italians: 1,300 of them. Next came Swiss, 292, Germans, 246, French, 228, Dutch, 139, British, 66, Belgians, 42, Austrians, 34, Americans, 34, Australians, 30, Spanish, 27, Canadians, 17, Norwegians, 14, Swedes, 13, Danes, 5, Irish, 5, and Polish, 5. Nations with three or fewer pilgrims include Portugal, Vietnam, Estonia, Croatia, Hungary, Russia, Finland, South Africa, Chile and Argentina. Almost all were heading for Rome, but each year there are several driven souls making their way to Jerusalem, Santiago de Compostela and Canterbury.

Danilo has logged 22 pilgrims walking to Canterbury since 1998, against 20 to Jerusalem, and 16 to Santiago de Compostela; no one, as far as he knew, had undertaken the journey to and from Rome on foot. I learned later, however, that a retired Australian lawyer and serial long-distance walker, Andrew Judd, had come this way a few weeks before me on a return journey from Rome to Canterbury via Santiago de Compostela, but it was on a ferry from Santander rather than from Calais that Andrew had made his English landfall. Much later, in our very different homeward journeys, our paths would cross again.

The old house at Soprarivo is in every sense, therefore, a crossroads; and Danilo has enshrined its position as an epicentre of contemporary pilgrimage with a cast bronze plaque on the wall of his house, on which moulded lettering and numerals announce the distances to Rome, Jerusalem, Santiago de Compostela and Canterbury. It told me I had 1,313 kilometres to go to the See of St Augustine.

The two youngsters sent on their southward way, it was time for me to depart. Danilo gave me a slice of homemade fruit tart and refilled my water bottle; my pilgrim passport duly endorsed with his *Transitus Padi – Caupona Sigerico* stamp, we returned to his launch. Assisted this time by Pierfrancesco, Danilo's nine-year-old son who is already on his way to becoming a skilful boatman, we quickly cleared the sand-banks and skimmed upstream – the 'wrong' way – to the new landing stage at Corte Sant' Andrea, where Danilo normally picks up pilgrims. He accompanied me to the top of the steps for a farewell embrace at the place where he normally says hello. Everything was back to front. I was leaving Emilia-Romagna, and I was leaving a friend. It was a sad farewell.

"I'll be back," I promised him, "but perhaps next time in a car!"

My feet now firmly on Lombard soil, I set off along the embankment of the River Lambro, the little town of Orio Litta to my right across an eternity of maize. The track was long and treeless, and down it came a file of pilgrims, their arrival signalled by a telltale cloud of dust in the midday haze. With each one I exchanged friendly greetings. Danilo, good for him, would be busy this afternoon.

Joining the main road at the village of Lambrina, I decided again to skip the vagaries of the Via Francigena and press on directly towards

Pavia. It was quick work, and I arrived in Belgioioso at three-thirty, just in time to check into the only hotel, La Locanda della Pesa, before it closed for the afternoon. I had walked 40 kilometres since Piacenza and journeyed three times across the River Pò, and I was hot and tired. Revived after a shower and a siesta, I spent the afternoon chatting to locals in the London Café, whose name bore no relationship at all to the town's medieval castle just across the street, whose walls were studded with Ghibelline merlons. The word on everyone's lips was "*crisi*". Italy was hurting, weighed down by a sluggish economy and anxiety about the future of the euro.

"You guys were so lucky to stay out of the single currency," a farmer told me.

"Yes, but we are still in a mess. It will take years to clean up after Tony Blair and Gordon Brown. Neither of them were businessmen. At least you had Silvio Berlusconi."

They liked that. The old rascal may have been caught repeatedly with his pants down, but, here in northern Italy, he was seen to be business friendly, although that vision was perhaps a mirage.

The next day's walk to Pavia was completed by 9.15 am, the short hop unexpectedly enhanced by a morning back among the rice-fields. On my way to Rome, the monotony of Italy's paddy fields had got to me, but when I saw them again I could only gasp with delight at those carpets of fresh green shoots, diced up into regular squares by flowing irrigation canals, and brushed in a golden glow by the morning sun. I ambled joyfully between them along the lanes and farm tracks that led through to the Ticino Park and to the suburbs of the city before the heat and mosquitoes could take hold of the day, encountering nobody but a young German pilgrim who wanted to take a picture of the anti-pilgrim walking the 'wrong way'. She carried a shepherd's crook, and one knee was bandaged up. Would she ever get to Rome, I wondered?

After checking into the Excelsior in Pavia, just outside the centre, and dealing with my laundry, I had the rest of the day to renew my acquaintance with the city of a hundred towers. This is how Pavia was known in the 16th century, although there are just a few left today clustered round the old university. My first port of call was not, however, to one of these old defensive towers, but to the tourist office where I was keen to turn back the pages of the pilgrim book that I had signed on my way to Rome. The office is on a piazza off the Corso Cavour, and I was greeted by a tall, courteous Somali. How wonderful to see the visitor centre in one of Italy's great medieval cities in the hands of a migrant from the Horn of Africa; the city's fathers are moving with the times.

He dug out the book from a cupboard and handed it to me with a reverence more suited to a priest serving communion.

"Not many pilgrims ask for it," he said.

"Well, if the book is out of sight and not out on a table, how would they know about it?" I asked. "Surely, nobody is going to walk off with it!"

No surprise therefore that the vellum pages of Pavia's pilgrim book, in such contrast to Danilo Parisi's encyclopaedic *Liber Peregrinorum* a few kilometres to the south, had lapsed into disuse. In the preceding month, only eight people had signed it, and there were not many pages to leaf back through before I found my original entry – "*Brian Mooney, a piedi di Londra a Roma 14 Luglio 2010*".

This time the words spilled out more effusively, and in English.

"Brian Mooney," I wrote, "on the return leg Rome-London. I came 'down' this way from my home in Coggeshall, Essex, via St Paul's in London on 14th July 2010, arriving in Rome on 11th August. In the intervening two years, the waymarking has been much improved."

A dentist's assistant called Sarah, owner of a bulldog and a poodle, pummelled me back into shape and tended to my sore limbs with a massage after lunch. Her mix of domestic dogs baffled me, and I also couldn't help thinking of all those patients about to submit themselves to her boss's dental drill wondering what lay beneath her white coat.

FOUR
Aiming High

It was still dark in Pavia when I crossed the Ponte Coperto the following morning to retrace my steps of 2010 along the sandy track on the south bank of the River Ticino, for much of its way deep in forest. The river ran still and shallow, braiding through a maze of sandbanks on which pelicans already stood guard ready to scoop up their breakfast. Nothing stirred onshore, but as the light grew the Fidenza pilgrim, peeking out of the scrub on intermittent waymarks in his modern Via Francigena livery, kept me sure I was on course.

After a few kilometres, I left the river near the hamlet of Canarazzo, emerging onto a narrow lane, banked high above the rice-fields to make it passable in floods. There, from the top of the dyke, I could now make out a distinct white band to the north. It was not cloud: Italy hadn't seen any in weeks. Far beyond the rice paddies and the elm and plane trees hovered the snowy corona of the Alps.

It would be seven days' marching before I reached them, but I had been stealthily sneaking up on them, planning my campaign with care. The simple option would have been to return via the Grand St Bernard, the classic pilgrim and Via Francigena route over the Alps, the one favoured by Hannibal and Napoleon, this being the easiest and most direct crossing; and, at 2,469 metres, one of the lowest. But I had no appetite to retread that path, and had set my sights instead on the Théodule Pass that joins Cervinia with Zermatt. The route is 46 kilometres longer, and more than a thousand metres higher, but I was drawn irresistibly by the proximity of the Matterhorn, a mountain I had once climbed. That youthful ascent had left me under the spell of this iconic arrow-headed peak, which the French call Mont Cervin and the Italians Monte Cervino – a derivation, it is said, of either the Latin word for forest, *silva,* or the Italian word for stag, *cervo.*

Passing a side street named Via Cervinia on the first day of my walk in the suburbs of Rome had given me a sort of premonition that I would cross the Alps that way – nothing short of superstition, I admit, but long-distance walkers have time to feed on irrational thoughts. I had shared my ideas about crossing the Alps that way, a few days later, at La Locanda Monticelli with the French couple who were making their way to Rome with their three little daughters in a donkey cart. It so happened that Edouard and Matilde had chosen the Théodule Pass on a previous journey they had made on foot to the Holy Land, traversing now war-ravaged Syria in more peaceful times. Edouard assured me that there was a *piste cyclable* along the Rhône Valley on which, once over the Alps, I would be able to make a rapid descent to Lake Geneva, but he warned me that there was a treacherous stretch up the Italian side of the valley from Châtillon to Cervinia.

"There is no footway as such, and the road has some scary tunnels," Edouard had explained. In fact, as it turned out, he was wrong. But he was not alone in believing that there was no footpath up to Cervinia.

That just left the glacier. There is no permanent snow or ice on the Grand St Bernard Pass, making it straightforward to cross in the summer, but the Théodule straddles a glacier with crevasses down which an unprotected hiker could fall and disappear – only to emerge complete with yellow rucksack 3,000 years later. I wasn't about to jeopardise my journey by crossing its icy crust without the right equipment and – more important – without a guide. The days between had given me a lot to think about, and much to arrange.

Now, with the Alps in sight, I set my mind to finalising these arrangements. I had first to settle the day that I would get to Cervinia, and from that, when I would actually make the crossing. I had already arranged a provisional booking for a guide through the Zermatt Guides Office; soon it would be time to firm this up.

Into this equation, I now found myself factoring another person, Ros, a university lecturer in Oman, whom I had first met in 1994 on the North side of Everest. She was keen to join me over the Théodule Pass, but a lot depended on whether her husband, Lew, who was recovering from a heart operation, would be fit enough to travel with her to Chamonix, where they were to spend part of the summer. To share the alpine crossing with an old friend would be a joy, but it threw in other uncertainties. Under an eagle's wings, Chamonix and Cervinia are no distance, but the bus journey is slow and awkward. Then there was the weather; in late summer in the Alps it has a knack of suddenly turning bad, potentially leaving us stuck for a few days in a mountain hut. There were lots of things that could go wrong in that distant line of white that now danced on the horizon in front of me.

Meanwhile, closer to hand, I had more vistas of rice and maize. I walked all day by lane and dusty farm track, once more enjoying the almost dazzling effect of sun on green shoots and sparkling light on irrigation channels, their borders of low shrub bright with red berries. My universe of green was given measure and incident by the occasional stand of plane trees, or by some great Lombard barn, or by an abandoned field-labourers' *cascina*, its roof tiles long caved in, but the brick walls standing, ghost-like, high and proud.

I stopped in Zerbolò, a small town I had much admired on my way to Rome for the way life carried on despite its being sliced in two by the elevated A7 Autostrada. The Café Oasis, where I sat outside for my breakfast – lemon juice and an excellent cake – looks up at the perpetual motion of the motorway, its din muted by glazed side screens which are engraved with swallows in flight.

If Zerbolò was a compromised tranquillity, the real thing awaited me a few kilometres to the west at the Sanctuary of the Madonna della Bozzola. Its large church and convent stand where, according to tradition, in 1465 the Virgin appeared to the young-deaf mute child,

Maria di Garlasco, resulting in a miraculous cure, and the place at once becoming a hub of pilgrimage. Even in the 19th century it was drawing large numbers, sufficient to pay for the church to be dressed up with a new elaborated facade. At mid-morning, as I walked up to it on grassy tracks between the rice paddies, it was utterly deserted. A side door was open, but there was no one beneath the cavernous dome; only the flickers of candlelight under the bronze statues of the Madonna and her child namesake attested to any evidence of human life. But it was cool, and I sat quenching my thirst from the plastic bottle I had refreshed from a tap outside; at least the Virgin supplies free water!

By now I was well to the north of the Via Francigena, intending to leapfrog two of its stages in one day by avoiding the town of Garlasco. I had stayed there on my way to Rome, and it didn't seem to warrant a return visit. I therefore made my way to the rather prettier town of Gambolò with a view to reaching Motara, of which I had good memories. That meant a long day – 45 kilometres – but the town-centre hotel I had stayed in on my journey south was a worthy destination. The slightly antiquated air of the Albergo della Torre, with its bedroom ceiling fans and primitive shower facilities, suited my rustic mood, and there was no doubt, the second time round, of the excellence of its *trattoria.*

It was one more day before I was fully out of the Pò Valley, and for most of the 34 kilometres I covered from Mortara to Vercelli I was struggling: from early on the heat was way up on the previous days, and this last day of rice-fields was not only featureless but also perplexing. The farm tracks bordering the irrigation channels splayed out in multiple directions, each unmarked intersection leaving me guessing which way to go. Even though I had passed this way two years before, I couldn't recall a single landmark till at last I spotted the large red brick farmhouse and its barns at the hamlet of Nicorvo. It was like emerging from a desert, except that I was greeted by something extra-terrestrial – a tractor propelled by four giant wheels, with shiny spuds like the teeth of a circular saw, towing a trailer sprouting two prodigious crop-spraying gantries. The winged locust drove straight at me, before, in a flash, turning and plunging down the bank into the rice-fields.

My next encounter was entirely human; a group of young Italians marching down the narrow lane close to the town of Robbio. They were doing the Via Francigena the hard way, weighed down with packs carrying tents and food; even the youngest was using a walking pole.

"But you are going backwards," one of them said, questioningly.

"No," I replied. "I am going home."

The town of Robbio had struck me with its hospitable air the first time I walked through it. Then it had provided me with a welcome bench outside the little Romanesque brick church of San Pietro; this time, I upgraded and sat at a table outside the Bar Roma, enjoying a lemon juice and a *melanzane* sandwich, directed there by an elderly man's insistence that it was the only place for a pilgrim to take his elevenses in Robbio.

Nourished and reinvigorated, I found myself picking up remembered features from 2010 as I made my way on the road to Palestro before striking south towards the River Sesia, which flows into the Pò from the north. In its higher reaches, fed from alpine glaciers in the Valley of Valsesia, the river is a gushing torrent popular with canoeists and rafters, but in the flatlands of the Pò plain it has grown sedate, with waters now sluggish and turbid; joining the Sesia along its embankment, and, shaded from the blazing sun by eucalyptus and willow, I made my way to the outskirts of Vercelli.

It was early August, approaching noon on a Sunday, and the medieval city was empty. Anyone walking to Rome today will have Vercelli firmly etched on the mind as the arbitrary point at which Volume II of Paul Chinn's three-volume Lightfoot guide ends and so begins Volume III, the final stretch to St Peter's. Living life in reverse, I could now dispose of Volume III and start Volume II, which would take me across the Alps, through Switzerland and into France. In practice I would only be consulting it for a few more sections, but the swap-over was a moment to savour. Just as on first sighting the Alps, I felt I was making progress.

I stayed at the Hotel Matteotti, not ideal, being by the bridge just across the Sesia and a longish hot walk into the city centre. But after a shower and a rest I was ready to re-visit the Duomo and the even more striking Romanesque Basilica di Sant' Andrea. Then, best of all, was my ice cream and cool beer at a café terrace in the Piazza Cavour, the perfect prelude to a relaxed supper of home-made pasta with *zucchini* and prawns.

I wasn't to know it, but 30 kilometres later the next day, August 9th, I would end up in a golf resort. I had walked the *strada provinciale* to Santhià, my intended staging post for the night. But my progress among the last of the flat rice-fields had been so swift that I was well ahead of my usual staging hour. Besides, I had no good memories of Santhià; I had been served revoltingly raw garlic in the town's only hotel, which suffered from its proximity to the railway junction. Here, where seven rail routes converge, even the Via Francigena has to deflect and follow a seemingly endless steel bridge two storeys above the lines. A pause long enough for refreshment was in order, though, before pressing on – with some relief – into the foothills of Piedmont.

But by noon, after 30 kilometres, I had had enough. A phone call to an enticing sounding hotel on the shores of Lake Viverone had proved fruitless: but then I found myself at the entrance to the Cavaglià, a large ochre-coloured colonial style hotel with its own golf course, and decided to investigate. Playing golf, I have come to know many such resorts; they have a certain ambience not usually associated with booted walkers. The girl at the reception in the far corner of the generous foyer looked up with a degree of surprise, disguised behind a warm smile. The hotel wasn't fully booked and, even without playing a round of golf, I would be welcome to stay. Alicia had spent time in London; she was interested in my story and – later in the day – she was to come to my rescue.

My room looked onto a lush fairway rising between ilex and silver birch towards the bunkers and flag at the ninth. This was my first hint of sloping ground since entering the Pò Valley a week before. The temptation to hire clubs and tee off for a round was countermanded by common sense: the hot work of it, and the risk, however remote, of injury, the very reason that a few years earlier I had sacrificed the fun and thrill of skiing to my even bigger passion for long-distance walking. In any case, an afternoon by the pool was not a bad alternative, and I lazed under a sunshade, dipping in and out of sleep – and in and out of the pool – until late in the day. It was a good place, marooned on a golf course, in which to receive an SMS text from Harry with news that he had arrived that same day in Rome.

Back in my room, I experienced one of those uncomfortable moments that come, I imagine, to all long-distance walkers. I had been keeping a close eye on my boots, my most important piece of kit, expecting that they would need re-heeling sometime before crossing the Alps. When I inspected them that afternoon I was taken aback. It was like a driver discovering a puncture; the hot macadam of the Pò plains had melted down the heels. A few days before, there had been plenty of rubber left to burn; they were now reduced to their cores. This abrupt revelation was all too familiar. It had happened with equal suddenness on two occasions on my way to Rome; one day the boot is fine, the next it is rotten.

After a quick calculation, I reckoned that with luck the shredded cores would get me to Cervinia, and with such eventualities in mind I had already stored the number of its tourist office. I called and asked, is there a *calzolaio* in town who could repair my boots?

"Good heavens, no!" replied a helpful female voice. "Everyone here is far too rich to bother with boot repairs."

I managed to get from her the number of Cervinia's main mountain-sports shop. I would buy a new pair, but they had to be the same. I have grown accustomed to walking long distances with one particular make – no other would quite do. I phoned and asked whether they stocked Meindl boots.

"Good heavens, no!" replied the store manager. "Meindl are made in Germany."

"I don't understand. You Italians drive German cars, so why not stock German boots?"

"Because even in the euro crisis there are limits to Italian dignity," responded the manager. "Italians are happy to drive German automobiles, but they wouldn't be seen dead in German-manufactured boots."

I had collided with European boot politics, and it left me with a big problem; how and where to repair my pair, or indeed replace them, to get me over the Alps. I shared my crisis with Alicia at reception. Harry, by now most probably on his second cask of wine from the Alban Hills, had told us in Gambassi Terme that the Via Francigena has its angels. One such was about to put herself in my way.

Did she have any idea whether there were cobblers in Ivrea, where I was headed the next day?

"Not in the town itself," she replied. "But there is a cobbler who works in the Carrefour supermarket at Burolo on the outskirts of town."

I could have kissed her! I would actually be walking that way.

This unofficial angel did me one more favour, plopping the hotel stamp onto my pilgrim passport and authenticating my unexpected halt at a golf resort; the UNA Golf Hotel Cavaglià monogram thus sits casually on the same page as the Via Francigena pilgrim logo from Pavia.

Dinner, strangely enough, was served in the clubhouse of the golf course, a wooden colonial style pavilion surrounded by a terraced verandah from which there were panoramic views of the fairways. Two members were still playing as night fell. From my wicker chair on the terrace I felt I had been transported out of Italy, perhaps to New Orleans, or even to the venerable Kurmitola golf course in Dhaka, and when the menu was laid on my table my imaginary quartering of the globe was complete; everything on it was good ole Texan cuisine.

Firmly focussed on getting to the Burolo supermarket, I was away the following morning and beginning my climb into the wooded Piedmont foothills by 5.25 am. For the first time since leaving the Apennines I felt that familiar tug on my calves as I ascended above Lake Viverone along the narrow lanes of a succession of pretty hillside villages – Roppolo, Viverone, Piverone and Palazzo Canavese – where, after so much raw flood-plain brick, the churches and campaniles were all built of the distinctive local sand-coloured stone. I had been through them before, but this time, and seen from the south, they seemed more imposing, set now against the backdrop of the morainal hills emerging ahead of me which began to dwarf the lake, glistening below in the dawn light.

On another day I might have kicked myself for missing the vineyard track to the ruined Gesiun, a tiny chapel dedicated to Saint Peter, and perhaps on my southward journey one of the most haunting structures I had encountered, but my eyes were skinned for the turning to Carrefour at the Burolo shopping centre.

Just as Alicia had assured me, I found Roberto, a swarthy man dressed in blue sweat shirt and jeans, bent over a clunky green lathe in a cubby hole close to the superstore's café. I unbooted and presented the damaged pair for his inspection.

Cobblers, like all artisans, are the same the world over; they will throw up their hands in horror and protest that the job is either very difficult or downright impossible. After that, as if reluctantly offering to perform a miracle, they come up with the solution. Roberto was true to form.

"These need complete resoling, and I don't have the kit to do that," he said.

"Well, what can you do?"

"Fix a new heel."

"As it happens, that's just what I need."

The ritual boot dance completed, I slipped away in my stockinged feet to the store's café to get a coffee each for the two of us. Roberto was pleased by my gesture, and we chatted amiably while he fixed my new heels. I noted he used both glue and nails – the first time I had seen such old fashioned technology applied to a modern boot.

He handed them back with pride.

"The nails are for extra security. They will get you over the Alps."

"And then what?"

"They should be good for England."

Roberto wasn't quite right about that, but his alpine assurance worked wonders for my morale. He had done my Meindls proud.

And now, re-heeled, I was ready for Ivrea: a very different city from the one I had visited two years previously. That is to say, my 2012 experience of it was to be a revelation. On my first visit, I had confined myself to the old city and the cobbled streets around the cathedral and castle. Ivrea's distinguished modern history as the capital of the typewriter, or at least of the Olivetti typewriter, had all but passed me by. Looking back, I now find it amazing that I could have visited and written about Ivrea with scarcely a mention of Olivetti, and I owe my understanding of the scope of Ivrea's debt to that once-great company to a chance encounter with an enigmatic but engaging young Ivrean woman called Michaela.

Olivetti is a remarkable story of both industrial and architectural innovation. Two generations built up the business until by the 1950s and 1960s the company was producing about one third of the world's typewriters and calculators and employing 24,000 staff worldwide, more than half of them in Ivrea. Olivetti didn't just sit on its laurels; it was an early pioneer in electronics and of the personal computer, and Adriano Olivetti, the son of the founder, was also an innovative builder of factories, offices and housing for his staff on the scale of a Medici. But Adriano's untimely death in 1960, combined with the disastrous acquisition of the American manufacturer Underwood and the advance of the microchip, set in trail the great firm's slow dissolution. Weighed down by debt and outpaced by cheaper competition from Asia and Silicon Valley, the company was taken over and effectively closed down as a manufacturer in 2003.

Michaela lives in one of the most unusual Olivetti buildings – an amphitheatre of duplex flats just across the Dora Baltea River, dug out of a hillside behind Via Jervis, on which stands the company's state-of-the-art 1950s glass fronted and trellised factory. The buildings on Via Jervis were commissioned from Italy's top architects, and today form part of an exciting open air museum of town planning and urban architecture; the products may have disappeared into history, but Olivetti's buildings remain as its lasting legacy.

Stretched out on the massage couch at Michaela's duplex, I gazed up through a glass domed ceiling light to the bright blue above, while an entire window-wall, subtly dished, looked onto a grassy bank; the apartment itself was cut out of the round like a slice of cake, making everything in it a little off square – including Michaela, who told me how these flats had been built for Olivetti executives, and how she had studied to be a doctor, and how – apparently connected with the collapse of Olivetti – something had gone badly wrong for her.

"Everybody has their hidden histories," she said without elaborating.

A younger Joanna Lumley in Italian, she was beginning to arouse my interest. I wanted to prise out her secrets; but none of my probes got any further, except in our shared loved of mountains. She, too, had climbed in the Alps.

"I made it up Castor some years ago, near where you are heading," she said.

"Wasn't that the mountain which lost its top?" I asked, recalling the dramatic collapse of the summit ridge.

"Yes, you can never really trust a mountain – a bit like men. Now turn over."

"You must have been good at anatomy, Michaela," I said, drifting into a profound sleep, troubled only by visions of those high peaks ahead.

The following morning, 11th August just after 5.30 am, I walked from my hotel to the station and found a friendly bar; fortified by a breakfast of tea and croissant, I headed briskly out of Ivrea, passing on the way the horseshoe of Olivetti flats where Michaela would surely still be fast asleep. I gave her a wave and, after crossing beneath the A5 autostrada, took a lane due north which instantly presented me with a wall of mountain tops set on fire by the rising sun.

Just two years before, I had walked out of this valley with a sense of relief and excitement – the Alps behind, Italy ahead. Now I was experiencing the same sharp emotions in reverse, and as I ticked off the villages that morning – Calea, Baio Dora, Quassolo and Quincinetto – I reflected on the twin gifts that had come my way. Not only had I been fortunate enough to have the time and health to walk all the way to Rome, I was now being blessed with the chance to do it over again the 'wrong' way. I had been given time to go back in time. Maybe this is as close as we can ever get to re-living life.

All the while, the valley was closing in, the hills either side rising ever higher, until I reached the narrow neck at Pont St Martin, where the Roman Bridge over the River Lys guards the entrance to the Val d'Aosta and where the Italian tongue becomes inflected with French. Though I had booked to stay at the hotel overlooking the bridge, it was too early to stop, so after dropping in to cancel my room I walked on up the valley that I had found so lush and delightful on my way south.

Below the hanging gardens of vines, the rock-hewn Roman arch at Donnas looked even more imposing. A stretch of original Roman road runs through the arch, its paved stones worn into runnels by the tracks of passing wheels, and I walked through it as if embraced by an old friend. Soon after, I stopped to chat to a Dutch pilgrim, a blonde woman in her fifties, dressed sensibly in shorts and carrying a light pack. Like me, she was staying in hotels, and for some reason she told me that she had booked into one on the outskirts of Pont Saint Martin.

"You could do better," I said. "The Hotel Ponte Romano is the best spot – right by the bridge." I hadn't erased the phone number, and called them to say that the room I had just cancelled would be needed after all, for a Dutch lady. I wonder if it worked out.

She, in turn, had a favour for me.

"Don't follow the track," she told me. "It has been blocked by a landslide."

The Via Francigena had indeed been diverted to a lower track nearer the river, but to anyone coming from the south there was no indication of that. The diversion notice had been posted only to alert those walking towards Rome; no one had given a thought to the possibility that someone might actually be coming from the 'wrong' direction. If she hadn't warned me, I would have run into a wall of fallen rock and trees trunks, and lost valuable time.

It was through the narrow Gorge de Bard in 1800 that the swash-buckling young Napoleon had managed to sneak his army undetected at night, on his way to defeating the Austrians at Marengo and expelling them from Italy, despite its approaches being protected by a forbidding castle that commands both road and river.

The Via Francigena winds past its lower bastions by the entrance to the panoramic elevator that takes tourists to the alpine museum and the prison cells in the upper bailey and keep. The donjon of Bard, which sits astride a rocky buttress of jasper, dates in part from the 9th century, and it became so strategically important in later times that the Emperor Charles V accorded the Bardi the right to mint their own coinage. The sentries, who were perhaps sleeping off a night on the town when Napoleon slipped by, may not have been the first to be caught napping here by an invader: legend has it that the town's name derives from 'Bardus', or 'Barrio', the last elephant of Hannibal's army, said to have died here during the great Carthaginian commander's march on Rome in 218 BC.

The Hotel Stendhal, just off the main street in the centre of the borgo, commemorates one of France's greatest creative writers, and it had clearly enjoyed a previous existence as a semi-grand town-house. I dropped in out of curiosity. The restaurant invokes the writer's 'real' name, Henri Beyle. Was there any actual connection, I enquired? No, they replied, there was no record that Stendhal ever stayed in the building, but he came to Bard as a young officer in Napoleon's army. The author of *La Chartreuse de Parme*, a tale of political and personal intrigues in the city-state in Napoleonic times, would no doubt have appreciated this re-working of history. His Parma is a fiction, and by that token the hotel in Bard, too, can be excused its literary licence.

The town's older houses are like miniature towers, jostled together to form its streets and lanes. I walked down the steep slope to the River Dora Baltea and crossed over to Hône on the west bank, where the Albergo Bordet provided my berth for the night. From the thickness of the walls and the sturdiness of the shutters, I now knew for sure that I had arrived in the mountains.

The afternoon found me in the little park formed around the Torrente Brenve where it cascades into the Dora Baltea, its walkways built up on reinforced concrete flood-walls, the perfect viewpoint from which to take in the sub-alpine summits that were now all around me. The A5 autostrada sailed above, high on its stilts; back down the valley the multi-layered castle at Bard brooded menacingly in the afternoon sun.

At the park's lower end I had passed the memorial to Mario Colliard, a partisan shot by the Germans on 1st September 1944. There are hundreds of such memorials in Italy, and whenever I find them I always try to learn what happened. Colliard is commemorated with a photograph set into a black marble plaque; a young man in a white poloneck jumper under a smart jacket, he has a toothy, innocent grin and his light coloured hair is brushed back in the slick, un-parted sweep that was fashionable in the 1940s. But there is not much information, except that he was part of the Garibaldi Brigade, named after the 19th century hero of Italian Unification. The plaque was erected on the tenth anniversary of his death and promises "to keep alive and resplendent the flame of liberty", pledging that his heroic sacrifice will never be forgotten in Hône. I spent the rest of the afternoon enquiring about him – even at a village open-air barbecue. No one seemed to know. This was sad, and I could not help wondering what Mario Colliard, approaching 90 today, would have made of his sacrifice in the light of the economic crisis that had left Italy in the summer of 2012 in the hands of an un-elected Prime Minister, Mario Monti, or what he would have thought of the dishonour Monti's predecessor, Silvio Berlusconi, had visited on his country.

But something of him does live on in Hône: the village's main street has been named in his honour. In it, I alighted on a restaurant with the enticing if enigmatic name of Antichi Saporo di Ravo Filomena. It is owned by the local cooperative and I am not certain whether Ravo Filomena was actually there, but this humble village restaurant gave me one of the finest meals I have eaten in Italy – the tomato salad, the fagiolini and the garlic sauce with my pasta were so fresh and so delicately flavoured that I lingered late into the evening savouring every mouthful.

Next morning I gave myself a few minutes' lie-in before making a final bow to the unknown partisan in walking down his street to clear Hône. A 25-kilometre haul took me to Châtillon, and for the first half of the day I walked along minor roads on the western side of the Dora Baltea, sometimes dipping down to the grassy river bank. This was no longer a familiar 'Italian' landscape; I was walking by meadows of hay and buttercups under hillsides knotted with deciduous forest. It was a day of castles: on the west bank the flamboyant medieval structure at Issogne and the more austere four-square bastion at Verres, and across the valley to the east the dramatic hilltop fortress of Montjovet. I crossed the river and climbed high into an abundant country of orchards and vineyards from where, missing a waymark and losing my way, I had to drop down into the town of St Vincent, cutting a path on an untracked hillside of chestnuts.

Val d'Aosta, the spa town, once famous for its mineral springs, had served me well for an overnight stop, but this time I halted only for lunch before continuing up the valley to Châtillon. The two towns are strung out along the northern slopes of the Val d'Aosta; with the A5 autostrada and the main railway converging in a narrowing gap there is a sense of being hemmed in. The traditional pilgrim route continues up the valley to Aosta before addressing the Alps by way of the Grand St Bernard Pass; Châtillon, however, was where I would make my break-out, leaving the valley and the Via Francigena and heading into the high Alps.

It was a Sunday and the town was pretty much dead. I booked into a nondescript hotel near the centre and spent the afternoon snoozing in the sun in a deserted playground. All my focus was on the challenge ahead – trekking up the Val Tournenche to Cervinia and climbing over the Théodule Pass, a total ascent of 3,000 metres.

FIVE
Alpine Diversion

Everybody had told me that the walk up to Cervinia would be a tough stage. The French couple Edouard and Matilde, outside Rome a month ago, had warned me that I would have to contend with the main road and that I would have to walk on narrow verges and face the headlights of oncoming traffic when it came to the unavoidable tunnels and snow galleries. At Castel Fabiano, Elisabetta had consulted a computer programme that displays online maps of Italy's footpaths and mountain trails. None had shown up for the Val Tournenche. In the hope of more local knowledge, I had also double-checked with the tourist office at Cervinia. The only way up on foot, they had all said, was the *strada Statale* 406.

I was away at 5.45 am – later than usual because it seemed sensible not to start until daylight, when I would be more visible. The first tunnel was just above Châtillon, but I only had to share it with one truck. By the time I reached the one at Berzin, however, the Monday morning traffic was out in force. A track to the west of the road – in fact it was a section of the ancient route up the valley – appeared to offer an alternative. It took me through the hamlet of Lilla where an elderly farmer, Franco, was loading his scooter trailer with empty milk urns. He looked almost too frail to lift them. I asked him about the continuation up the valley, and he told me that the track itself came to an end, giving way to a path from which, by crossing a bridge, I would rejoin the main road. Looking across the valley I could see the outlines of a long tunnelled section through which I had no wish to walk. After about half a kilometre I reached a barrier at the end of the forest track, just as he had told me, and then searched in vain for any sign of a way across the racing torrent of the Marmore that roared through a deep gorge below me. I inspected the scene more carefully and among the turmoil of water splashed boulders I could just make out the stone abutments of a long-vanished bridge. To cross here would entail some serious scrambling, as well as the danger of falling and being swept away. It just wasn't on. I walked back down to the farmyard, trying to be philosophical. If the road was my only option, I could perhaps lose a few kilometres, and then maybe I could find a way of walking over the tunnel roof. Franco was still standing there. He was having difficulties starting his three-wheeler.

"You again," he said. "You must like my farm."

"There was no bridge," I said.

"Oh yes there is, I'm absolutely certain of that."

A defining moment! I was now determined to find that bridge and to avoid at all costs walking through the long road tunnel. Franco, I decided, would have to show me. I explained I was walking from Rome to London; could he possibly help me by driving me back to the spot where the bridge should be? I wasn't about to cheat on my own rules – I had walked it all twice, hadn't I? Franco's immediate reaction was "Sorry, too much work to do this morning". Somehow, without too much wheedling, I managed to persuade him to change his mind. Was there an urgency in my voice which convinced him that it would be simpler to get rid of me by dumping me at the top of the track? Certainly he did not appear to be impressed by my walk; indeed, I wondered if Franco had ever been either to Rome or London; he looked as if he had rarely left the Val Tournenche, and the end of the track could well be the top of his world.

"OK, hop in," he said.

I slung my rucksack onto the trailer beside the churns and jumped onto the bench seat next to Franco. After a few choking false starts we set off up the track that I had just walked down. I was heading into the Alps in a phut-phut, an unglamorous way of marking the near half century since I had first stuck out my thumb on a French road to embark on my youthful hitch-hiking adventures across Europe and Africa.

We were soon at the barrier, and I got out, expecting Franco to show me a hidden path into the gorge; instead, he pointed to the trees above the track. I had been looking in the wrong direction. Unmarked it may have been, but the path was clear and well-worn.

"Follow that," he said, "and you'll come to the bridge."

I heaped thanks on this kind man and cursed my own stupidity. It had never occurred to me to look up.

A little further up the gorge, there it was. I crossed and resumed my tramp on the main road, which now began to wind round the contours in a series of hairpin bends, at each of which I took the precaution of switching to the outer side. That apart, it made for easy and even pleasant going as the valley opened into an ever-expanding arena of spectacular mountain tops.

The Val Tournenche rises in progressive steps, each one comprising a narrow Shangri-la of meadowland dotted with slate-roofed wooden houses. The last cultivated layer is the great amphitheatre of Valtournenche itself that spreads its limbs in a comfortable arc, with a single spire rising above the cluster of buildings to announce the town's head-of-valley status. Above it I could just begin to make out the highest layer of all, the summits above Cervinia. Below the town, I took to a footpath at the lakeside and followed it all the way up to the church. The weathered timber houses with their glistening slate roofs along the main street were as Swiss as they were Italian, already with that distinct alpine character. Here we were at 1,500 metres, of which I had climbed 1,000 since Châtillon. I stopped in a bar for well-earned refreshment, but I should also have stopped by the Tourist Office; a visit there would have spared me a few kilometres more of road slogging.

It was only when confronted with the final dark tunnel at Les Perrères that I realised that there was, after all, a footpath all the way up to the head of the valley. Just short of the tunnel, I spotted two ladies moving gingerly around boulders by the roadside. I broke into a trot to catch them up. Was this by any chance a footpath that would lead me to Cervinia?

"Of course," one of them replied. "This is Number One!"

Had I but known it, Footpath Number One starts far down the valley at Antey St André, and I could have saved myself a lot of grief had I realised that it was there. But I had the belated pleasure of real hill walking for the final few kilometres from the little sanctuary chapel of Notre Dame at Perrères right up to Cervinia, in particular savouring those steps during which the massive hunk of the top of the Matterhorn hove into view before me. From the Italian side of Le Cervin, the Matterhorn's summit is less pronounced – the iconic arrowhead is unique to Switzerland – but she still casts her spell. I walked towards her, drawn back 22 years to when I had reached the summit, and tugged forward by the promise of crossing to Switzerland in her shadow.

In all my previous visits, I had swooped on Cervinia from above and in winter, skiing one of the finest blue runs in the Alps from the Théodule Pass. From that viewpoint, Cervinia has few pretensions; it is a largely concrete development dating from the 1920s, when the hamlet of Breuil was renamed Breuil-Cervinia to cash in on its ringside views of Le Cervin, as the Matterhorn is called in this French-speaking part of Italy. The upstart name, Cervinia, has since eclipsed Breuil, and although it may lack the old fashioned alpine charms of Valtournenche or of Zermatt, it has prospered because it is superbly located as a gateway to the high Alps. My path to the resort took me round the edge of one of the highest golf courses in Europe before arriving at the café-lined Via Carrel, packed with summer trippers lunching at outdoor tables. The place held out an unpretentious dignity; besides, nothing man-made could upstage the majestic backdrop of the Matterhorn.

I had booked into one of the few old timber built hotels, the Punta Maquignaz, the surname of the pioneer alpine guides, Jean Joseph, Baptiste and Daniel, respectively father, son and nephew. The Maquignaz trio originated the techniques of climbing with pitons and ropes on one of the twin summits of the Dent du Géant in July 1882 to achieve the first ascent of a peak that the great English mountaineer, Albert Frederick Mummery, had pronounced "absolutely inaccessible by fair means". In the lobby of the Maquignaz, I was greeted by a friendly stuffed Polar bear, and by its beautiful assistant, Valentina, from far away Ukraine and therefore well equipped to empathise with one who had just made the distance, on foot, from Rome. I was glad to settle in for two nights and take my first day off since the beach at Marina di Pietrasanta two weeks before. If all went to plan tomorrow, Ros would arrive sometime around midday.

I spent the remainder of the day regrouping and recouping; from the comfort of a bench back by the golf course outside the Cervinia Guides Office I gazed up at the late afternoon clouds billowing and dancing around the summit of the Matterhorn. Climbers would by now be safely off the summit ridges, heading down to the huts. Its sheer presence brought back memories. I had made it to the top without the need to use either ice-axe or crampons. At the time, I was based in Israel, and I had flown to Switzerland from Tel Aviv. I must have brought the Middle Eastern sun with me; it was one of those rare summer days, 30th July 1990, when the upper bands of the Hörnli Ridge were not compacted with snow and ice.

There had, however, been an unexpected sequel to my climb. I filed a story for Reuters centred round the 125th anniversary of the first ascent by Edward Whymper, based both on my own experiences and on an informal interview with the veteran Zermatt guide, Richard Andenmatten. I had chatted to him in the Hörnli hut the night before our ascent. That year, he told me, the Matterhorn had already claimed the lives of ten climbers who had all attempted the mountain without a guide. If you want to stay alive, he had insisted, your best chance is to be roped to a guide.

"Of course, you can't stop people if they want to throw themselves off the Golden Gate Bridge," Andenmatten had said. "And we can't close the mountain to reckless amateurs who want to risk it without a guide."

In his 30 years of climbing the Matterhorn, no one had been killed with a guide, and that's how I pitched my story, which was published extensively, as far away as the *New York Times.* But it proved to be a lesson in never saying never: the following season, two climbers were lost on the Matterhorn along with their guide.

Not that they were the first paying customers to fall down the Matterhorn. Three Englishmen, Lord Alfred Douglas, the Rev Charles Hudson and Douglas Haddow, together with the Chamonix guide, Michel Gros, tumbled down the north face when Haddow lost his footing while the party was descending from the summit after the first successful climb of the mountain on 14th July 1865. The four of them were roped to Edward Whymper and two more local guides, a father and son both called Peter Taugwalder; but the rope parted and, for years, suspicions lingered that the senior Taugwalder, or even Whymper, had severed it. Modern scientific analysis has restored their reputation; the old natural hemp rope was quite simply not strong enough to hold four falling men. The body of Lord Alfred was never found; he lies somewhere in a long-closed crevasse on the Matterhorn glacier.

Later that evening, I found a chalet restaurant with a semi-indigestible name, La Maison Jean Bich de Pers da Mario. It is run by the daughter of a former Italian mountain guide, and she personally cooked me a dinner of pasta *aglio e olio* strong enough to fuel me there and then back to the top of the Matterhorn.

The night in bed, knowing that there was no need to get up and go anywhere, was bliss. My only expedition the following morning was to a novel experience – a high-tech laundromat. During walks across Europe, I had grown accustomed to the classic 'steam-driven' machines requiring a mix of coins to extract and dispense the correct amount of washing powder or liquid, and then still more change for the dryer. But the technology of coin-operated washing machines has moved on since the first one was installed in Philadelphia in 1947, and here, on a terrace of shops above the town's main supermarket, was a fully automated system: these glistening new machines provided their own washing powder. Operating them, though, presented the same challenges as the flight deck of a Boeing 747, but eventually, with the help of a summer resident who was a regular user, I did manage to wash my clothes, the only casualty being the big white kerchief I had worn every day to protect my neck from the hot Italian sun. It went into the machine, never to re-emerge, but I didn't need to replace it: I was heading north.

Noon brought my reunion with my friend Ros. It would be easy to be frightened by her CV: she has a Ph.D. in American literature, and she has attempted Everest three times; that is where we first met in 1994, high-altitude friendship forged on the Rongbuk Glacier on the way up to the North Col. We had kept in touch. Forget her doctoral thesis, her studies of Saul Bellow, and her extensive writing on literature and travel: Ros is a serious mountaineer. She has Mount McKinley in Alaska, Mount Vinson in Antarctica and Mount Kenya in Africa under her belt, and she has roamed the tops of the Andes, the Pamirs and the Alps. In between expeditions, she has taught for many years in the Gulf, first in Iran, then the UAE, and most recently in Oman. She has a variety of retreats, and when I let her know of my plans to cross the Alps from the south in late summer it was from the one in Chamonix that she arranged to intersect with me.

I was eagerly looking forward to meeting her again in her natural habitat. For someone who has climbed so high and survived such a tough environment, Ros is as slender as a feather. In the Himalayas, I once accused her of floating up mountains. When I spotted her at the bus terminal, she looked even thinner, her long dark hair combed flat like a newly rolled lawn, not a blade out of place; the trim rucksack and light blue fleece only emphasised her small frame. The boots alone betrayed a sense of mission.

"The buses worked perfectly," she said, "they all left fifteen minutes earlier than scheduled!"

"That sounds like my walk. I am always leaving earlier than I plan. Your job is to slow me down."

"I'll do my best," Ros replied, her face melting into that wrinkly smile contoured by years of exposure to Middle Eastern and high-altitude sun that had so drawn me on the Rongbuk Glacier.

"You haven't changed," I said. "Still as beautiful as you were all those years ago in Tibet."

"Well, there is a bit less of me. I had a brain tumour removed last year – the size of a baseball."

We were jostling our way down the main street among the crowds of trippers up in Cervinia to get their fix of the Matterhorn. I mumbled an awkward query in response to that bombshell.

"Are you still all right at altitude?"

"We'll find out, but don't worry; I have never felt better."

Sitting in an armchair in the lobby, under the gaze of the polar bear and the watchful eye of Valentina, Ros recounted the adventures of her tumour. The worst part had been the constant headaches, as doctor after doctor failed to pick up that there was anything seriously wrong. The brain scan came only after months of failed diagnoses.

"The operation was an instant cure. The day the tumour was removed I felt, quite literally, like a weight had been lifted from my mind."

We moved on from medical reports and caught up on recent news, the day filtering away pleasantly as we swapped stories about different countries where Ros had taught and those others, now far away in time, where I had worked as a journalist. Finally, towards the end of the afternoon, I briefed her on the plans for our crossing of the Alps.

Simple as it was, the strategy I had hatched hinged on teaming up with a guide at the appointed time. He had a prior arrangement to rope a party up and down the Breithorn, the easiest of the local 4,000-metre peaks, and, after seeing them back into the cable-car at the Klein Matterhorn, our guide would descend to meet us at the Théodule Hut, at the head of the pass we were to cross, at 1.30. That gave us ample time to climb the 1,500 metres from Cervinia to the pass, and also provided us, the following morning, with the time for an early but leisurely breakfast, served by Valentina who had already been out to buy us fresh bread.

The Théodule Pass had fascinated me ever since I had seen Roman coins found there, now on display in the museum in Zermatt alongside the rope that snapped during the Whymper party's fatal descent of the Matterhorn. The coins, spanning from the second century BC to the fourth century AD, indicate that the Théodule was used more than 2,000 years ago as a trading route from the Ligurian ports and the western Pò plain to the Rhône and Rhine valleys. At that time Europe was warmer, and no glacier occupied the upper pass. It continued in use right through the Middle Ages until a new miniature ice age set in during the 16th century. It was only around this time that the pass seems to have been permanently named after Saint Théodule, the missionary from the Orient, who brought Christianity to the Valais and is today celebrated in Switzerland as the patron saint of winemakers. With Europe again apparently entering a warm phase – whether caused by man or part of the natural cycle – the glacier over the Théodule Pass is once more receding, but there is still enough of it left to warrant hiring a guide.

Following breakfast at the Punta Maquignaz, my new companion and I were away by 7.15 am, scrambling over rough ground to pass a large block of holiday apartments and joining the main path to Plan Maison just above the Hotel Cime Blanchi. I registered the light regular footfall on the stony surface as Ros settled into her measured stride up the steepening valley of the Torrente Vielle. The sun was rising into a cloudless sky; the forecasted rain had not materialised. It was good to be going again in company, especially with a comrade whose biography includes an essay titled: "Physical and Spiritual Journeys in Mountain Literature: the Mountaineer as Tourist".

With each step uphill we moved closer to the giant pyramid of the Matterhorn, the Italian ridge with its awesome trio of summit pinnacles etched against an alpine blue sky. Exposed to the blast of the sun, the sheer southern face of the gneiss rock mountain was laid bare, with only patches of snow and ice clinging to the lower gullies.

At 2,450 metres, we stopped at Plan Maison, the 'half-way' house café. During the winter season this is a busy hub of chair lift routes; in summer it is a bleak and barren spot, with scarcely a blade of grass on the worn tracks around the building, a utilitarian cross between village hall and old time cinema whose corrugated roof and large Coca Cola banner did it no favours. The interior made up for initial impressions; we were the morning's first customers, indeed the first hikers on the mountain, and when I indicated to the barman that I had walked all this way from Rome he reacted warmly:

"We don't get many people coming up here who can say that. In fact in all my 20 years here you are the first!"

It was as good as a hero's welcome, and as he served us our elevenses it suddenly dawned on me that I was leaving Italy; a critical stage in my journey home was nearly completed. The Swiss border was only 1,000 metres higher and a few kilometres further on. Ros and I drank our tea and I signed a card for the café recording my journey, which had started in St Peter's Square just over a month ago – 32 days, to be precise.

A broad track bathed in bright morning sun led up to the col. The hut was just visible in the dip below the peaks of the Testa Grigia and the Klein Matterhorn further to the east, but over them cloud was gathering. Far below us, we could now see the shining surface of Lago Goillet set into the floor of the upper valley, itself ringed with an immense cirque of untamed rocky pasture. To our left the Matterhorn loomed ever bulkier as we continued up.

Ros pointed to the numerals of the 3,000 metre mark laid out on the track ahead, a multi-coloured signpost of stones artfully spliced like a correctly laid jig-saw. A little higher up, a small chapel was open and we went inside to pay our respects. But this was no longer a sacred shrine. Stacked against the stone altar were bunches of snow poles to mark the track in winter.

I noticed that Ros, who had set out with a Leki pole, was beginning to lean on it. Indeed, as we got higher, she was slowing. But she was too much of the old fox to be concerned about that. Ros had tramped higher and further than I would ever go.

"Are you all right?" I enquired.

"Yes, I am just pacing myself."

In any case, at this juncture there was time to play with. Later in the day, perhaps, our pace might be more important. Nearing the top, at around 3,200 metres, we passed a couple from England and swapped stories. They had just come over the col on one of the great high alpine walks, the circuit of the base of the Monte Rosa, and they appeared to be astonished that I had walked all the way from Rome.

"We thought we were going some by touring the Monte Rosa, but Rome is almost unbelievable," said the girl.

By the time we reached the col at 3,300 metres above sea level, cloud had veiled the sky, it was cold and mist eddied round the rocky buttresses. The hut perches on a crag at the neck of the col, but what I saw took me by surprise. The ancient wooden contraption I had so often used in my skiing here had been replaced with a structure of gleaming factory-made panels; I had been looking out for the old familiar Dakota and there stood a brand new Airbus. Leaving the murk and chill, we stepped inside to find a spacious café and welcoming food counter. One or two hikers had come up from the Zermatt Valley, including a pair of hardy mountain bikers who were planning to cycle down to Cervinia. The preparations for their descent gave the place a sense of excitement. Midday left us almost an hour to wait for our guide, and Ros was looking a little pale, so I ordered celebratory dishes of pasta for both of us. This would be the one time on my walk home that I would have a full lunch, but we needed the fuel for the long descent to Zermatt. I called Gail with a birthday greeting, and marked my exit from Italy by getting my pilgrim passport stamped with the hut's Italian logo – *Rifugio Teodolo*.

No doubt it was the cloud's doing, but our guide Rudolf Steindl turned up early; so I added another dish of pasta to the bill. The choice was a surprise, since in my experience Zermatt guides are used to wolfing down meat and cheese. The explanation is simple: Rudolf is Austrian.

Good mountain guides have the grace of a ballet dancer. Dressed in a trim wind jacket and skin-tight salopettes, Rudolf moved with economy of effort, each footfall crunching lightly and cleanly into the crusty ice of the glacier.

"We won't use crampons here, and I won't rope you up either," he announced, displaying practical mountain craft as he bent down to retrieve some broken snow poles from the ice. "We can use these, and, Brian, you can take my Leki."

So with bits of old stick we glissaded rather inelegantly down the icy slope towards the Gandegg Hut, 300 metres below. In the narrow band of ice and snow, strewn with the detritus of decades, there were no signs of crevasses. The strip is all that is left of the once expansive Théodule Glacier – but Ros and I were grateful to have our guide, especially one like Rudolf who was in tune with the changing conditions of the terrain and ice.

"Centuries ago, this was an open highway, and if the glacier keeps on retreating it will become one again," said Rudolf. I didn't press him for an explanation. I believe in natural cycles, but I wasn't going to spoil the day with a debate about man-made global warming.

Rudolf left us at Trockener Stegg, another busy ski junction from where a cable car soars to the summit of the Klein Matterhorn. He would take another down to Zermatt; we would descend on foot. The sky had cleared, and there were now glorious views to the east towards the Monte Rosa massif. Soon Zermatt came into view, an almost invisible blob at the bottom of the valley like something seen through the reverse lenses of a telescope. We had to drop 1,600 metres, a seemingly endless spiral down winding rocky paths while the summits of the Zermatt Valley danced before us, and it wasn't long before I noticed that Ros was struggling.

On her arrival, she had indeed pointed out that she was out of practice at walking, especially at altitude, and wondered whether she would be up to the crossing; nevertheless, she hadn't wanted to miss the opportunity that I had suggested just two weeks before. We had already completed the hardest part of the descent, but unfortunately lack of training had caught up with her.

"I am all right," she insisted. "I just have to take my time."

That remained her mantra throughout the afternoon's long descent. It was like being back with Gail in Tuscany, only now I had an experienced mountaineer faltering at my heels. With the uneven and halting crunch of our boots punctuated by my barks and grunts of encouragement we, little by little, inched down the rugged trail, Ros taking ever longer rests. At times, she seemed to stagger, as if her legs were giving way. Was this a fall-out of the operation? If I could get a signal, should I call for help? No, it was just the effect on muscles unaccustomed to steep descents, she retorted; her face torn in strain, she kept going until after a few short surges she finally reached the top of the Furi gondola.

"Now, look, Ros," I said. "*I'm* the one who has to walk all the way; *you* don't. You've done brilliantly and you have done quite enough."

I left her to swoop gently down the meadows and wooded ravines to the centre of Zermatt while I raced down the path to meet her. On the church with its conical spire, the clock was striking six as together we struggled up the road next to the River Vispa towards our hotel. It had ended up being a tough day for both of us.

I celebrated my arrival in Switzerland with a swim. We had booked into the contemporary chalet-style Hotel Metropol, where I had been staying for many years, and it has a pool with a panoramic view of the Matterhorn. The hotel is owned by Gabriel Taugwalder, bearer of the same family name as Peter Taugwalder who, with his son, lived to tell the tale of that first fatal ascent of the Matterhorn with Whymper almost 150 years ago. Gabriel may sometimes seem a bit grumpy, but his wife Franziska is tall and graceful; in her youth, she was regarded as one of the most beautiful women in the Valais, and she still turns heads. Franziska used to give my children bars of chocolate when I brought them here skiing; instinctively she must have known that they needed a special treat after another hard day on the slopes with their father. Ros would have appreciated the gesture; while I swam, she contented herself with a shower and bathed in the warm glow of a good day in the hills.

Both restored, and ready for our farewell dinner – and to say all the things kept back by the concentration of the day – we set off for Le Vieux Valais. What remained from many previous visits was the authenticity of the pizza oven and the Italian cuisine; the premises had undergone the same sort of upgrading as the Théodule Hut and it was as bright and clean as IKEA furniture. This evening was our last chance to talk. I would resume my early starts in the morning, while Ros could lie in before making a leisurely return round the mountains to Lew and home, with a tremendous walk under her belt. She was still game for a little *divertissement*, though. When Whymper made it back from the Matterhorn, no doubt in shock, he put up at the Monte Rosa Hotel, and we strolled there for a nightcap. I steered Ros to the hotel's upstairs wood-panelled reading room to show her a letter preserved inside a glass case:

"Dear Leo: You tell me that Zermatt is holding a mountaineering reunion to celebrate the centenary of the first ascent of Monte Rosa and of the opening of the Monte Rosa Hotel.

I still retain vivid memories of the peaceful valley of Zermatt and of its glorious amphitheatre of great peaks, when we were both there 61 years ago, as well as my own ascent of Monte Rosa.

Except for the Wetterhorn, I did not follow up that first youthful introduction to mountaineering, but my experience was enough for me to understand the joys you and others have found in the high hills. So I hope your fellow mountaineers will accept my best wishes for the success of your reunion."

The letter is from Winston S. Churchill, and was written by him from Downing Street on 20th June 1955 to his old political ally Leo Amery. The young Winston had obviously also appreciated the long walk which the climb had entailed. In a letter from Zermatt to his mother in 1894, he had noted: "more than 16 hours of continual walking. I was very proud and pleased to find that I was able to do it and come down very fresh."

Though she wouldn't have been aware of these words, I hoped that a memory of the 15th August 2012 along those lines was what Ros would take back from Zermatt with her.

1. To Rome by donkey cart.

2. Foot treatment at the thermal springs near Viterbo.

3. Vines and olives above Lago di Bolsena.

4. Radicofani – gateway to Tuscany.

5. Jonathan and Gail.

6. Approaching Siena.

7. Gail and Hugo, a former Italian P.O.W.

8. Harry and the author.

9. Uncovering the past at Pozzeveri.

10. A Botero horse in Pietrasanta.

11. Waymark at Fornova di Taro.

12. Danilo and the author.

13. The Matterhorn from Cervinia.

14. Ros and the author descending the Théodule glacier.

15. Tom and Voltaire.

16. The *Pleurants* in Dijon.

17. Towpath on the Canal de Bourgogne.

18. A French fisherman.

19. Entrance to Paris.

20. Approaching the cathedral of Notre-Dame.

21. Monsieur Amidou's boot repairs.

22. Jon by the yew tree at All Saints Waldershare.

23. Arrival at Canterbury Cathedral.

24. Back in Coggeshall at the Church of St Peter ad Vincula.

SIX
SWISS ROLL

AT THE MID-POINT OF AUGUST, I WAS back on my own, and would be for the foreseeable future – until Dover, in fact. Walking from Zermatt down to the Rhône Valley is not for the faint-hearted. In sections where the path follows ancient terraced trails, it can feel more like the Andes than the Alps: Indiana Jones country of narrow tracks suspended over gorges with vertiginous drops to the river or railway below. I was descending more than 1,000 metres, but the descent was never even; a dip of 200 metres would be followed by a stiff climb back up to almost the same height. And it proved a long day – 40 kilometres.

I started in rain, the first downpour since I had left Rome. In waterproof jacket and hood, I couldn't complain: at this altitude, rain might be boring and uncomfortable, but back on the Théodule it would have been snow. In any case, it petered out soon after I left the woods above Täsch, and within minutes the day began to notch up another record in Swiss summer heat waves.

For much of it, I had open views to the steep eastern slopes of the valley, villages and houses clinging to the hillsides among meadow and forests, snowy peaks towering above them. I measured my descent by ticking off the names of the villages I had heard so often in recorded announcements in that lilting Valais Swiss German while riding the rack railway up the valley to Zermatt – Randa, Herbriggen, St Niklaus, where I stopped at the station for lunch, then Stalden at the big fork to Saas Fee, and finally to the Rhône vineyards and the town of Visp.

I arrived in Visp exhausted. I had descended nearly three kilometres from the Théodule Pass in just over 24 hours. In need of rest, I headed straight to the tourist office, where two nasty surprises awaited me. First I purchased a map of the cycle route that I intended to follow down the Rhône Valley, and then I asked about accommodation. I would in fact need two maps to get to Martigny, and each one cost 28 Swiss francs, the equivalent of 20 pounds. The girl serving me responded to my raised eyebrows, and did her best to recompose them.

"But this is Switzerland," she said, as if that alone was a good enough excuse to charge three times the price of a map in any other country.

Next, I asked if she could book me a hotel room for the night.

"You won't find anything in Visp. You'll have to take the train to Leuk or Brig."

Again she caught my look.

"But this is the summer," she countered, deploying the logic she had used to explain the expensive maps. Hotel rooms, like maps, were finite in the Swiss summer.

"Look, I've walked all the way from Rome," I said, "I've crossed the Alps on foot, and I'm not leaving Visp on a bloody train. If you can't find me something, I'm going to sleep outside on the pavement."

I was so tired that I could have curled up there and then, and I was probably also, at that moment, giving off anti-pheromones of exhaustion. Whether prompted by my threat of tousled vagrancy in a Swiss commune or my proffering of the pilgrim passport for her to stamp, the girl went off to make a phone call and, coming back to me, announced that she had persuaded an elderly lady, who normally takes lodgers by the week or month, to give me a room just for the one night. It was on the sixth floor of a simple apartment block close by on a street called Müchlackerstrasse. I couldn't have asked for better. The room was equipped with a shower and a kitchen, and after sorting myself out I had just enough energy to stumble to a restaurant in the central Kaufplatz, where I was served filling pasta and a generous carafe of local white wine by a trim blonde woman of Visp who attributed her very decent English to the wild oats she claimed to have sown in the English town of Uxbridge, near where I grew up, in the 1960s.

"I was living near there then," I said. "It was a non-stop party."

"What a pity we never met."

Being clear of the Alps meant once again that it was warm enough, at 6.00 am on the 17th August, to breakfast at a table outside Visp's Bahnhof. The Upper Rhône Valley was waking to another hot day, and I had laid in an extra bottle of water against the hard grind ahead on the *piste cyclable*, which Matilde and Edouard had told me about at La Locanda Monticelli. The alternative would have been a roller coaster on the hillside footpaths through villages and vineyards along the south-facing slopes of the valley. It was a choice between the best of rural Switzerland, with its meanderings and ups and downs adding even more kilometres to what had already been an extended loop over the Alps by Zermatt, and a fast even path on the more shaded side of the grit-coloured river. I opted for speed, and, besides, I could always look up and enjoy the views.

But it wasn't all plain sailing. In August 2013, they were still working on sections of the *piste cyclable*, so at times I was forced away from the river. Even so, I was making swift progress as expected, and clipping along at over five kilometres an hour, when I came up against a fence blocking the way. Now, in the old days, with fences you had a choice: obey, or climb over or squeeze through and take your chances. But the technology has advanced, so that the fences they erect now at the sides of motorways and high-speed railways actually do the job of keeping people out. Here, straddling my path on the Rhône embankment, I faced one with mesh that offered no footholds, with a cornice of spiky blades two metres and more off the ground: hands off! Crawling through the undergrowth to the bank in the hope of getting round it, I found the security contractors had thought of that, too; the fence reached all the way to the fast-flowing river.

I had noticed a few tents on the field below the embankment – a summer campsite no doubt – but my assumptions changed as I realised the clientèle consisted of apparently spaced-out youths of both sexes. I managed to engage one of them, and yelled across to him.

"How do I get across here?"

"You can't. The path has been closed for the festival."

I looked at the encampment with renewed interest and then surveyed the ground beyond it – a sea of blue, green, orange, red and yellow tents as far as the eye stretched. This was no holiday camp. Despite the impenetrable barrier on the embankment path preventing me from getting out of it, I had somehow stumbled into a rock festival.

"How the heck do I get through here?" I asked more urgently.

They pointed to a spot a long way back on what turned out to be the far side of the camp, where they said there was a gate. I dropped down the embankment, entered the camp's perimeter and trudged across an extensive water meadow on which the festival goers had pitched their tents. There was hardly a sound; at this early stage of the day most of the occupants were fast asleep. The few awake were sitting by the open flaps of their tents sunning themselves and smoking sweet-smelling substances.

I reached the gate, anxious to be on my way. It was by the public road that would lead me back to the riverside village of Niedergampel in a long diversion away from the river around the encampment, and I walked out in the company of a few festival goers. They turned right along the road, towards the station at Gampel, and I turned left and resumed my broken journey in the opposite direction towards Niedergampel until I heard a loud shout, and two uniformed and armed security guards stepped in front of me. They barked at me in German. I was still just in German-speaking Switzerland.

"You cannot go that way," one of them said. "The road is for cars, not for people on foot. You must get back inside the compound."

"But I don't want to; I want to get *out* of it."

"Then you must go to Gampel and leave by train. The way ahead is barred to festival-goers for their own safety."

It dawned on me that, with a rucksack on my back, and dressed for what I was doing, I was being confused with the festival-goers. At a rock festival even my big walking boots were not so out of place. Nasty images of Switzerland, not just a land of cuckoo clocks, began to hover, for example that of Logan Mountstuart, the principal character of William Boyd's *Any Human Heart,* held incommunicado in a Swiss fortress for nearly two years of World War II. My mantra from skiing and climbing in Switzerland was that the Swiss, especially the Swiss Germans, improve with altitude: the higher up, the more civilised. The closer to sea level, the less agreeable they are, and the more inclined to the crueller streaks of their Teutonic German cousins. Here I was a mere 600 metres high.

I looked around at one of the festival hoardings. *Open Air Gampel 2012* offered a Dantesque eternity of entertainment: 32 groups in the line-up, among them Placebo, All Time Low, Eagles of Death Metal, The Joy Formidable, Trigger Finger, and Stress. The festival lasted until Sunday; today was only Friday. I entertained the quite dreadful thought that I could be trapped here for the weekend.

"But, look, I want to walk to the next village," I insisted.

"You can't. The road is closed."

"But I am nothing to do with the festival."

"You are under our care now, and during the festival the road is closed. Now, move on."

I was tempted to take him literally and run for it, but, would you believe, they were armed. Arrested, I would then have to waste hours talking my way out of a police cell, or, worse, discover whether Mountstuart's incarceration in the novel was actually based on reality. I tried a different tack. I took off my rucksack and extracted my pilgrim passport.

"Please look at this," I said, showing the guards my credentials, "I am a pilgrim walking from Rome to London."

Either they didn't understand, or didn't wish to.

"But Rome is that way," said my chief tormentor, pointing down the road towards the station at Gampel, where they were telling me to go.

How was I going to explain in bad German that I was a pilgrim, going the 'wrong' way, returning from Rome? I was becoming quite desperate, and my arm lashed out and, as it did, I caught a butterfly.

"Now look here," I insisted, "people have a constitutional right to walk on roads in Switzerland. You can't stop me."

That, miraculously, seemed to do it; the mere mention of the country's constitution had unblocked the way, although I still have no idea if what I said is strictly true. The guards stood aside, and I walked on, quickening my pace as I passed the fenced-in encampment, which was the size of an airfield, in case they changed their minds and came after me.

So, having escaped the living hell of a Swiss rock festival, I regained the riverside at Niedergampel, and the embankment path took me without further incident to Leuk with its castle commanding the hillside. Here I would again have to make a choice between a quiet country road snaking along the upper slopes among vineyards, or the *piste cyclable*, but now on the side of the N28, and demarcated on the hard shoulder of the main road by its yellow painted line. I decided to stick with the cycle track. Headfirst into oncoming traffic, such as it was, I walked comfortably to Sierre with two delightful encounters along the way. A cyclist stopped and asked me where I was going. This is a rare occurrence; cyclists don't usually have time for pedestrians. He also asked whether I ever felt threatened on the road.

"Good heavens, no!" I said. "At least I can see what is coming towards me. You cyclists have your backs to the enemy."

Later, I passed a roadside kiosk where a boy was selling juicy apricots, a local speciality. I picked out two of the most succulent looking and offered him money, but he refused to take any, and wished me well on my hot way.

All the while, I was enjoying majestic views of the vineyards and the craggy buttresses that flank the southern side of the Rhône Valley at the foot of the outliers of the Bernese Alps.

Sierre, or Siders in Swiss German, marks the language-divide, but German Switzerland had one more trick to play on me before I was back in French-speaking territory. I headed straight for the town's tourist office at the Bahnhof to check hotels in Sion. I didn't want a repeat of last night's near-fiasco in Visp. I also asked how far it was to Sion. Twelve kilometres at most, they said. That would do me fine, so I booked a room there. Leaving Siders, I rejoined the Rhône embankment path only to see that the fingerpost to Sion read: 19 kilometres. That extra hour made for one of my longest days: it was gone five o'clock when I got in, having walked 44 kilometres on what turned out to be the hottest day of that summer.

In Sion, I stayed in the heart of the city in the appropriately named Hôtel du Rhône in Rue du Scex, but I could make it no further than the hotel's terrace for dinner – a rather good *spaghetti alla carbonara* and a cardboardy apple pie. The local red and white wines were so fizzy and fresh that they could have been decanted straight from a spigot in the hillside vineyards I had walked past. Re-mobilised by a quantity of both, I strolled into the old town to see the Romanesque cathedral and to pay my respects to the nearby gothic church of St Théodule, first bishop of Sion and patron of the alpine pass that Ros and I had safely traversed.

The Rhône flows southwest as far as Martigny. To follow it, therefore, meant a deviation from the direct route to England, like the back step in a waltz, while the straight line from Sion would lead me across the Bernese Alps, an arduous undertaking. From Martigny, where I would rejoin the Via Francigena and the direct route from the Grand St Bernard Pass, the Rhône makes a bold 90 degree turn to the north towards Lac Léman. After playing one map against the other, I opted to stay with the river. Not a bad decision: all that Saturday I would have the excitement of approaching this great elbow-shaped bend with the rising wall of the Mont Blanc Massif slowly taking shape ahead.

However, the day got off to a bad start. I came down to breakfast a tad before the official opening time of 7.00 am. The man behind the closed glass door was setting out the various dishes for the buffet service, and I knocked. Having seen me, he continued working, so I knocked again: he stormed out and swore.

"What do you think you are doing? If this was a train it would leave at seven, not ten minutes earlier."

"But this isn't a train, and I only want some cereal and juice."

He calmed down and let me in.

Reflecting once more on the Swiss obsession with time and punctuality, I put together a perfectly adequate breakfast without further troubling him. Being early in this country, I thought, is just as big an offence as being late.

Back down on the river I was struck by another Swiss obsession: doubling up on instructions. This part of the Valais is famed for its fruits, as I had seen yesterday with the apricots, but now along the path passing through the Commune de Vétroz I kept reading notices warning "*Interdit – Le Vol des fruits et légumes*". I spent a lot of the day wrestling with the logic of forbidding theft; perhaps in some cantons of Switzerland it is permitted.

The bridleway followed the levée of the Rhône for most of the way down to Martigny, the crags of the Bernese foothills defining the terrain. Either the flow of the river had slowed, or my pace had quickened. When I had joined it at Visp, the river was running far swifter than I could walk, but I was now keeping pace with the current as it settled into a sedate five kilometres an hour. My problem was water. It was another searingly hot day, with no cloud, no breeze and my thermometer registering 38 degrees, and despite an abundance of probably suspect fresh water at my side I came close to dehydration before being able to refill my water bottle at a chicken farm.

The brackish water of the river was almost certainly not for drinking, and besides, it would have been dangerous to scramble down the steep banks to scoop up even a mouthful. The Upper Rhône is a strange river; it is more like a sluice, and does not become a full-bodied river until it has made its way across Lac Léman, from where it flows into France and down to the Mediterranean, for many centuries one of Europe's great trading arteries. But here, as the Rhône forces a passage through a narrow gateway of mountains, there are no boats; indeed, periodic notices remind the rule-obsessed Swiss that boating is prohibited. That day, the only signs of life on the walking-pace current were birds swooping and diving. I could hear marsh warblers and nightingales chirping among the thickets and reeds along the embankment, and, if I was lucky, could spot them darting across the water.

'Fully' was a thoughtful name for the medieval town that sorted me out for lunch with two large tumblers of iced tea and a big cheese sandwich. From there I approached Martigny along a rugged path on the cliffs which descend almost to the water's edge at the axis around which the river makes its right angled turn to the north. Only a short 32 kilometres from Sion, it was a dramatic setting in which to rejoin the Via Francigena.

Once again, I intersected with my outgoing journey. The city of Martigny was in a festive mood: the Place Centrale was given over to a fairground, and with cold beer in hand I sat on the terrace of a café watching children and their parents on the carousel. The parents, of course, were having all the fun. I had ended up in the same centrally located Hôtel de la Poste, where I like to feel that the gravel-voiced receptionist, in fact the husband of the owner, recognised me. I certainly remembered him, and he again provided me with smiling service – breakfast at 6.00 am the following morning, 19th August.

Martigny to Villeneuve is another long haul – 42 kilometres to the shores of Lac Léman, and once again I was walking to a deadline. Tom Netter was meeting me in Lausanne the next day. Tom lives near Geneva and I had arranged to stay with him at his home; it would be my first non-hotel night since leaving Jonathan and Elisabetta at San Fabiano outside Siena four weeks ago. In the old days, deadlines – and Tom and I – went together. We met as young international reporters in Warsaw in 1980 at the beginning of the Solidarity Revolution which would help sweep away Communist rule from Poland and, ultimately, from the rest of Soviet-controlled Eastern Europe. Despite working for rival organisations – Associated Press and Reuters – we had become close friends. Tom had moved on from journalism into the United Nations and had ended up with a permanent post in Geneva. I would take the lake steamer from Villeneuve and meet him in Lausanne.

But that morning I started out from Martigny on the back foot. Fast macadam tracks down the Rhône Valley had sprung me a visitor – a blister on my left big toe. Till now, I had always believed that blisters were things that happened to other walkers and that I was somehow miraculously immune to them. Beyond wearing two-skinned 1,000 Mile Socks and a comfortable pair of boots with a wide last, I take no precautions against blisters, and most of the time I walk great distances without suffering from them. On the rare occasions that one does appear, I drain it, and put it on 'ignore', invariably finding that the pains of the morning are not those of the evening. But this one had continued to niggle, so I turned up the ignore dial and bent to the road with renewed determination. My foot would recover during the day with Tom.

I followed a succession of country lanes out of Martigny before rejoining the river, now heading decisively to the north. A rugged footpath up the escarpment took me to St Maurice and thence down to the riverbank as far as the turning to Aigle; I was retracing my steps from two years ago, feeling that same deep nostalgia that had so overwhelmed me on setting out from Rome, but this time my feelings were tinged with a gentle glow of satisfaction. For heaven's sake, I was halfway home. Though a light breeze took the worst off the heat, it still sucked me dry; I had to call at a house below the embankment to ask for water. The experience was as expected: an initially hostile reception, followed by warm displays of hospitality as bottle after bottle of freshly cooled water was offered, along with a kindly Godspeed for the remaining thousand-odd kilometres.

The landscape now changes dramatically, and just before the village of Chessel the river loops to the west, where I left it to cross the lateral canal and head out over the now flat farmland to Villeneuve. Here the river punches free from its great alpine gateway, and for the first time since leaving the Pò Valley I struck out across a featureless web of maize fields. But the distances weren't to be compared, and I was soon mingling with the tourists sunbathing by the lakeshore in the playground atmosphere at the little port of Villeneuve.

Wanting a room overlooking the lake, I had booked into the Hôtel du Port on the basis of its name and location. On my last stay in Villeneuve, on my way to Rome, I had found a delightful hotel in the main street, but with no views through its shuttered windows. Now that I was leaving the high mountains, I was eager once more for open vistas.

The receptionist threw me: why did she have to stamp my pilgrim passport, and what for?

"There is no rational explanation," I said. "Put it this way: I am walking the 'wrong' way from Rome, and no one will ever look at it, but still, for my own record, I am keen to keep it up to date."

My reply confused her even further. I think she was anxious lest I was trying to trick her into applying the hotel's stamp to some fraudulent document, but she suspended her native Swiss suspicions and stamped it anyway. My room was a treat. From the window, I could see across to the Château de Chillon and Montreux and, in the far distance, the silhouette of Vevey shimmering in the afternoon haze. I swam in the lake, and that evening dined over its gently lapping water at the Oasis restaurant on the little pier. With no more big hills to climb, and a rest day in the offing, I renounced my staple pasta dish in favour of the restaurant's speciality, lake trout.

I always carried a stout envelope, ready to mail home maps and notebooks, and, after sleeping until six, I parcelled up the second volume of Paul Chinn's Lightfoot guide with the maps which had guided me through the Alps. A last look told me that Chinn calculated Rome was 1,101 kilometres from Villeneuve. My daily log from Rome, recording my longer way over the Alps, came to 1,077 kilometres, and I was happy with the tally. I had on occasion taken short cuts when walking in Italy, and after all that distance I wasn't going to argue over a couple of dozen kilometres. So when the post office opened promptly as the church tower clock struck eight, I popped my package off before returning to the Grand Rue in search of a haircut. I had been on the road for nearly five weeks and there was a lot to snip off. A chatterbox of a girl attended to it at Eden Coiffure, asking whether I was "just visiting" Villeneuve. When I explained that "just visiting" had involved walking half way up Italy and over the Alps, I could feel the scissors and comb in Marie's delicate hands freezing, as if she sensed danger, evidently convinced that she was cutting the hair of a lunatic. I left her a generous tip, the gesture no doubt reinforcing her impressions of this strange foreigner's derangement.

Shorn of that heavy shag, I strolled to the jetty and sat on a bench sunning myself, content just to be still. The pistons of the Sulzer engines in the steamboat *La Suisse* could do my leg-work for the next hour-and-a-half: I had opted to re-cross Lac Léman on the elegant paddle steamer, built in 1910 and embodying all the grace of the Edwardian era in her sweet lines. Once on board, I perched myself within the arrow-head gunwales of the elongated prow, and there I stayed as we set off over the eastern end of the lake. We steamed in and out of Chillon, rounding the castle beneath its ramparts – although Jean-Jacques Rousseau, Lord Byron and Gustave Courbet would scarcely have approved of the way this fabled romantic landmark is now framed from the waterside by the motorway soaring overhead on stilts. We steamed on round the head of the lake to Vevey and Lausanne, and between there and Ouchy, as on my earlier crossing, the rhythmic throb of the engines and the gentle wash at the bows sent me into a deep sleep.

I didn't wake until we had berthed at Ouchy. This is the port below Lausanne which almost saw the last breath of a young English visitor: the same Winston Churchill who, a few days before, had reported to his mother on the successful climb of the Monte Rosa. Swimming from a rowing boat a mile offshore, he and his companion were blown out of reach. In his memoir, *My Early Life*, he recalled the stark peril they faced:

"I now saw Death as near as I believe I have ever seen Him," Churchill wrote. "He was swimming in the water at our side, whispering from time to time in the rising wind which continued to carry the boat away from us at about the same speed we could swim. No help was near. Unaided we would never reach the shore ... I now swam for life. Twice I reached within a yard of the boat and each time a gust carried it just beyond my reach; but by a supreme effort I caught hold of its side in the nick of time before a stronger gust bulged the red awning again."

Young Churchill had climbed the Monte Rosa because it was deemed safer than the Matterhorn, which he had wanted to scale, and a few days later he was nearly drowned. What would have happened to Britain in 1940, had that puff of wind come on sooner and stronger?

I walked up Mont Jorat by the side of the metro funicular, adjusting to the unaccustomed traffic and bustle of a big city as I reached the boulevards and shops. Tom would meet me later in the day in the city centre at Place Riponne; but before that I had stuff to do. My first stop was Lausanne's best book store, the Librairie Payot, to check the availability of French maps as a precaution in case the consignment Gail was sending me, covering Lausanne to Paris, failed to turn up at the *Poste Restante*.

Place Riponne had that morning been taken over by a battalion of Swiss homeless, some with cans and bottles in their hands – neither threatening nor particularly friendly, although my ageing rucksack and Meindls fitted me in rather well. Easing past them, I entered the post office, passport at the ready, anxious to find out whether my new maps had arrived. Last time, on my way to Rome, I had been asked to show my ID before despatching a similar package home. Maps, it had seemed in 2010, were deemed dangerous items in Switzerland. But post office passport control was asleep this time, or maybe maps had been taken off the list of dangerous items. The man at the counter had no interest in asking me to prove that I was the rightful recipient; perhaps he was convinced by the huge grin I gave him when I recognised Gail's leggy italic writing. I opened the package with the relish of a child attending to his biggest and best Christmas present.

From Place Riponne it was a short walk up to the Cathedral of

Notre-Dame where I could present my pilgrim passport for its ritual stamp. On the lake passage, I had given some thought to the question posed at Villeneuve: what were these stamps for? In my heart I knew that they had nothing to do with real pilgrimage, since the true pilgrim makes his or her own internal journey, for which there are no stamps. Mine were simply the colourful and picturesque trappings of an outer journey; even so, I didn't quite want to let go of my connection with the pilgrim route, and I clung to the notion that all such long journeys on foot remain in some sense pilgrimages.

It was lunchtime in the cathedral, the equivalent of the seventh day. I had to wait under the high gothic arches of the cool interior for half an hour before the shop at the western end re-opened, but my wait was rewarded, and not just with another pilgrim stamp. The lady attending the desk showed an instant understanding of my journey.

"We have many who walk from Lausanne to Rome and even to Santiago, but hardly any come back this way," she said. "It must be so fulfilling to retrace your steps."

On my way through Lausanne in 2010 I had wanted to visit the Musée des Beaux-Arts, only to find it closed for major refurbishment. Instead I had the excitement of discovering the Collection de l'Art Brut – an astonishing display of work inspired by mental disorder. So after lunching on the terrace below the cathedral I climbed the steps to the imposing Palais de Rumine to make good my omission. But the museum was once again closed; I had forgotten it was a Monday. There was nothing else to do in the short time before Tom arrived, so in a town house in the nearby Rue Valentin I surrendered myself for a massage in the hands of a Brazilian girl called Daniela.

"I've never seen a pilgrim before," she said.

"I am not sure if I am one," I replied. "I fear I am just using the word."

I had time to drink tea and send postcards before Tom swept into Place Riponne at the wheel of a large Chrysler with Swiss diplomatic plates, his vehicle announcing not just an arrival but a presence. Tom is a big man and he does everything to scale. He can work round the clock, and then fly half way round the world and repeat the process until a job is done. He can drink, not just round the clock, but for weeks on end. He smokes two cigarettes at once, and he eats with a relish matched only by the magnificence of his cooking. Women have loved him in equal measure. From the rookie journalist I had first known in Warsaw, Tom had risen to a high rank at the United Nations – and he had a life style to match.

The first thing that struck me when I slid onto the leather upholstered passenger seat beside him was that Tom had increased. Even with his driver's seat pushed back, Tom's ample stomach reached out towards the steering wheel. Other parts had changed, too. There was less of that brown hair, and more of a pronounced balding gap in the centre of his square-set head. The beard was now all white. But the baritone American burr, the musical flow of words, and the humour were all on parade. Tom hadn't changed; there was just more of him.

We drove in the direction of Geneva, in the lee of the Jura Mountains I would soon be crossing. Tom's village of Céligny, set among vineyards and forests, has retained its rustic character for all its closeness to the city and the lake; it is largely a cluster of old stone manors and farmhouses centred round a large pollarded plane tree, and there is a wonderful silence. It is often defined by those who lie buried in the cemetery not far from the single nave church: the Italian economist Vilfredo Pareto, father of the 80/20 theory; and two celebrated Britons, the novelist Alastair Maclean and the actor Richard Burton. Tom, who has lived in Céligny for more than a decade, harbours no plans to join them; he still talks of returning to his native America and of settling in a homestead in New England.

We stopped by a local supermarket; Tom, stocking up on goodies and grog for dinner, sent me to the bar where I dipped into a beer and the local paper. Along with the news that Switzerland was sizzling in an unusually hot summer, I read that a former Miss Switzerland had just scaled the Matterhorn with a guide, declaring that she had no inkling there was so much beauty in the Alps. I would have used my time better visiting the in-store cobbler which Tom had pointed out on the way in; a glance at his booth showed that it was well equipped, and I would soon have reason to regret not having parked my boots there.

"He's terrific," said Tom. "There is nobody left in Geneva who can repair boots like him."

I spent two nights with Tom and his American Puerto Rican partner, Jeannette. Physically his opposite – slender and petite – she also works at the United Nations. Their flat is a bit cramped and my sleeping quarters were not quite five-star – my bed was an inflatable mattress laid out on the floor, which I had to pump up during the night. But it was marvellous not being in a hotel, and the wine, food and conversation filled me to the brim with good old-fashioned contentment.

Happy to let my host snore on the following morning, I spent a taxing hour or so, phone in hand, sorting out my route across the Jura and booking hotels. I would be off piste, leaving the Via Francigena for a succession of passes about which I could find very little information. I plotted my route from what I could read on the maps and from the availability of accommodation, and that was a problem. I was walking into a part of Switzerland where hotels and bed & breakfasts were thin on the ground, and I couldn't help wondering why.

With Tom awake and breakfasted, I declared my ambition for the day. I wanted to visit the château that Voltaire rebuilt and used as his headquarters at Ferney, just across the French border. François Arouet, Voltaire's birth name, had long inspired me, but in the many years of visiting Geneva and passing the gates of his domain I had never yet set foot in it. He settled there in 1758, conveniently close to the border in case he needed to slip across into the safety of the Canton of Geneva. That was standard procedure for Voltaire; he spent a lot of his life having to flee into exile simply for daring to speak out. For his 21st century students, one of the most disturbing features of this daring is that he would probably run into similar problems today. He had the courage to challenge Judaism, Christianity and Islam – lampooning all three of these monotheistic religions in the satirical novella *Candide*, written the year before he moved to Ferney. It's not as if he rejected a Supreme Being, he just couldn't accept what he saw as man-made religions. This was heresy in the old regimes of 18th century Europe, and is regarded in the same light today in, for instance, many Middle Eastern and mid-Western American communities.

After the French Revolution with its anticlerical mindset, Ferney was renamed Ferney-Voltaire in honour of its literary patriarch. The philosopher's house, a sunny stone building with Palladian portico and wings and classic shuttered windows, is now owned by the state, and, after being knocked about over many generations in private hands, it has been transformed by France's Fifth Republic into a respectable literary and historical memorial. Voltaire, who held open house for Europe's elite, would perhaps have complained, however, that it is today only possible to visit the château in an organised party. A tolerant man, he may not have approved of the queues. Tom and I patrolled the gardens, tired and dowdy in the summer heat, kicking our heels, waiting for our group to muster by the chapel Voltaire built as his mausoleum. Tom lit a cigarette and pointed to the sage's chutzpah in the inscription over the chapel door: *Deo erexit VOLTAIRE* (erected to God by VOLTAIRE), an outrage to some because his adopted name was written in the larger characters.

There was an element of smoke and mirrors about what we were shown, a charge that can be levelled when you visit the home of Voltaire's equally sparky English contemporary, Horace Walpole, at Strawberry Hill. The actual rooms that Voltaire inhabited have been changed around, but we could tread the same parquet as the great man. The guide tested our patience by tackling us with trick questions: how, for instance, did Voltaire make his fortune, she asked? None of her French visitors had the answers, but I remained silent and bit my tongue, holding back my own modest knowledge of the writer's life, knowing that he had cashed in on state lotteries and set himself up as a private banker. But my dander was aroused when, in one of the principal salons, she drew our attention to the 'human rights' causes that Voltaire had espoused, among them those of Jean Calas, Admiral John Byng and Jean François Lefevre de la Barre. She made all of them out to have been triumphs.

Without wishing to play down Voltaire's courage and conviction in taking up these cases and in daring to challenge authority with his naked pen, I pointed out to our guide that they were all actually lost causes. Voltaire did succeed in obtaining a posthumous pardon for the Protestant merchant Jean Calas, barbarically tortured and put to death in Toulouse in 1762 for murdering his son for converting to Catholicism. But he was less successful in the cases of the British Admiral Byng and the French nobleman de la Barre. Byng, court-martialled for "cowardice" in disengaging from the French in a naval encounter off Minorca, was executed in 1757, despite Voltaire's pleas for his life. Byng's execution by firing squad on his own quarter-deck in Portsmouth Harbour is immortalised in *Candide* with the priceless observation about George II's England: "In this country it is considered useful now and again to shoot an admiral to encourage the others". The wily philosopher also failed to save the young de la Barre from having his tongue wrenched out in Abbeville in 1766 and being put to death, in the most part for failing to genuflect as a church procession passed him.

When we reached the chapel I gave our guide something else to look up. She trotted out the story that Voltaire had wished to be buried in the chapel, but that he had died in Paris and that his body was smuggled out of the city and interred in the abbey of Scellières in Champagne, only to be brought back in triumph to Paris after the 1789 Revolution and installed in the new national acropolis, the Panthéon. One story asserts that the hero's marble sarcophagus was later pillaged by monarchist fanatics after Napoleon's downfall; and Voltaire's remains – minus his heart and brain, which had been separately embalmed – were dumped on waste ground outside Paris. I put this particular version to our guide, and she looked blank. She promised to check it out.

Voltaire, in any case, is widely held to have had the last laugh. On his deathbed, asked by a priest whether he was ready to denounce the

Devil, he is reported to have replied: "This is no time to be making new enemies."

That evening, Tom and I left Jeannette to finish some work at home and dined outdoors at the Auberge de Céligny, the modest village restaurant. We had Swiss beef and the local red wine – *Clos de Céligny* – and by the end of the second bottle we had re-visited the more insane moments of our time as young journalists in Warsaw where we were among the small band of Western correspondents who reported the Solidarity Revolution from its outset at the Gdansk shipyards all the way through to the imposition of Martial Law in December 1981. Tom had arrived in Poland with about the same preparation for the assignment as Evelyn Waugh's fictional journalist in *Scoop*, William Boot, who was plucked by mistake from the obscurity of the gardening column to report a war in Africa. Tom had been reporting a US State legislature shortly before the AP sent him to Warsaw allegedly because no one else wanted the job. Like Boot, who eventually got his scoop, Tom had risen to the challenge and become a legendary correspondent.

"Crazy days," said Tom.

"Yes, and the nights, too. You know, Tom, I feel rather like Winston Churchill and Harrow. He used to say that he was all for public schools, but had no wish to go there again. I don't think I would ever want to relive that Polish experience."

"Why not?" asked Tom.

"We were on the edge night and day for 18 months," I replied. "Life has never been quite the same since."

"Is that why you go on long walks, Brian?"

I didn't have an answer, but promised him I would think about it. I had temporarily put walking to the back of my mind, but the question had brought me abruptly back to thinking about the way ahead, and it reminded me that after 36 hours of normal existence I would be starting out again to embark on uncharted terrain over the Jura. We sauntered back to the flat, and soon I was down on my lilo, asleep, with Tom's question unanswered.

The news the following morning was not encouraging. Tom announced that there had been a terrific thunderstorm in the night, which I had somehow slept through. More storms were forecast, and as we drove back to Lausanne the Jura looked dark and threatening. Tom dropped me just before 8.00 am in Place Riponne at the same place where he had picked me up.

"Take care," he said. "You look nervous."

"I am."

My plan was to cut northwest from Lausanne to the town of L'Isle at the foot of the Jura. But I had been warned by the receptionist at the hotel where I planned to stay that there might not be room for me. The Swiss army was engaged on summer manoeuvres in the Jura – doubtless preparing for a French invasion – and the officers could just requisition the entire hotel. I wondered, if that was the case, whether they would lend me a tent. And so I struck out on the Avenue de Morges, stopping for tea and a croissant at a bar in the suburb of Rennes, the sole European among a crowd of coffee drinking Moroccans. Soon after, in the pretty town of Bussigny, I said a final farewell to the Via Francigena, exchanging its route into France that I had followed in 2010, for the higher tracks over the Jura slightly to the west and aiming for Dijon and Paris rather than Besançon and Rheims.

Getting started entailed a few early uncomfortable kilometres along a busy cantonal road where I was left in no doubt that, going about their daily business in the valley, the Swiss didn't like strangers walking in the path of their cars. But after crossing the River Venoge I transferred to footpaths and lanes, and, with the rising ground, the country opened out into undulating sweeps of arable fields which, with all their neat echelons of pale gold bales, could have been Wiltshire but for the near stifling heat. The village shop in Gollion provided me with an Emmental sandwich, and the village restaurant profusions of cold tea and a table outside at which to sit for a while. It was only when rather dressy customers arrived – Gollion is within Lausanne's catchment, and the menu is on the gourmet side – that the yellow rucksack and walking boots began to attract awkward glances.

The afternoon of my last full day in Switzerland was a gentle stroll along narrow deserted roads, sometimes no more than tractor tracks, that led me past large arable farms with red-tiled houses where it was hard to imagine that I was in the same country as the cities of Geneva and Lausanne, let alone one that produced the tough pastorals of Goffried Keller. Occasionally the road would dip, the serene arable slopes separated by sudden wooded dells into which the track would descend before emerging at another expansive headland. I was enjoying the idyll while I could: by now, the Jura were taking shape ahead of me, an unbroken range of shadowy heights that I would have to cross to reach France, and on which I noticed an ominous build-up of cloud.

L'Isle, 26 kilometres from Lausanne, lies at 1,200-odd metres at the end of a local railway line; it is where La Venoge has its source at the foot of the Jura in six different springs that combine to send the young river on its winding journey to Lac Léman. The springs also feed the ornamental lake in front of L'Isle's 17th century château, sometimes called the Little Versailles of Vaud. Built in 1696 by Charles de Chandieu, a Lieutenant-General of Louis XIV's Swiss Guards, the château is uncompromisingly and perfectly balanced in the French classical style, three upper and three lower windows on each side of a pedimented centre, from which paved flights of steps fan out to the park and the lake below, all under a thoroughly French mansard roof whose lines seem to rhyme with the contours of the Jura up behind.

Is that how my hotel got its name – La Balance – or was it just luck? It certainly wouldn't be my description of the place; an old coaching house, all its bedrooms round a central stairwell, and showers and bathrooms reached down a musty corridor, it is run by a family from Portugal. I was grateful to be there – at least the Swiss army had decided not to camp in L'Isle for the night – and dinner in the hotel dining room was turned into one of the jolliest feasts, all by the presence of another diner, one who was either wonderfully eccentric or utterly mad.

Patrick was a long-time denizen of La Balance. I had noticed him on arrival and had assumed from his blue denim jacket that he was some colourful local farmer. The face was smiling, with lively green eyes half-hidden behind a cascade of grey hair that curled round to mingle with a great white beard. This engaging profusion of untamed hair was topped with a black wide-brimmed Levellers-style hat, which stayed on even for eating. It was while I watched him attacking his steak that he cast me a friendly eye. I went over, and he poured me a glass of red wine, his hand revealing elongated, carefully filed fingernails. He was definitely not a farmer.

Where was I from, he enquired? I told him about my adventures, and then turned the conversation to him. He spoke in disjointed and often unconnected phrases, telltale signs perhaps of habitual drug taking, but over several more glasses I pieced together his unusual story. Patrick proudly showed me the Star of David on a silver chain round his neck.

"This is very important. This is my identity card. It never leaves me."

What a strange life. He was Jewish and born in Algiers, when it was still in French hands, and brought up in a wealthy family. As a young man he had written poetry, and he appears to have had a lot of fun. He travelled widely and spent time in London, but the music stopped – the money ran out – and he was now living in L'Isle in forced retirement; his family paid for him to be here. Though nothing seemed to extinguish that childish eagerness and his ever-ready smile, to all intents and purposes Patrick was an exile, and a prisoner of the hotel.

He would have been fast asleep when I crept away at 7.00 am on 24th August. The day had dawned bright, but I wasn't counting on it continuing that way. The forecast was for rain. The first thing I saw in the municipal car park was a cluster of windowless khaki vehicles – the Swiss Army had indeed set up camp overnight, and I was just thankful that they hadn't turned me out of the hotel.

I had one last big climb ahead over two high cols before descending into France; I fell in mentally to grind up the 600 metres from L'Isle to the first of them, the 1,840-metre Col de Mollendruz. A relatively minor height gain, this was my first serious ascent since the Alps, and my muscles weren't used to it; they had grown soft in the Rhône Valley. I left the main road at the village of La Coudre, branching off into the forest with certain misgivings. I could have done with a larger-scale map; but I needn't have been worried because the Swiss had been generous and practical with their Jura waymarks, and I managed to steer a course to the top. Emerging onto the col, I found myself greeted by a succession of deafening detonations. At first I thought it was thunder, but the gathering clouds did not yet look angry enough, and I quickly realised that I was hearing the boom of artillery. The Swiss Army had opened fire somewhere to the south around Mont Tendre, the highest peak of the Jura.

I descended by the main road to the Vallée de Joux, entering one of the enclosed upland valleys of the Jura that are renowned for two totally unrelated industries – watch making and cheese. At its heart lies the Lac de Joux, in winter a giant skating rink and in summer a holiday playground. I stopped at its head at the lakeside resort of Le Pont for a slice of pear tart and tea, which the café's *patron* insisted on serving me in a pot with its teabag in a metal clamp, as if to say that this was the way it was really done. The resort is strung along a beachside street, and facing it is an oversize concrete statue of the winged horse Pegasus protruding from the water. I sat and watched a young family at the jetty readying a sailing boat for a day trip, with an elderly Swiss couple next to me who rattled their newspapers at each other when they wanted to say something.

But now, after my eight days traversing Switzerland, it was time to cross into France; I downed my second cup of correctly brewed tea and walked on over the causeway separating Lac de Joux from its little brother, Lac Brenet, and set off back uphill for the day's final climb. Pulling away through the rock-strewn meadows above the lake I could see inky clouds closing round the summit of Dent de Vaulion behind me, and by the time I reached the French border it was raining.

The border is a ghostly place. It is no longer manned because Switzerland is part of frontier-free mainland Europe, and two wooden sheds either side of a limestone wall – the guard houses of the former border – are all that now remain, along with a notice informing travellers that they may not proceed without the necessary documents. I wondered how a migrant from North Africa would interpret such instructions. After the frontier I climbed to the Col de Landoz-Neuve at 1,260 metres, my highest point in the Jura, and with rain and wind now lashing me I felt cold for the first time since setting out from Rome. The northern sector of the range is deserted; I had as company only upland cattle in their fields bounded with dry stonewalls, their bells ringing sporadically. Even the occasional farmhouse appeared to be empty, and it was a relief to come away from the high passes and drop down through the thick pines of the forest of Noirmont to the valley of the River Doubs and my resting place for the night in the first settlement of the French Haut-Jura, the frontier-town of Mouthe.

SEVEN
French Nots

I HAD BEEN LONGING TO REACH FRANCE: IT was my Home Straight, the North-bound equivalent of entering Italy on my journey to Rome. I like to believe that I know France and the French well; I speak the language and have walked the length and breadth of the country on three occasions. I thought I knew the drill. But in the first week or so I had a succession of irksome experiences with the French which invariably resulted in outpourings of how *désolés* they were, and I began to wonder if I was carrying my own dark cloud of Gallic desolation with me.

Not that that was the frame of mind in which I approached my first night's destination! Mouthe, 32 kilometres from L'Isle, announced itself well before I came close: I could see the town rising in the distance over a flat floodplain of meadowland. "A chill synonymous with pleasure" was what it offered the visitor, according to a notice some two kilometres out, by the entrance to the forest park in the hills high above the town. Mouthe claims the unusual distinction of being the coldest place in France, having achieved the country's lowest ever recorded temperature, minus 41 degrees centigrade on 17th January 1985. In winter, it becomes a Mecca for cross-country skiers; what charms would it reveal on a hot drizzly afternoon in late August 2012?

I wondered if it had been a drovers' market-place, often the explanation of such places – Long Melford, for example, in England – but Mouthe's single wide street with its regular stone facades and a turreted

Mairie at the end is French town-planning at its most basic: rustic charm, but a bit sterile. I headed for the tourist office and the man on duty, Nicolas, explained the uniformity of the place, of which he was obviously a fan. There had been a great fire here in 1657, nine years before London's, which had devoured all the medieval timber buildings. I passed him my pilgrim passport, and he took great delight in bringing the Val de Mouthe stamp down on it. It filled half a page. He looked up and smiled. "Now you won't forget that you came over the Jura via Mouthe."

A prophetic insight? Soon there would be quite another reason not to forget Mouthe. I walked on down the Grande Rue to number 43, a simple town house which had a sign over the door, *La Chaumière*. It was a *chambres d'hôtes* run by Madame Marmet, and she had told me that she would be there to greet me by three o'clock. It was now two, so I removed my boots and settled down on the bench outside waiting for her arrival. That was the start of my travails. I glanced at the soles and noticed that the rubber heels, which Roberto at the Ivrea Carrefour had moulded and nailed to the boots, were coming loose. I could lift up the edges. This was serious. I had walked on them only for 367 kilometres, albeit over the Alps, and already they were knackered. I now had something meaningful to do to fill the time before Madame Marmet let me in: buy a new pair or find a mender.

There was a sports outlet nearby and I enquired if they had any mountain boots – the shop proprietor was *désolé* but the only footwear in stock was trainers and cycling shoes. Now there was a garage opposite, the sort of old fashioned outfit with pumps and workshops you used to find in the middle of most towns; it had probably only recently ceased to be Mouthe's principal source of petrol and diesel. I walked over, and into a dark repair bay stacked with tyres.

Could they apply some of the glue they used on tyres to the heels of my boots, I asked?

They looked puzzled. Accustomed to changing tyres, filtering oil and fixing new clutches, they had never before been asked to mend a pair of boots. I took one off, keeping my sock clear of oily patches, and half explained, half signed what I had in mind. A lot of *impossibles* and *désolés* followed – this was a garage where they repaired cars; they couldn't touch my boots because they could not guarantee the work, they didn't have the right size press, besides which the industrial glue used on tyres was not suitable, indeed it was positively dangerous. But by stringing out my tale of having walked from Rome, I eventually badgered them into giving it a go. A few minutes later, I limped back across Grande Rue in my socks, my thumbs acting on the freshly glued heels like the presses the garage didn't have, and rang the door bell at No 43. Still no reply. It was nearing five, and Madame Marmet had promised to be there at three. It was taking a serious turn. There was nowhere else to stay and, even in summer, at just below 1,000 metres, I did not fancy sleeping out in the coldest place in France, and felt I would rather give my retreads a night to cure before walking out.

I had Madame Marmet's mobile number, and I called her. A flustered, angry voice answered; she was on her way; why was I calling her in any case? I was happy to wait, I said. I had only called because I was anxious in case she had forgotten me. She was, after all, two hours late.

A further half hour passed before a car finally drew up; out stepped an attractive woman in her early forties. I smiled and introduced myself; Madame Marmet took my hand almost as if to brush it aside, and stood at her front door pouring out a streaming invective. What the French couple who came in during this made of it – they were also staying at No 43 – I don't know. It went like this (and some of its power gets lost in translation): How dare I call her when she was driving back from the hospital? Didn't I realise she had just had to undergo some urgent medical tests? Did I think I had the right to talk like that to her, or for that matter to anyone else? She was in a good mind to send me packing: she didn't like people like me, especially not foreigners like me. Madame Marmet was not only *désolée*, she was thoroughly *fâchée*.

I was *bouleversé*; in all my travelling through France I had never encountered such an explosion of anger from someone supposed to be my host. I demurred, apologised and fell silent. All I wanted was to check into a room and to continue pressing the heels of my boots. But I was so upset that after sorting myself out and settling into my room, which was actually a bunkhouse, I slipped out unnoticed by Madame Marmet and made my way back to the tourist office.

"Do you get many complaints about Madame Marmet?" I asked.

"Funny you ask," said Nicolas. "Yes, we do. She is known for her fireworks."

I described the manner of my reception. Nicolas promised to take it up. The incident coloured my stay in Mouthe and it even followed me to dinner. I dined at the *L'Oeil de Boeuf* across the street, and half way through dinner the French couple who had witnessed Madame Marmet's outburst came over to me.

"After you left, we told her that she should not treat clients like that."

Madame Marmet got up early to prepare my breakfast. She wasn't the same person; she was full of contrition, and I quickly discovered why. The tourist office had phoned, threatening to suspend her *chambres d'hôtes* from its approved list. It was Madame Marmet's turn to bite her lip; but I promised that I would call Nicolas at the tourist office when it opened later in the day to explain that it had all been a big misunderstanding.

The tyre glue had stiffened my heels, and ready for a final haul over the Jura I stepped out of Madame Marmet's house at 7.00 am into pouring rain. It rained all day. In fact, it didn't just rain; the *Haut Jura* was whacked by a violent electrical and thunderstorm, and I found myself walking straight through its path.

The day started easily, the rain still light enough for me to observe the country that I was passing through. The heels seemed to be holding, and I was back on a minor *route départementale*, perhaps my ideal way of walking in France. This was the D55, leading to the enticingly named village of Mignovillard. The road climbed a little over 100 metres above Mouthe, first through meadows crowned with limestone crags, then among the dripping conifers of a forest before finally emerging onto a plateau of high farmland, and here at Mignovillard I halted in search of elevenses. But the town's last café had closed years ago, and all I could find was a warmed croissant at the *boulangerie* that I munched in the shelter of its verandah. Starting to feel the cold, I stripped down to put on more layers; the heat of Italy and the Swiss valleys was becoming a dim memory. This was the moment to keep my pledge to Madame Marmet, and, crouched down under the eaves of the building, I called Nicolas. I did my best to suggest that Madame Marmet had meant no harm and that the misunderstanding may well have been my fault. But I was too late.

"That is very noble of you," said Nicolas, "but I have already reported the incident to my boss."

Leaving the village, I swapped *routes départementales*; the D107 soon plunged me back into a conifer tunnel, the *Fôret Domaniale de la Joux*, but not before I had noted thick clouds, almost football-shaped, rolling in low from the west; and now with the tall trunks either side of me yawing in the mounting wind, and the rain beginning to pelt down, I was becoming aware of real menace: sheets and jagged lines of lightning. I needed to find shelter, and quickly, but I looked around and there was none – no house, no barn, no hut, not even a decent ditch. The thunder came, explosions so close and so loud as to make me jump. Wet through and terrified, I had no option but to keep walking, counting the interval between the flash of lightning and the subsequent detonation of thunder, and trying to work out where I would be when the next one struck. The last place I needed to be was next to one of those 50-metre firs. I walked on through what is supposed to be one of the most beautiful pine and spruce forests in France, unnerved by the drumbeats of thunder, lashed by chilled rain and pursued by lightning. Had any car passed, I think I would have flagged it down. All afternoon the storm raged, and it wasn't until I cleared the forest and started downhill towards Andelot-en-Montagne that it showed any sign of easing. By then I had managed to find shelter in a logger's cabin, but I was so wet and cold that it made no difference; and I had decided to press on. Now came the first signs of human life for several hours; two cyclists pedalling up the hill towards me, Italians returning from London, which they had left six days ago. So pathetic must I have looked that one of them took out a mint and thrust it into my mouth.

"Here, you need that," he said. "We sat out the storm in Andelot-en-Montagne."

"I think I need more than a mint," I said.

But it was a kind gesture, and it was enough to carry me down into the valley. My first 24 hours back in France had not turned out quite as I had expected, but in the circumstances I think I was fortunate to arrive in Andelot-en-Montagne with little more to worry about than how to bale out my rucksack and where to dry my sodden clothes. And, moreover, my heels had survived the deluge.

Only later did I learn that a Pilatus PC-12 executive plane flying from Antwerp to Switzerland had crashed during the storm not far away, killing all four Swiss people on board. It was apparently struck by lightning, its starboard wing torn off before it impacted.

The *chambres d'hôtes* I had chosen for my night in Andelot-en-Montagne occupied a large old farmhouse at the top of the main street. The word Hotel remained painted on the wall, but it hadn't been that since shortly after the railway closed down. Now accommodating cross-country skiers and discerning summer holidaymakers, it is run by two elderly sisters, Madame Bourgeois and Madame Busson. The entrance was through the back garden and I was welcomed, dripping on the doormat, by a bony younger woman who turned out to be Françoise, one of their nieces. Summoning the last shreds of my humour, I told her that I had arrived soaking from Rome. Her reaction was the antithesis of my reception the previous evening in Mouthe.

"My goodness," she said, shutting the glazed door on the rain, "you had better get those wet clothes off at once. Well, not quite here. Let's get you to your room first, and then we will take your clothes to dry in the boiler room."

After my ill-starred first 32 kilometres in France, this was just what I needed. The old hotel was delightfully dated; my room, furnished with a brass bedstead, a simple wooden table and chair and an oversized armoire, could have been a 1950s film set. The shower was a trickle, but a warm trickle, and a great relief after the cold stuff outside. Washed and dried, I flung open the shutters. It was still sheeting, the water gushing off the gutters and streaming down the Grande Rue towards the market square and the *Mairie* at the bottom of the hill.

I emptied my rucksack, pouring out the water from its bilges, and put on my least wet shirt and trousers. Françoise led me through the kitchen to a covered yard and to the boiler, which would not have been out of place below decks in the engine room of a tramp steamer. It had pipes sprouting like the branches of an apple tree – and I should have taken in the smuts on them. But at that moment they were perfect; and I hung my clothes over the hot pipes like bunting, and was about to find a perch for my boots when Françoise intervened.

"You'll be needing newspaper to stuff your boots," she said, "obviously you are not used to drying them out."

"I've been spoilt with hot weather for the last 40 days. I had almost forgotten what rain looks like."

"Well, you have certainly made up for it today. And it looks as if the rain will be like this for a while yet."

Françoise nipped back across and returned with a few sheets of newsprint which she pushed tightly into the body of each boot. I saw they were all from *Le Monde*. Europe's leading dailies have their unofficial uses, and at home I find the *Financial Times* sets the best bonfires. I was beginning to fall for Françoise's charms, and, with her kind attentiveness to the unknown and perhaps deranged foot-traveller who had stumbled into her mountain-bound valley, I couldn't help asking myself what she wanted.

Holed up in my room, I slept the afternoon away to the thrum of rain. Presenting myself downstairs at six o'clock, I was ushered into the former hotel bar; renovated in the 1960s in the semblance of a Hall of Mirrors, it was now used as the guests' drawing room. A bar still filled the corner and, although there was nobody behind it, several beers appeared; while attending to them I learned something about the hotel from Thérèse, one of the sisters.

The Hôtel Bourgeois had begun as a staging inn; its heyday arrived with the railway in the early 1860s. Eighty years later, the German military had made good use of it during the Occupation, and Madame Thérèse said the local resistance was involved in numerous escapades and near misses. The hotel continued to prosper after the war, the *belle époque* for the new joint owners, Anne Marie Busson and her sister Thérèse Bourgeois, but gradually it fell on hard times and closure of the railway station in 1991 finally put paid to the business. But the sisters didn't want to give up, so they turned the place into an easier to run *chambres d'hôtes*. Creaky as it was, I was thankful that the valour and charm of the two old sisters had kept the Bourgeois name alive long enough for my visit. Two days in, this was the provincial France I had imagined to myself when approaching the Swiss border.

Madame Thérèse spoke of the country beyond Andelot-en-Montagne through which my path would take me tomorrow as some sort of El Dorado – lowland farms down in the valley where they cultivated crops and fruit in profusion scarcely imaginable up here in the Jura, where all you have is forest and cattle. Dinner with the other guests, served in the hotel's grand old dining room, certainly avoided any taint of the valley: local ham, local sausage, local cheese and Jura wine.

When I awoke at 4.00 am, it was still raining hard, and I listened to the rhythmic dripping for a few minutes and returned to my slumber, with the not unwelcome thought that if it went on raining I would rather sleep the day away. I stirred again an hour later, and something quite unexpected greeted me: silence. The rain had stopped, or at least petered out. I would face the day after all.

My clothes and boots were dry but soot-smeared; I would carry away a visual memento of Françoise in the form of smuts, but no matter; warm dry clothes make a good start to the day. After serving breakfast at the large communal table in the kitchen, Madame Thérèse saw me off with a parting present – two plastic bags.

"They're forecasting more rain," she said, almost apologetically.

I stepped into a still dripping world, with rain running off tiles and springing through leaking gutters. Patches of sky, however, reassured me that if the rain was returning it would hold off for a few hours yet. With a walk ahead of me well above my daily average, albeit downwards off the Jura, once out of Andelot I put my best foot forward. On clearing the forest at the village of Pont d'Héry, I joined the quiet D107, once again able to enjoy the countryside without cowering under a hood, and taking pleasure in the sounds, from either side, of cattle chewing the cud and the counterpoint of their bells. Though the dark band of the Jura was retreating behind me, this was still upland country, and now with every few hundred steps another expansive vista slowly resolved into a new framed picture. Closer to the road, the signpost to the village of Ivory caught my eye, and then a large oak tree: it had tumbled into the ditch with much smashing of limbs – no doubt the victim of yesterday's lightning. That was worth a photograph.

But at the very moment I put my camera away, I heard a snap and felt a jolt. The frame of my aged rucksack had torn through its supporting sleeve. This had happened before on my way south, when a seamstress in San Gimignano had carried out an emergency repair. I was still eight kilometres from the next town, Arbois, and I walked on with the loose frame digging into my ribs, cursing yet another irritating surprise and wondering if a solution could be found in Arbois.

The road dropped steeply, describing a long loop into the valley of the River Cuisance, the lower contours thick with vines and their hanging grapes. Arbois produces some of the Jura's best wines, including the sherry-like *vin jaune*, and it is no accident that the town's celebrated adopted son, Louis Pasteur, raised in Arbois but born in nearby Dôle, conducted his first experiments in microbiology here, and that his first major paper was on wine fermentation. However, it wasn't of wine or Pasteur that I was thinking as the town came into view in the fold of the valley around the conspicuous yellow-stone belfry of the church of St Just. I was nursing sore ribs, and hoping that on a Saturday there might be a tractor workshop or garage up to repairing my rucksack.

My friend Harry Bucknall, having arrived in Rome two weeks ago, had long left my airwaves. Since climbing over the Alps, there was no longer that evening radio call to look forward to. But what Harry had said at our dinner with Gail in Gambassi Terme had remained with me; that there are angels on the Via Francigena. If the Via Francigena is to be defined strictly by today's waymarked route taking in the stages of Archbishop Sigeric's journey, Arbois is way off course, but an extraordinary encounter was about to demonstrate that angels are seemingly not bound by precise geographical location. Entering the narrow streets of the old town, I noticed a saddle-maker and cobbler who also advertised the repair of leather goods. It was so dimly lit that I could easily have missed it. Then I looked again. The shop was called *Ange Répare* – Angel Repairs. Harry Bucknall's Via Francigena angels had spread their wings as far as Arbois.

There is nothing whimsical or falsely pious in the choice of name; it's that of the young proprietor, Angelique Jeanmougin. When I stepped in and approached the counter to present my rucksack, I could see her daughter playing in the back room. The aroma of new leather, and of the polished saddles and bridles on display, contrasted with the sour, rainy whiff of my own harness, and made me doubt that she would want to handle anything so crude, but this time there were no *désolées*. Angelique and her husband, her chief assistant, would fix my broken bag. He would saw off a length of the protruding plastic frame, and that would give sufficient purchase on the sleeve to stitch it over and keep it in place. In for a penny, in for a pound; could they possibly check my boots, too? Off they came; with one look at the heels, Ange pronounced them dead. They would fit new ones, and not just with glue, they would also nail them fast, and they would do it all on the spot. Within half an hour, I was back outside *Ange Répare*, miraculously reharnessed and reheeled.

After a celebratory croissant and coffee in the arcaded main square, and a bow to Dr Pasteur's house on the banks of the Cuisance, the road called, and the newly heeled boots were ready for a serious initiation. I walked hard for the remainder of the day along a gentle flood plain where water meadows fused into the grassy wetlands of the *Val d'Amour*, as far as the town of Mont-sous-Vaudrey; then cutting due west through the forests of Scey and Longwy until, just as early dusk fell and the long-held-off rain set in, I reached my destination for the night, the town of Chaussin. The fading light reminded me that high summer was drawing to a close; besides, I was inching my way ever northwards: I had covered 52 kilometres, a little over 32 miles, in ten and three quarter hours.

At the Auberge de Chaussin I found myself the sole guest, and although the owner did his best to serve a decent meal the one memorable part was a bottle of lightly chilled Arbois red wine – I had done with my mountains and felt I deserved it. The hotel wasn't up to early breakfasts, so the 26th August began with my sitting on the steps of the war memorial obelisk opposite the town hall, chewing a freshly baked croissant I had bought at the *boulangerie*. Among the names cut into the stone after the 1939-45 War were four local people who had been deported to German concentration camps. One stood out, that of Simone Michel-Lévy, a heroine of the French Resistance who was born in Chaussin.

In the 1930s, she had worked in the PTT, France's national post, telephone and telegraph service, becoming an expert in telephony. Simone's contribution to the resistance was vital in helping to set up clandestine radio communications and courier networks in many sectors of France. With her striking looks – cropped hair, generous lips and green eyes under arching eyebrows – she needed the camouflage of multiple codenames: Emma, Françoise, Madame Royale, Madame Bertrand and Mademoiselle Flaubert, suggesting a delight on Simone's part in *Madame Bovary* and her creator. In November 1943, in Paris, she was betrayed, arrested and brutally tortured before being deported first to Ravensbrück and then to the death camp of Flossenbürg on the Czech border, where she was hanged in April 1945, just ten days before it was liberated. She was 39 years old.

In her hometown of Chaussin, 67 years later, it was a dank August morning when I left the memorial to her and her comrades. I walked on up the Grande Rue past the modest house where she was born the daughter of a plasterer. It may be that people on foot are among the last guardians of the memory of such local heroes and heroines; cyclists and motorists pass by too fast to notice their memorials.

It was a day of three rivers. A back lane led over the first and smallest, the Orain, and next to the bubbling Doubs, which I crossed by an 1897 Eiffel-era metal bridge as the sun began to filter through the cloaking mist. The Doubs flows northeast and then southwest, describing the shape of a fencing-staple round a mountain spur, and I had briefly trodden its banks at Mouthe, close to its springs in the Jura. Down here, though, it occupies a broad alluvial plain which is crossed by arrow-straight roads. And here, half-way between the towns of St Aubin and St Jean-de-Losne, like an official endorsement of transition from hills to flatlands, an invisible frontier marks the divide between the departments of Jura and Côte d'Or.

Côte d'Or, or Golden Hillside as it would be in English, sounds like a piece of contemporary branding, but it is in fact one of the 83 *départements* created in 1790, a year after the French Revolution, when it was carved out of the former province of Burgundy; from St Jean-de-Losne, Burgundy was my business. I planned to walk through the heart of this warm land of lush vineyards and coloured roofs on the towpath of the Canal de Bourgogne. These French canals have cast a spell on me since childhood; in my early teens, in the summer of 1962, I journeyed through them by motor cruiser from Normandy to the Mediterranean, an unforgettable introduction to the hot sun and fine fare of the country. Years later, I found that the broad paths alongside them, the *Chemins d'halage*, make for relaxed and speedy walking. Once across my third river of the day, the Saône, from which the canal sets forth to link the Rhône and the Seine, I could put away my maps and look forward to several hundred kilometres of effortless progress. For the first time since leaving St Peter's Square 44 days before, I would not have to be watching out for the next turning, or the next signpost or waymark; nor would I be bothered by cars. All that was needed was to keep putting one foot in front of the other.

Once clear of the marina and boatyard, I set off briskly along the towpath for the few remaining kilometres to the first village on the canal, Brazey-en-Plaine. I had made that my destination for the day because, although with a walk of only 26 kilometres I had still had it in me to do the extra 25 to Dijon, I was content after the prolonged breakout from the Jura of the previous day, and resting in the sun would be pleasant. Besides, Dijon needs seeing in the daylight, and I particularly wanted time to visit one of its principal treasures – the group of *Pleurants*, or sculpted mourning figures, removed to the city's Musée des Beaux Arts from around the tomb of John the Fearless, Duke of Burgundy.

The hotel I had booked into called itself, somewhat grandly, the Shield of Burgundy – Le Bouclier de Bourgogne. It sat glumly by a roundabout on Brazey's outskirts, and when I arrived at 1.30 pm it appeared to be firmly shut. I knocked at the back door, and to my surprise and relief it opened. A woman, with drying-up cloth wound round her hair, stood in it. She was the *patronne*.

I was early, and she was *désolée*, but there had been a wedding party the night before which she was clearing up after, and there were no rooms ready for me. I would have to come back at six o'clock.

Was I, as perhaps at Mouthe, running once again into an unfamiliar face of France; ground down by years of state-run capitalism and socialist regulation, is it the case that the French have forgotten how to say yes? What was I supposed to do for the next four hours? I turned on my best charm, along with what had to be my trump card. How often, if ever, had she received a pilgrim arriving on foot from Rome? Not a flicker on the face in the door; by and large, Roman pilgrimage means virtually nothing in a country which, since 1945, has become overwhelmingly secular. Where, then, was the nearest hotel? St Jean-de-Losne, she said. But I've just come from there, I explained. She sighed – the penny or the euro equivalent had at last dropped, and she made a suggestion.

"Well, I have got a minuscule bedroom made up where you can settle in. But it is *very small.*"

She showed me upstairs to what was indeed one of the smallest hotel rooms I have ever seen; smaller, I am sure, than the average prison cell. In its confined space, I did my best to sort out my clammy and dirty clothes, trying all the time to avoid banging against the walls; hoping not to bump into the *patronne*, I then tiptoed down a corridor to the communal bathroom for a shower. It was now that she gave me my biggest shock, walking straight in, undeterred by my naked body, and informing me that she had just made up a room, and I would be welcome to transfer my things there. Step by step, from then on, our relationship improved to the point where I felt I could ask her for an enormous favour: could she kindly put my clothes through her washing machine, a service for which I was willing to pay a proper supplement? Out came a litany of reasons why this was *impossible*: not least, far too many sheets and towels to get through. But then, having faced me with the prospect of arriving grubby in Dijon, she suddenly relented: "but don't expect them back until tonight," she warned.

So leaving her my pile of washing, I strolled into Brazey-en-Plaine in the sum of my dry clothing for a well earned beer. I passed a by-road that reminded me that I was in *premier cru* wine country: Route de Nuits Saint Georges, 18 kilometres away. Perhaps it was Brazey itself, perhaps it was because it was Sunday afternoon, but the town appeared to have little going for it. The only bar was run by a couple from China, and the only attraction was the park at the Château Magnin, landscaped *à l'anglaise* by a mid-19th century political figure and governor of the Bank of France, with a spreading lawn, remarkably kempt, fringed by sweet chestnut, oak, cedar and wellingtonia. Back at the Bouclier de Bourgogne, the *patronne* cooked me a surprisingly good dinner, chicken followed by prune pie, and by breakfast the next morning we were the best of friends; and so, decked out in freshly laundered clothes, I returned in buoyant mood to my new waterside world on the *chemin d'halage.*

Over the canal, banked above the meadows, a steamy mist arose, and against the early morning chill I had put on a fleece for the first time since crossing the Alps. The going was good, though not perfect. Burgundy is the home of many marvellous cathedrals and churches, built of a distinctive grain coloured limestone; but some of the chippings and leftovers from these great buildings seem to have ended up as the canal's towpath. In some sections where the path has not been rolled off and tarmacked for cyclists, the surface has irritating loose chips and flakes which, when they caught the edges of my soles, caused me repeatedly to curse Burgundian stone.

It was in these stretches that I thought how much easier the barges and cruisers had it on the water – except that to travel the 242 kilometres from end to end, Saône to Seine, they would need to negotiate no less than 191 locks. Little wonder, then, that there weren't many of them: in fact during the six days I spent walking the canalside I can't have counted more than two boats a day. That's scant traffic for a waterway that took three centuries to build, being finally completed in 1833. By then, sadly, it was already prey to the new fast mode of transporting goods, the railway network. But *Voies Navigables de France (VNF),* the subsidised state agency in charge of the country's inland navigations, does an incomparable job in caring for the Canal de Bourgogne. The people VNF employs are priests dedicated to a unique water-borne world and its environment.

On the 25 kilometres to Dijon just one boat passed, *La Petite Folie,* an old working barge converted into a floating hotel. English-speaking guests assembled on the deck as its freshly painted black hull emerged from lock gates.

"Now which lock are we at?" enquired one of the guests.

"Does it really matter?" I nearly hollered back to her. It's not that one lock is the same as the other – far from it, the landscape changes all the time – but rather that time and place become irrelevant on the Canal de Bourgogne. It's timeless and enchanting practically all the way.

For the rest, I shared the canal with herons that alighted at the waterside and seemingly enjoyed a far greater strike rate than their prayerful rivals, the fishermen, patiently bent over still rods on the bank. As I approached Dijon, I had reason to thank cyclists, not a thought I am generally prone to when I see them on public footpaths. But the towpath had been resurfaced for them, so I could fairly race the final few kilometres, and I was in the city centre by midday.

Even though my attire and rucksack were decidedly out of place, the three-star Hôtel des Ducs had caught my eye, and that is where I had made my booking. On presenting myself shortly after noon, I was met with a frosty reception. They were *désolés*, but check-in wasn't until three o'clock. In 2010, I had grown used to the 36-hour week and its effect on French provincial hotels, but this was a first for a city centre establishment, and I asked to see the manager. He was considerably younger than me. How could a prime city hotel operate so inflexible a system? Someone must surely have checked out early? Take myself: I would be leaving at dawn the next day. I threatened to look elsewhere, but the manager insisted that the room would still have to be paid for and that in any case, in the month of August, I wasn't going to find anywhere else in Dijon. It may not have worked back in Brazey, but at last I played the Roman pilgrimage card, and this did the trick: they would make up a room for me as soon as possible. When I got to it, it was modern, bright and spacious, and it had a wonderful view over Dijon's rooftops, and I was damned if I was going to let my stand-off in the hotel foyer colour my visit to the city.

The *Pleurants*, the cluster of miniature alabaster figures made for the tomb of Jean sans Peur had long haunted me. John, Duke of Burgundy, and known as the Fearless, had been treacherously assassinated in 1419 by men of the Dauphin, the future Charles VII of France. The figures were installed a generation later at the foot of his tomb, representing a procession of mourners. The sculptor was a Spaniard. What had first struck me many years before was that though most of the faces are hidden – for example, the group of cowled Carthusian monks – each figure contrives to convey a particular sorrow, expressed through gesture and the complex drapery of the outer garments. Some of the most impressive are precisely those whose faces are most hidden. Over the last two years, hooded figures had become part of my life; I had been following the cowled pilgrim on Fidenza Cathedral to and from Rome in all the variations in which the Via Francigena waymarks recast him, and although the figures on the Fidenza frieze were carved several centuries earlier than Juan de la Huerta's highly sophisticated sculptures, mainly of the 1440s, I could not help but be drawn back to them. I found them again in their temporary home in the Musée des Beaux-Arts. Under museum illumination and in glass cases at eye level, they lost something of their dark mystery, but those veiled faces still spoke across nearly six centuries.

The hot August sun beat on the city all afternoon, so I took a walk up the Avenue du Drapeau to submit myself to a Dijonnaise lady who on the phone had promised me a 'special' Burgundian massage. The treatment was as good as her word. The avenue outside her apartment was being ripped up for a new tramway – a trend in France, where cities are reverting to trams – and the freshly-laid tracks and overhead cables were in range of a Sherman tank, parked at one end as a monument to the battle for the liberation of Dijon in September 1944. The tank has a hole through the turret: it had taken a direct hit that killed its three French occupants, and it is perhaps one of France's more unusual World War II memorials. After getting my pilgrim passport stamped at the Cathedral of Saint-Bénigne, I just had time for a second visit to the *Pleurants* before drawing the day to a close at a terrace restaurant in Place de la Libération.

The young manager of the Hôtel des Ducs, having tried to delay my check-in, seemed still not quite *au fait* with his own organisation, insisting that no breakfast would be available before 7.00 am. The night porter, who appeared to know what really went on in the hotel, assured me, however, that he would have something ready earlier. Indeed, he did; I was away by 6.45 am.

To the west of Dijon, the range of hills is cut through by the River Ouche. This gave the old canal surveyors a natural course, which I followed on an easy tarmacked section of towpath. After the village of Fleury-sur-Ouche, the river turns abruptly south into a gorge, and the canal makers once again could not resist a ready-made route although it entails a considerable deviation for boats and land-travellers alike. Since, however, I was heading north and west, and had already, early in the day, spotted the first road signs to Paris, I decided against giving up all that hard won ground by going south; and so shortly after Fleury, at the village of Pont-de-Pany, I broke away for higher ground and headed due west directly for Pouilly-en-Auxois. Now every town and village seemed to be hyphenated – a sure sign that I was back in *la France profonde*, the lost world of the French interior.

The other sure sign, on which I hadn't reckoned, was the sudden dearth of cafés and *boulangeries*. I had hoped to restock on water at Pont-de-Pany, but none was available. The hotel had closed down; and even the lock keeper's house was deserted. But at the very top of the village, I spotted a pharmacy. There they filled my water bottle and kindly gave me an energy drink.

"You might need that," said the lady at the counter. "You won't be able to buy any food in these parts. All the shops have gone."

This was a feature of the next few days, and I sometimes went hungry. Though my short cut worked out well, it had started badly with a long, lonely march uphill on a solitary farm track alongside the A38 motorway. It was a pain, pushing uphill once more, when I thought I had done with it; and to make matters worse it started to rain. I took shelter in a barn, munching a few nuts, before pressing on to the hilltop village of Sombernon, where lunch meant sitting on a bench in pouring rain, negotiating an out-of-date Mars Bar and glugging warm Coca

Cola – all there was to scavenge from what appeared to be the only shop. The absurdity of long-distance walking was suddenly borne in on me, and I found myself dissolving into laughter, and it made me feel a whole lot better.

The day improved. From the higher ground of treeless arable land I started to enjoy expansive views to the west, and even the sun returned. The D16 *route départementale*, which I had swapped for the farm track, ran side by side with its 21st century replacement, the A38, and for a while I had the sensation that I was actually walking on a French motorway, especially when I passed directly under one of the giant scenic signs which, unlike their British counterparts, the babyish brown and white country-house icons, always look so enticing. This one was for the Château de Commarin.

Western Burgundy spread out below me, its fields and hedgerows extending to the distant Morvan hills, a thin dark band on the far horizon. Down in the dip of the valley was my destination for the night, Pouilly-en-Auxois. It had been a hard cross-country 42 kilometres, but there I would rejoin my canal, which arrives in the town after emerging from one of the engineering marvels of the whole navigation, a 3,300 metre tunnel.

My first call at Pouilly-en-Auxois was to the tourist office that is housed in one of the town's old pigeon towers. I told the lady in charge that I reckoned I had walked further than most pigeons could fly. She quickly disabused me:

"Don't you believe it, I heard of one which flew all the way from Paris to Istanbul."

That put me firmly back in my place. I liked Pouilly-en-Auxois; it sits comfortably on its rise above the tunnel linking the twin river valleys of the Saône and Yonne and can be taken in at a single glance, just a church and a market square. I put up at the Hôtel du Commerce and was well fed on *foie gras* and *penne*, accompanied by a local Burgundy. It was doubly reassuring that tomorrow I would be reunited with my water course, which was as good as a direct compass line to Paris.

EIGHT
WATER COURSE

ON THE MORNING OF THE 29TH, IT WAS a short hop back to the towpath at Pouilly-en-Auxois where it resumes after the two-mile canal tunnel. The water emerges from darkness into an impressive brick-lined dyke that reminded me of the moat around a Vauban fortress. The tunnel exit is shaded by tall plane trees, and I waited for a few moments in the dawn light before photographing it in the hope a boat might appear to animate the scene, but it was too early in the day. There was a stuttering of life around the canal basin a little further on, with a few boat owners up to greet the red-gold sunrise.

Leaving the line of moored boats at the port, I plunged into the green artery of the canal and its tree-lined towpath and marched towards the heart of Burgundy. For the first time since setting out from Rome, I saw hills in the distance that I did not have to climb. My way was now gently downhill, descending from the highest point of the navigation, until, for a few kilometres, it kept step with the tranquil waters of the young River Armançon; both it and I were aiming to meet the larger Yonne. The only obstacles preventing me from opening up into fifth and sixth gear were loose Burgundian stone and shingle on the towpath. But there was plenty to enjoy: the towpath had been thoughtfully planted with a medley of poplar, oak and plane, and in the fields either side muscular white Charolais cattle were contentedly fattening up to become *Boeuf Bourguignon.* I clocked my progress by the locks, each with its kilometre signpost; most were guarded by simple cottage-style houses, some now given over to holiday lets, but a few still occupied by multi-tasking lock-keepers who use moped or van in order to attend several locks in quick succession. Like old railway stations, the best locks have colourful blazes of well-tended flowers. This particular morning, the only aquatic activity was from the birds and insects. Not a single barge or cruiser made its way past me, and there was only one visual incident: rising above the canal at the village of Saint-Thibault was the exceptionally tall church of Notre-Dame, an exuberant work of Burgundian Gothic known locally for its soaring nave and tower as the cathedral of the fields.

On a day of good walking, my only problem proved to be food. I had planned to re-stock at the invitingly-named village of Pont Royal, which has a bridge and a little canal port graced, as I surveyed it, with a sleek red, black and blue liveried barge. She bore the English name *Who Knows*, and it should have been a warning. The canalside *chambres d'hôtes* was shut; so was the local restaurant, though there I spotted movement in the backyard. I went over to ask the young *patronne* if she had some bread to sell.

No, she said emphatically, she was *désolée*. The family had just returned from their annual holiday, and there was no food on the premises. Did she not have just a tin of something I could buy? This triggered another *Non;* now angry and loud. The neighbours, an elderly couple, had heard the raised voice and came out from next door to investigate the commotion. I was on the point of retreating when the lady beckoned to me.

"Come into the kitchen," she said. "We can spare you some bread."

I entered their house though the narrow kitchen door and she took a *baguette* out of the freezer, and cut it in half.

"I am afraid that is all we can spare, and you will have to let it unthaw. We can't get fresh bread here any longer," she explained. "The nearest shop is nine kilometres."

"My God, this really is *la France profonde*," I said.

"*La France profonde*?" she scoffed. "You should try the Vosges!"

I went on my way doubly grateful – for the kind gift and for its being Burgundy, not the mountains of eastern France, which I was traversing. While the hot sun brought the frozen bread back to life, I walked on to the hamlet of Braux. It was a little way off the canal, and had all the charm of lost Burgundy, a few stone farm houses and cottages at the foot of a valley; and I was about to meet another of Harry's angels. Needing water, I knocked on one of the cottage doors and to my amazement was welcomed by a retired farm labourer. He said he was proud to have lived all his life on the land, and pressed on me a bottle of fresh water and a handful of his own garden tomatoes. We spent several minutes chatting cordially in his sitting room before I retraced my steps to find a canalside bench to feast on cool Burgundian water and a succulently fresh tomato sandwich.

The Canal de Bourgogne continues downhill from Braux on a ladder of 40 locks – an average of one every 200 metres for eight kilometres. It would have taken a horse-drawn barge at least a day to lock through them all; and a modern cruiser not much less. But there were no contenders; by the end of the day, before I turned off the canal for the village of Pouillenay, I had seen just one vessel underway in 34 kilometres, a pleasure boat called *Martin-Pêcheur* – Kingfisher.

My evening's resting place, Pouillenay, was a village slightly away from the canal, built round the stream of La Lochère. It was by now late afternoon, and the phrase 'one-horse town' immediately came to mind when a farmer rode past me on the bridge crossing the stream. An hour later, when it had clouded over and I was installed in the modest Hôtel Macaréna in the central square, the same man rode up to the terrace bar, hitched his horse to the railings, and came in for his drink.

By then, there had been a small misadventure. I had sat for a long time in the shower basin letting the water wash over me. I failed to notice that some part of me was blocking the modest downhole, so that, on emerging from my bathroom, I found a runnel of water crossing the bedroom and flowing under the corridor. I did my best to sop it all up before daring to appear for my evening beer; nobody saw me, or at least, not a word was said. Dinner, a bit later, was a plate of Pouillenay duck, its excellence made unforgettable by the accompaniment: a spectacular lightning and rain storm, through which I was singularly glad not to be walking.

By morning the storm had passed, but I had altogether different problems. No one had turned up to serve breakfast and, to my disbelief, I found all the outside doors of the hotel locked. So I prised open a window in the restaurant and dropped down into the car park, jumping out of the hotel. It made for an inelegant, if practical, exit from Pouillenay, but I wasn't too bothered about missing breakfast. I had learned my lesson and stocked up the previous evening on apples and chocolate.

They kept me going as I resumed my canalside jaunt. Around me, the countryside now flattened into an unbroken mesh of hedged fields in which more white Charolais cattle fanned out, looking from afar like the fieldsmen of an English village cricket match in their best whites. I halted at Montbard for a late breakfast, a good cheese sandwich at the station hotel. This, it suddenly struck me, was the first industry-driven town I had encountered since Ivrea; and what's more, it is still at it. It had begun with iron foundries; the steel sections for France's high-speed trains are manufactured here in the Brenne Valley, and they account for Montbard being a stop on the TGV network. The timetable showed you could be whisked into Paris in one hour and five minutes, in almost bewildering contrast to the slow passage of the canal, and to my own even snailier pace on foot.

"You cannot be in a hurry if you cruise this canal," a German nomad with clipped grey hair told me at the lock at Fontenay. Pipe in jaw, he was out walking his black Labrador close to where his canal barge, *Joie de Vivre*, lay moored beside the old forge. "I have been pottering down the *Canal de Bourgogne* for ten years and I still haven't quite got to the end of it."

We live in a world of relative speeds, even us walkers. Bernard, retired to his native region from insurance broking in Paris, was my next towpath encounter, and definitely a saunterer.

"I have been watching you," he said. "You're a fast walker."

The canal rejoins the River Armançon at the town of Buffon, from which Montbard's most renowned son took his title, Comte de Buffon. Georges-Louis Leclerc began his career as an academic botanist, writing a 36-volume history of nature and re-designing the royal gardens in Paris for King Louis XV; but, like Bernard, he too felt the pull of his native Burgundy, returning here to experiment with metallurgy and set up forges. The flagship of his enterprises, *La Grande Forge,* in Buffon itself, on the banks of the river, and in full sight of the canal, is now a museum commemorating this visionary industrial pioneer, who had the good fortune to die just one year before the 1789 Revolution. The forge, and its workshops and living quarters, were conceived on the same scale and with something of the architectural grandeur of the Cistercian abbeys of Burgundy, with which he would have been familiar.

The museum shop gave me the opportunity to refill my water bottles. Standing at the entrance were two attractive women half my age; we got talking – they were heading my way – and before I knew it the three of us were walking together. They were both teachers of English, thrilled to meet someone who spoke the language they taught, and intrigued by the distance I had walked. I began to wonder when the bell would go on our extra-curricular lesson in English grammar, this unexpected canalside flowering of the *Entente Cordiale*. But then, rounding a bend, we came in sight of a berthed motorboat at the same time as it blew an impatient blast of its hooter at us. It was theirs. We said goodbye, and the two *instructrices* clambered back on board to continue their cruise with their partners, whose four eyes remained fixed on the stranger with a distinct air of disapproval.

Beyond Buffon the Armançon valley gathers in, defined by a steep escarpment from which limestone used to be quarried on an industrial scale and barged out by canal. Cry-sur-Armançon still has its working quarries, and a signboard on the towpath proclaims that Burgundian stone did not just embellish local cathedrals, churches, castles and manors; it was also used on many buildings in Paris – and continues to be used there – and as far afield as New York's Metropolitan Museum of Art and Riyadh's international airport. Conversely, a little further on, a rival notice asks you to consider that as well as supplying best Burgundian structural limestone to the world, the Commune of Cry-sur-Armançon is also home to a distinctive blue violet – *Cryacus Violetta*.

On my approach to a bridge, a peculiar sound alerted me to a novel form of canal maintenance – a reed-mulcher. Reeds are a problem, growing in from the banks to restrict the fairway, and this shallow-draught vessel, driven by paddles and akin to a dredger, gobbles up the reed beds and turns the fibres into mulch. I climbed up on the bridge, watching the boat munch its way towards me and exchanging waves with its two-man crew.

It had been a long drag – 46 kilometres – and it was wonderful to round the curve of the towpath and see the lock, and the hotel named after it, at Chassignelles straight ahead. I had spotted the Hôtel de l'Écluse many years back. A simple two-storey building flanked by plane trees with, upstairs, a scenic window onto the lock from its dining room, it had always seemed to be perfectly located for a canal walk, or for a layover on a canal cruise. I was right. It provided me with a comfortable room overlooking the canal and its lock.

It had rained in the afternoon, but by the evening the sun had returned: it was still warm enough to sit out for dinner on the waterside terrace, and I celebrated the canal, and the fisherman I had passed, by ordering the *cassolette du pêcheur*. Before leaving the following morning I wrote in the visitors' book: *une bonne étape* – a good stopover.

The last day of August had dawned cold. I had already begun to notice the leaves from poplars and planes spiralling down to the canal, and on the water surface there was less life – fewer skimming water-boatmen, herons and kingfishers. The frogs still croaked in the early morning, but the season was changing. I was now on a section of the canal that I had walked many years before, and which was the key to my present route; Gail and I had stayed in Ancy-le-Franc visiting its 16th century château, a lovely example of Italian Renassaisance influence.

It was our short stroll together along the towpath towards the lock at Rapille that had left me determined to return one day and walk the entire canal. Little had changed, though the old mill by the bridge, a wreck when we saw it, had been saved by being converted into apartments. The towpath, too, had been partially resurfaced, though there were still sections of loose shingle that continued to catch my boots.

From Rapille on, the canal was tied to the contours of the River Armançon, which made for many twists and turns, and so to give my feet variety and to save time, I cut across one of the larger loops, heading by road to Ancy-le-Libre. This entailed a stiff climb, but it opened up views of the rolling country, until a willow stream led me, by a beautiful lane, back down to the towpath at Argentay.

On this stretch of the canal I found major repairs being carried out; a bright yellow Volvo digger was piling in new corrugated steel plates to protect the eroded bank. I couldn't help flinching at the economics of continuous work on this scale. The French state must be forking out a fortune to keep its canals going; good for it, but how much longer could it afford to do so? The affable lock-keeper at St Martin assured me that traffic was up 50 per cent on the previous year, but that's 50 per cent of a still minuscule number – a trickle, bringing in only modest revenue when set against the high cost of infrastructure and maintenance.

These thoughts were amplified when I learnt about a natural disaster afflicting another of France's major canals, one that was likely to spoil its appeal for up to two generations. I had hoped to restock at the canal port in Tonnerre, avoiding the town itself, which was some distance from the towpath. I was out of luck; there was no sign of shop or bar by the port. The one vessel moored at the wharf was a modern 15-metre motor-boat with the intriguing name *Raconteuse of Ipswich*. I approached her out of curiosity, and her skipper, generously answering my needs with a doorstep of bread and good cheese, told me how *Raconteuse* had first been commissioned for film making on the River Orwell at Ipswich, and had since been plying the canals of France.

Done them all, he said. So have I, I replied, but most of them on foot.

"Have you heard what is happening on the Canal du Midi?" he asked.

This is the oldest and most revered man-made waterway in France, linking the Atlantic to the Mediterranean.

"They are chopping down all the trees because they have been infected by some deadly fungus."

"They will have to grow new ones," I said.

"Yes, but they will not be full trees in our lifetime; for us the Canal du Midi will never be the same."

I could picture the effects. The 175-year-old plane trees create a wonderful arched canopy the length of the canal, and, if my informant was correct, all 42,000 would most probably have to be cut down and replaced. I ate my sandwich reflecting glumly on how the removal of those doomed plane trees would leave the canal stripped bare, and I walked on, having given Tonnerre and its shops a miss. Perhaps this was undeserved; it may well be that the birthplace of the Chévalier d'Éon deserves better than the guidebook description of it as a largely dull town. Its scion put a term in the dictionary, though you won't find it there now: eonism, meaning the adoption, by a male, of female dress and behaviour. The Chevalier, under the name of Mademoiselle Lea de Beaumont, spent much of his adult life as a spy in Russia, but his later years, in Regency London, ended in poverty when he died, aged 82, in 1810.

Perhaps there was something erotic in the air or the water in this part of France, because I got the distinct impression that my hostess at the *chambres d'hôtes* where I stayed in Flogny-la-Chapelle had designs on me. Or, maybe, tired by another 44 kilometres, some of it towards the end of the day in the rain, I was just confused by her charm and hospitality, and also perhaps by the name of her establishment – *Le Rêve et La Clef*. Or was it the nearly full moon that night? Tall and comely, Madame Grosjean is an interior designer. The room in which she installed me, on the ground floor of her pretty town house with its own courtyard and garden, purred with luxury and with her own creative energy. The sumptuousness extended to the bathroom and its magnificent bathtub. Nothing had been overlooked, down to the separate sockets on either side of the king-sized bed. Which one to use for my phone charger? Nothing was too much trouble for Madame Grosjean, as she put my dirty clothes through the washing machine, explaining as she worked the dials that her husband was away in Paris, and that she was on her own tonight. Also, she added with a smile, I had no reason to worry about the weather tomorrow. It would be better. In fact, under her roof, I would have nothing to worry about whatsoever.

On my return from the pizzeria – all that Flogny had to offer – Madame Grosjean was sitting alone in her room downstairs. The curtain was open and as I passed she looked up with an air of expectation, an invitation.

Drawing a veil over the previous evening, Madame Grosjean had been right; the first day of September dawned clear and bright and I was in fine fettle. I was nearing the top of the Canal de Bourgogne, and well on my way through France. A French guidebook to the towpath, written with great humour by Josette Chevolleau and Jacques Clouteau, seasoned hikers with a penchant for travelling with donkeys, estimates ten days for covering its 240 kilometres – eight-and-a-half, if really pushed. Admittedly with a couple of loops cut off, I would be on the banks of the River Yonne after just six days.

This last day provided more scenic delights – the aqueduct over the Armançon at the ancient Gallo-Roman town of Saint-Florentin, and the pretty town of Brienon-sur-Armançon, where I stopped for a cheese sandwich and to inspect the unusual circular *lavoir* – its open domed roof like a miniature Globe Theatre. Thereafter, in its northernmost stretches and with a broad plain to play with, the canal departs from the winding river and makes a beeline for Migennes. And now I found myself gathering speed as I counted down the kilometres, half aware that all the while the heels of my boots were chafing on those last loose Burgundian stones.

Approaching the final lock alongside the railway provided a real sensation of arrival; with the wide expanse of the River Yonne in sight, Migennes was both a junction and a terminus. At the quayside, I dropped in at the tourist office, and, with the town's stamp in my pilgrim passport, walked round the canal headland to join the Yonne. After a week of confinement to the narrow world of canals and towpaths, and of walking beside rivers which were not much more than youthful streams, it was liberating to be once more by a wide open river, especially one whose waters flow into the Seine, and on to Paris and Normandy. I could almost scent the English Channel.

I had given myself a short day of 32 kilometres, and checked into the hotel on the banks of the river at two o'clock. My room at the Rives d'Yonne was over a private jetty, looking across sunlit water to the sandy shore of the tree-lined west bank. I could hear the water lapping as it flowed slowly beneath my window: something like paradise.

That is, until I removed my boots and was confronted with an awful realisation. The rubbers on both my heels were flaking off, one of them virtually dangling. The *chemin d'halage* chippings had prised out the nails and torn away the glue binding. I recalled my miraculous find in Arbois, *Ange Répare*, where Angelique had fitted new heels. I worked it out; that was only 270 kilometres ago, and I made a mental note to tell Harry Bucknall that Via Francigena angels can have their limitations.

These boots were going nowhere. I was in a hotel some distance downstream from Migennes, and it was well into Saturday afternoon. Without my old Meindls mended, or a new pair, I was grounded. I explained this to Lydie Faguais, the *patronne*, and she did her best to help. There was a cobbler at the local Leclerc: the usual taxis were unavailable, and very generously she enlisted the sous-chef's help. This kind man, from Quimper on the Atlantic coast, whisked me to the outskirts of town to drop me at Leclerc's doors before heading away for his afternoon off while I hastened to the shoe-repair booth, easily spotted but ... it was closed on a Saturday afternoon. Two ladies at the adjacent footwear counter observed my distress.

"He is not back until Monday," said one of them.

"Is there anywhere else which repairs shoes?" I asked.

"Yes, at the Intermarché in Joigny."

"How far is that?"

"It's just down the road, about ten kilometres from here."

My heart sank to the level of my boots, but there was nothing for it: I would have to get back into Migennes and find a taxi to take me. Stepping outside into the hot afternoon, once again I encountered one of Harry's angels, an elderly man sitting at the wheel of an old blue Citroën. I was aware of grey hair, lively blue eyes and an open face; he didn't seem to be doing anything and so I put my head in at the passenger window and asked if he would be prepared to give me a lift to the station.

"Yes, sure, hop in."

I couldn't believe it. Was this actually France? We quickly exchanged names. Monsieur Serge Motter had been a fireman, and he happened to live, not in Migennes, but in Joigny.

"Ah! That's actually where I want to get to," I explained, and I told him about my broken boots and my walk from Rome.

"No problem," said Serge, "I'll take you up to the Intermarché in Joigny. I know the cobbler there. He's a good friend."

Serge was, indeed, a man with angelic qualities. He talked about his life as a fireman, and, as we drove past the newly built fire-station on the outskirts of Joigny where he had worked his final years until retirement, he said something which I won't easily forget.

"We were there to serve, and I go on serving. It's what we do."

The Intermarché at Joigny proved to be one of those retail worlds set apart from any settlement; I tried to imagine what it would have been like to hack my way there on foot. Once we were through the giant car park and into the hyper-emporium, Serge led me directly to his friend, Michel. He was there, and his repair counter was open. I showed him my boots, and he nodded his head while inspecting the damage.

"Who the hell fitted these heels? This cannot be the work of a French cobbler!"

Not wanting to let down French cobblers, and intent on preserving the honour of Arbois, I answered circumspectly: "I have come from Italy. You know the Italians, lousy with football and lousy with boots."

That was a good start. Michel made his prognostication.

"You might get to England in these – on your hands and knees! They need a complete new sole, and I cannot do that today, but to keep you going I am happy to put on new heels with glue and nails that will hold."

"That'll do me fine," I told my second angel of the day.

Serge insisted on waiting till my boots were ready, and I bought us both a coffee before he drove me back to Migennes after first making a scenic tour around Joigny. The hilltop above the terraces of the Côte de St Jacques gave me a spectacular panorama of the Yonne and the meadows and vineyards along its banks. Thanks to Serge's kindness, I had a bird's-eye reconnaissance of the way I would be taking tomorrow, following the borders of the river to the city of Sens. Though he refused, of course, to take any money for his time and trouble, he did ask me to send him some memento from my own local fire service. This I did, three weeks later: but before that I was destined to run into him one time more.

Back on the river terrace at the Hôtel aux Rives, I celebrated my escape from near disaster with duck and cherries for dinner – *aiguillette de canard aux griottes*. At the next table were four nuns from a local Sacred Heart convent, marking a birthday. One of them told me about her time in Rome; too close to the engine room, she said. A little further along were four English tourists who had moored their chartered boat under my window. Long into the night I was aware of them chattering over clinking glasses. I slept fitfully, worrying about my boots; never in my forty-odd years of long-distance walking had I encountered such problems with heels. I was beginning to wonder if I hadn't developed some unusual boot-destroying lollop, and whether this repair would be any better.

Breakfast, at dawn, was green tea and bread in my room. I was off by 6.30 am, and, following the riverbank for a few kilometres, I found myself back on the road that Serge had driven me down the previous afternoon. Steaming into Joigny, just by the arched river-bridge, I spotted a familiar Citroën parked on the quayside. Serge was standing by the door, grinning broadly, waiting to wave me goodbye. We exchanged a fond embrace.

"Please tell Michel that his heels are great. I'm all set for Paris and home. All thanks to a kind fireman."

The Côte St Jacques above me, as I left Joigny on the quiet D959, had given its name to a hotel with a three-star Michelin restaurant where guests were stirring for their breakfast as I passed by. The lane quickly brought me to the right bank of the Joigny Canal, a navigation which cuts out a large loop around a shallow section of the Yonne, and along its innocent *levée* my new-heeled boots were about to meet an unexpected nemesis.

Crunching up the towpath, I spied a serious angler with a portfolio of rods and extra crooks stacked in a tray beside him. He was corralled by buckets and boxes. At my approach, he kindly lowered the extended pole on which his rod was cantilevered above the water and let me pass. I thanked him and then noticed that he was not alone. Every fisherman in the *Département de Yonne* seemed to be on the bank, a row of them stretching the length of a platform, their cars parked all along the track at the foot of the embankment below them. This was a fishing competition, although there were no notices to prepare me for it, and as I moved down the line each competitor courteously lowered his rod to let me through. Each one, that is, until I reached Monsieur Masson, so intent on his rod and line that he failed to see me coming. He had what appeared to be an extra-long extender whose handle fully blocked my passage. Carefully, I lifted my front foot over it, but just as it was touching ground my lazy back foot snagged the end with its heel, and, with a loud thwack, like a bolt released from a crossbow, the man's delicately balanced fishing gear was hurled into the air and dismembered.

Swinging around on his canvas stool, Monsieur Masson looked up in bewilderment. His rod and extender, which he had been lovingly tending in his hands, had been shot from his grasp; its sections lay on the bank all round him, some even in the canal.

"I am so sorry," I said, lamely.

"Sorry," he yelped back. "You will be sorrier than you know when I have finished with you. That is a carbon super-extender and it cost hundreds of euros. My God, you are going to pay for this."

"But it was an accident," I insisted. "I caught your extender with my rear foot, and surely you can just put it back together."

No longer the sedate angler, but a Frenchman whose domain had been invaded, Monsieur Masson rounded on me in all his fury.

"Of course I can't just reassemble it, you fool! This is very special carbon and you have broken it. You were reading your map, weren't you? It's in your bloody hands. You walkers are all the same – just vermin."

I felt insulted and saddened, and I was pretty darned sure he wasn't fighting fairly. It looked to me as if the various sections could be reassembled, but I wasn't going to argue on that point. Instead I tried to make him understand that it was a genuine accident, and that I wasn't carelessly reading a map – indeed, my glasses were still there in my pocket. But he wasn't having it, and summoned the official in charge, a young woman of about 30. Instantly making clear whose side she was on, she demanded to see my *papiers* – my ID card. I was no longer merely in the company of weekend anglers; I was being threatened with citizen's arrest. Had I made a move, they would have grabbed me and set me at the mercy of a regiment of angry French fishermen.

A wise man would, at this stage, have bitten his lip. Instead Monsieur Masson came out with more invective.

"Pouf, he probably doesn't have any documents. These wretched vagabonds never do."

If he had used his eyes, he would have registered by the expensive sports watch on my wrist and the newly heeled pair of boots on my feet that I was no tramp. But his unthinking prejudice had shown me the way out.

"No, I am afraid I don't have any documents to hand," I said. My passport was nesting safely in its usual place, on my back, deep in my rucksack. "But I tell you what, give me your card, and when I get home I will contact you."

"This is a complete waste of time. You don't think for a minute that I believe you?"

If he had only thought, he would also have come to the conclusion that I must have some document. How else would I leave France and cross the Channel to Britain? In any case, he trotted muttering down the *levée* to his car, emerging in haste with his card, which he thrust disdainfully into my hands. It said he was Lucien Masson, a professional chauffeur and member of the National Union of Blood Hounds, from Châlette-sur-Loing, a town some distance away.

Now it was the turn of the officious girl. She demanded my address. I gave her half of it, fairly confident that without a full postcode they would never be able to track me down. I slipped away feeling thoroughly dispirited. A genuine accident had blown up into a collision of two cultures. I festered on it for days, and back in England I did indeed write to Monsieur Masson, suggesting that he had been needlessly aggressive, and that he had been equally in the wrong because he had blocked a right of way on which there should be unimpeded passage. I also once again rebuffed his highly offensive claim that I had been walking along nonchalantly reading my map.

So France was still throwing unpleasant surprises at me. I wondered what would come next, and it wasn't long before I found out. Leaving the competing anglers to their towpath, I crossed the narrow metal bridge at St Aubin-sur-Yonne and turned north up the D3, with the river now on my right. I crossed briefly again at Villeneuve-sur-Yonne to buy a pastry at the *boulangerie*, surprisingly open on a Sunday, and then returned to the towpath that would lead me to the cathedral city of Sens.

The River Yonne was serene, its surface giving off a near perfect reflection of the tree-lined banks, the sky pure blue, the sun pleasantly hot, when somewhere ahead of me on the bank I heard loud music. It was issuing from a Ghetto Blaster, and around it I saw smoke rising and, in the hazy cloud, a girl dancing wildly. The smoke was from a camp fire, smouldering in front of what might have been a bright yellow car but which, as I drew nearer, I realised was in fact a tent; and the flailing girl was stark naked.

"Hello," she beckoned to me. "Want to dance, want to fuck?"

I looked around the camp ground: empties on the grass, and behind the open flap of the tent two male feet. The rest of her partner was inside. They had evidently been having a good time, and she was left soaring high from wine or drugs, or both. Keeping going, I glanced anxiously at the tent to make sure her man wasn't lurking there, ready to mug me.

"Oh, don't worry about him. He's fast asleep and he can't get it up."

"You are having quite a party," I said, looking back. "But I really have to get on."

"What's the hurry, *mon chéri*," she called after me. "There is always time to fuck."

She had used the French word *baiser*, not so blunt as its English equivalent; in some respects she was quite right, but for the second time that day I found myself breaking into a gentle trot. My eventful 44 kilometres brought me into the centre of Sens at 4.30 pm in the afternoon, and for the remainder of the day I let the city envelop me like an oasis of normality.

I had booked into the three-star Hôtel de Paris et de la Poste, a stone's throw from the Cathedral of St Étienne. Taking its directives from the Abbey of St Denis, this is the earliest Gothic cathedral in France, and what I saw and heard beneath the delicate three-tier elevation of its nave and flying buttresses restored my sense of being on pilgrimage. I have the verger to thank. He stamped my pilgrim passport and, on learning that I was walking to Canterbury, his eyes lit up with tremendous enthusiasm. Canterbury Cathedral had been inspired by Sens, and it was their master-builder William of Sens who had presided over the re-construction of its choir after a fire. But there was an even more special link between Sens and Canterbury, which the verger insisted on showing me, leading me up the stone stairway to the Treasury. Here in well-lit glass cases were priceless treasures, original vestments worn by Thomas à Becket, the Archbishop murdered on the steps of his altar in Canterbury Cathedral in 1170 by knights of King Henry II, whose tomb became one of the great medieval pilgrim shrines.

During the 1160s, Becket had resided for four years in Sens in self-imposed exile. From the ecclesiastical garments on display, the martyred archbishop clearly had style – and stature, too. The dark blue silk chasuble is decorated with a rich orphrey border, and the alb has lavishly embroidered cuffs. The maniple and stole are threaded with gold. Becket obviously liked to make an impression, and may even have seemed ostentatious. But the most striking feature of the garments is their scale. Becket's white pontifical sandals would fit a size 12 foot today, and the alb and chasuble are for a man well over six feet tall. Maybe, as well as being driven mad by the serious disputes between church and state, the ill-tempered king was simply jealous of this showy giant of a man.

A little later, I returned to the cathedral to experience the great trumpet-stop of its 18th century organ in an afternoon recital by the visiting Italian organist, Maurizio Salerno, playing a sequence of Sweelinck, Buxtehude, Bach and Mendelssohn, and I found myself drifting off; my dreams troubled neither by anglers chasing me with rods nor by naked girls dancing on the towpath.

Sated by the music, I completed my visit to Sens, and my homage to the cathedral's unknown master-builder and his great invention, the flying buttress, by dining on the terrace of the restaurant by the west door, *Aux Pieds de la Cathédrale*. The surrounding square has a number of ancient timber-framed buildings that told me, at long last, that I was back in Northern Europe.

As I left the Hôtel de Paris et de la Poste early next morning, September 3rd, to walk to my triple-named destination, Montereau-Fault-Yonne, the receptionist came flying after me, waving a piece of paper.

"You haven't paid your bill," she said.

"Yes, I did. I paid it last night." I replied.

We returned together to the front desk so that she could peruse the previous night's transactions. There was my payment – for a single Armagnac. To save time in the mornings and to give me the freedom to leave when I want, I always make a point of settling my hotel bills the night before. Last night I had asked the girl serving me to make up my bill, and she had evidently misunderstood me, and, stupidly, I hadn't checked the printout from my card. It must have been a good nightcap; I had only paid for the Armagnac. The mistake was quickly and amicably put right, but I began to feel the charges mounting against me: rod wrecker, failed *baiseur* and now brigand.

As I walked out of Sens on the D23, every car and truck in the Yonne Department seemed to be stacked against me. Monday morning rush-hour, relentless at times, forced me across the ditch to wade through stubble; it was my fault for being on the road, but needs must: the *levée* footpath of the Yonne appeared not to be walkable here, but after about five kilometres I turned off onto quiet back roads where I spent the day walking to the mouth of the river through a succession of pretty villages. Though marred by a few more 'French Nots', the day would be made memorable by my meeting with an amateur philosopher from Morocco.

Luscious apples hung from the trees in the orchards of the Parc de Nolon; passing the gates, I asked a farm manager if I could purchase a few. She was *désolée*, but she was not authorised to sell the fruit. Not even a single apple, I asked? Not even one, said she. A little later, in Serbonnes, I entered the village post office intent on mailing home the maps and guidebook I had used from Dijon. The girl at the counter was *désolée*, but she could only take parcels for local delivery. But surely she could have it consigned to a sorting office for mailing abroad?

No, I would have to hand it in myself at a major post office; local PTTs were not authorised to take international consignments. I wondered what Simone Michel-Lévy, the PTT operative and Resistance heroine from Chaussin, would have made of such bureaucratic piffle.

It took a Moroccan immigrant who runs a shop on the outskirts of the village of Michery to put these fresh irritants into context and restore my humour. He was from southern Morocco; his shop was a large warehouse on a plot looking over the Yonne, and it sold everything from potted plants to whisky. A village shop in rural France today is a rare sight, and this one was bright and clean and looked brand new. I stepped inside to buy some lunch. Nothing was too much trouble; the father and son who work the shop together *en famille* made me a cheese sandwich and produced fresh fruit and juice, a feast for my takeaway lunch. How long had they been there? Their reply surprised me – 20 years. The father asked me in turn where I was walking, and I told him about my journey.

"You are doubly fortunate," he said. "You have the health and the time. Most who get to your stage in life, when they want to go off and do something noble such as a long walk, are no longer fit enough."

He had put my recalcitrant apples and parcels firmly in their place, and I continued along the valley in search of a suitable bench on which to savour his cheese sandwich. I found one by the steps to the church of Saint-Georges in the village of Vinneuf, a worthy throne on which to enjoy my Moroccan lunch. This proved to be my farewell to limestone Burgundian churches; soon afterwards I exchanged the *Département* of Yonne for that of the Seine-et-Marne, and at Misy-sur-Yonne I quit the road, rejoining the riverbank to walk the last of the day's 38 kilometres by woodland and marshes to Montereau-Fault-Yonne.

That name is perhaps the city's greatest distinction: Fault is a corruption of the verb to fail or fall and denotes the point where the Yonne spills into the River Seine. The place appeared down-at-heel, with many shops shuttered and closed, even the tourist office. But there was a *pharmacie*, which sold me a much-needed pair of nail clippers, and a

Japanese restaurant in Rue Danielle, where I enjoyed a meal of fresh sushi. I stayed in the centre, for just €40 – almost my cheapest night in France – at the dingy Hôtel Marigny above a *bar tabac* in Rue des Fosses, and woke the following morning to the distinct rumble of planes landing and taking off at Orly Airport. That familiar urban growl told me I had left *la France profonde* and was back in cosmopolitan Europe.

Where the Yonne meets the Seine, an equestrian statue of Napoleon stands guarding the promontory at the confluence between the two bridges. He is taking no chances; his Marengo faces east, while his tri-corned head is turned north to Paris and his outstretched right hand points defiantly to the south. It commemorates one of the French Emperor's last victories, in 1814, an engagement in which his army overran a force of Austrians and Prussians, but his is not the only memorial here. A marble plaque on the Yonne Bridge marks the spot where, four centuries before, the Duke of Burgundy, John the Fearless, whose stone mourners I had visited in Dijon, was cut down and assassinated by partisans of the future King Charles VII. The collegiate church by the bridge claims to house the slain duke's sword, but when I walked past just before 7.00 am on Monday 4th September the doors were still firmly shut.

The second bridge took me across the Seine; the home run was beginning. I turned left along a quayside whose multi-coloured confection of *bijou* houses, with shuttered windows and dormers peeking out through their red-tiled roofs, no longer quite belong in the riverside setting. Cut into the woodland of the hill above them are new suburban villas overseen by a multi-storey white apartment block. The Seine would be my companion for the next two days; whether walking its banks or criss-crossing it sweeping meanders, I would get to appreciate, as nowhere so far in my journey through France, how its riverside slopes are prime residential land.

For the moment it was the east bank that I followed, and once I had cleared the river port there were remnants of a towpath. Not more than a century ago, horse-drawn barges still worked the length of the

Seine, and they needed an unimpeded towpath. But the intervening century has made incursions; I was to discover that, unlike the River Thames that can in principle be walked on a towpath from sea to source, it is no longer possible to walk the Seine all the way on its natural bank. The path wove among thickets of hawthorn and bramble; overhead skeins of power lines converged on a large EDF electricity station before warping across the river in an array half a kilometre wide, which darkened the sky. A rare barge chugged past; but otherwise all that moved in the river was its own current pushing slowly downstream. After the blight of industry, I came out to a lonely oxbow backwater, tucked into a wooded hillside, which had become a graveyard for abandoned barges, some still in the water, their hulls stripped to the ribs by rot and rust, and others parked on the hard. There was no sign of life except for the rhythmic pulse of a single generator running like a ghost ship with no visible cables. I quickly put this eerie scrap yard behind me and stopped at the cheerful village of Champagne-sur-Seine for an orange juice freshly squeezed at a Turkish restaurant. From there I headed inland and uphill to cut over a spur and rejoin the river at Vulaines-sur-Seine.

During his later years, the poet Stéphane Mallarmé made Vulaines his home. Remembered best today for mordant sound bites such as "The flesh is sad, alas, and I have read all the books", or "Everything in the world exists in order to end up in a book", the inventor of symbolism in poetry was invariably a puzzle and always a challenge to translate, except perhaps into music, his influence extending from Fauré and Debussy to Pierre Boulez. His quayside home is now a museum, and tangled memories of grappling with his poetry at Oxford without a musical shoehorn hastened my step. I would give the house a miss. On the other side of the river now was the majestic and unenigmatic Forest of Fontainebleau, and I crossed to the west bank and entered it.

Walking the busy D138, the ancient *Route de Bourgogne,* is probably not the best way to appreciate the glades and dense stands of oak, beech, hornbeam and birch of this former royal hunting ground. The road streamed with traffic, but walking into it I had a sense of moral superiority: the forest gave the distinct message it should only be visited on foot, and sure enough at a road intersection I encountered a bunch of French *randonneurs*. At eleven o'clock, they had already done with their hike and were gathered round their cars, drinking bucks fizz from plastic mugs. The September sun was baking hot and I had worked up a thirst and was running low on water. I approached them for a refill. These Parisians, kitted in the latest gear, walking and drinking to celebrate a birthday, didn't take kindly to the interloper and grudgingly offered me half a cupful of their orange juice. From my being alone and manifestly foreign, they had taken me for a tramp. When I told them I was walking into Paris they burst into guffaws.

"You would be better off rowing into the city on the River Seine," one suggested.

I answered indignantly. "You are mocking me, and with all your cars parked here, you are mocking yourselves. You don't know what real walking is."

They were shocked. They hadn't expected to be upbraided for driving to the Forest of Fontainebleau, but that's what they got for their unfriendliness. More thoughtful *randonneurs* might even have put me right about negotiating my entry into Paris, something that was already bothering me.

The pretty riverside village of Bois-le-Roi, with the opulence and extravagant trim of is waterside villas, provided me with a sandwich lunch, which I ate on the main square. Here I crossed the river once again to regain the left bank, which I followed down to Melun. The first sight of the city from upstream was forbidding – high walls and barred windows: the imposing former convent on its island is now one of France's larger prisons.

But soon I was welcomed by the narrow streets of the old medieval quarter, clustering around the fine Gothic church of St Aspais. I wasn't stopping, though, except in the tourist office for a pilgrim stamp. My destination, which would round the day off at 36 kilometres, was the southern suburb of Le Mée-sur-Seine. I was approaching Paris, and my days of finding picturesque town-centre resting places for the night were behind me. I was now engaged in a strategic exercise, positioning myself to steal up on the French capital without colliding with six-lane motorways and TGV railway lines, and so I checked into a convenient place on a roundabout, the thoroughly bland Hôtel du Mée.

The garden terrace just about preserved the illusion of being far from a big city, and it was warm and pleasant enough to eat my dinner there, but breakfast at 6.45 am the following morning reminded me that I was after all on the edge of a metropolis. In the French provinces I had invariably been the sole breakfaster: now I shared the tables with a dozen or so suited businessmen, all readying themselves for a day's work. Dressed merely for a day's walking, my 54th since leaving Rome, I felt positively guilty among the pressed shirts and ties.

The local authorities had thoughtfully laid a *piste cyclable* all the way down to the Seine at Boissie-la-Bertrand, and from there I had the river practically lapping at my boots. My route was alongside the D39, passing the sprawling conference centre of the Campus des Berges de Seine – an important institution that announced the approach to a capital city – on the way to the Pont Choiseul. From there another *piste cyclable* took me through woods to Seine Port. I had worried for many days about approaching Paris on busy roads; now I was falling in love with cyclists. From Seine Port, where I picked up a picnic sandwich for lunch, a delightful country lane threaded the edge of Rougeau forest on the finger of foreshore below the cliffs, a scattering of fields and woodland on which old houses and riverside cottages intermingled with lavish new villas.

The towpath resumed at the lock by Morsang-sur-Seine, and for the next few hours I had the river on my left almost without interruption. The other constant in the middle distance was the hum of the *Autoroute du Soleil*, just beyond the river's west bank. Here on the east bank the only hint of those monster highways were the concrete spans of the Paris Orbital Motorway – *La Francilienne* – under which I walked beside grassy meadows. Below Evry, I sat by the lock and weir, enjoying my cheese sandwich, the whole scene rendered timeless, like the floating image of an Impressionist painting, by the dazzling reflections of the sun. Time itself dissolved: I recalled passing through the same lock in the motor yacht as a teenager on that journey through the French canals, exactly half a century before.

The idyll was cut short when I found, somewhere after the bridge at Soisy-sur-Seine, that I must have missed a turning or maybe a waymark and gone sailing on up the towpath. When it came to a sudden end at an inlet with no bridge over it, I wasn't too bothered, and made my way to its head: a long detour, but the footpath, when it resumed, was well trodden. But once again, at the edge of a grove of beeches, it came to a dead end before an even wider inlet. I was seriously adrift, and to get back on course I had to make another lengthy detour across a freshly ploughed field. I was heading towards an alien world of tall apartment buildings. At its far edge was a sports field separated by a high mesh screen. Once again, as in Switzerland, I had the opportunity to admire the thoroughness of modern fence-makers. The top was well beyond my reach, and the lack of footholds suitable for my no-longer childish boots would almost certainly have resulted in a broken ankle on my way down. On the other hand, following the perimeter was going to entail a really long detour back to the bridge where I had gone wrong. It was growing late; I was hot and tired. Hesitating, I walked a little further along the fence and spotted a gate. It was bolted but I gave it a try – just in case. To my utter relief, it opened for me.

I walked through the sports centre out into the suburbs of Draveil. Wouldn't it be nice, I thought in self-mocking anger, if a hotel turned up round the next corner? Yes, it would, replied the same angel that had left the gate open for me. I got out my BlackBerry and entered 'hotel' next to my location on Google Earth. Two blocks away was the Hôtel Comfort, and it had a room for the night. The hotel was in a suburban street, and the room was compact, but I didn't care. A final 36-kilometre push up the Seine, with a few frustrations thrown in, had brought me to the gates of Paris, and I strode out to celebrate with two long, cool beers and a dinner of pasta and prawns at a nearby Italian restaurant. All I had to do tomorrow was cross the river once more and walk into the city.

NINE
Spaced Out

The brief entry for 6th September in my diary records simply "a dream walk into Paris". But this disguises the anxiety I felt setting out from Draveil, as I turned left onto Boulevard General de Gaulle in front of the lake and park and crossed to the west bank of the Seine at Juvisy-sur-Orge. I had visions of being ensnared in motorway intersections; on the map these ring the southern approach to Paris with impenetrable barbicans, and I could also see that ahead of me in Juvisy was an extensive junction of railway lines which threatened to put Clapham into the shadows.

It was just before seven, another hot and sunny day in the offing; already there were barges plying the river. My apprehensions proved needless: I turned right on the bank onto the pavement of a road that hugged the river and set me right for Paris. The gift of the day was that from then on, apart from at street crossings, I never needed to leave the safety of a pavement all the way to the city centre and the Cathedral of Notre-Dame.

Closer to Paris, the banks of the Seine took on a new character: the well maintained barges moored along the quayside were lived in or dined on; they flew bunting and had flower gardens and even the occasional palm, or yucca, growing from a tub. The road took in one last bite of country before the houses recolonised the road and climbed up the gentle slopes around Athis Mons, the town that flanks the southern runway of Orly Airport. At Villeneuve le-Roi, parting from the river, I took a childish delight in walking directly under the southern flight path, getting closer and closer to the shiny metallic underbellies of the passenger jets taking off into the rising sun. It was equally exciting to leave the planes behind and edge my way into the warm embrace of Parisian suburbia: first Vitry-sur-Seine with its splendid contemporary sculptures, then Ivry-sur-Seine, Paris's China town, and finally the *Boulevard Périphérique* ring road. Crossing it at last, I entered Paris through the Porte de Choisy. The modest roadside sign announcing Paris was almost an anti-climax: it could have been marking the entry to any village in France. I had somehow expected something grander: a roll of drums at least, or a blast of trumpets.

Walking into the centre of Paris, having journeyed all the way there on foot from Rome, filled me with a sense of awe and joy. It had taken me 55 days to cover the 1,651 kilometres, and, as I crossed the Place d'Italie and descended the Boulevard de l'Hôpital, I felt as if I was being carried on a magic carpet.

Passing the *Gare d'Austerlitz* and the *Jardin des Plantes*, which the Burgundian Comte de Buffon had laid out in his first career as a botanist, I turned left onto the river bank and walked slowly up the cobbled quayside taking it all in. At first just the top of the two-tier *flêche* of Notre-Dame was visible above the Parisian roofs and then, where the river turned by the Île Saint Louis, the full east end of the cathedral came into view, the buttresses sheering away from the upper walls like the legs of a giant spider and the tops of the west towers filling the sky over the steep lead roofs of nave and transept. On the Quai St Bernard, I stopped two young Americans visitors from Chicago and got them to photograph me with the cathedral in the background. They were happy to oblige, but when I told them what they were commemorating they seemed to have no idea of the distances in Europe. Rome, for them, was just round the corner.

It was a moment for misbehaviour. I made a quick calculation of the queue at the west doors of the cathedral and decided I merited fast-track. Nobody challenged me, and I stepped into the darkened interior that has greeted foot weary pilgrims for nearly 1,000 years and approached one of the information booths to present my pilgrim passport.

"I have arrived from Rome on foot," I told the girl in a half whisper.

"Oh, that is so wonderful," she said, taking it from my hand to apply the cathedral's stamp. "What a marvellous journey. I welcome you to Notre-Dame."

It was simply said, but enough for me. Replacing the passport in its pocket inside my rucksack, I walked down the nave to the south transept, and there under the great rose window casting its coloured lights over the carving of the Virgin and Child, I picked a votive candle from the rack and lit it.

It was just after midday. I had completed the final 25 kilometres of my journey into Paris in swift order, which gave me the rest of the day and all of the next for sightseeing. My hotel, Les Degrés de Notre Dame, was just across the river on the Left Bank. A typical medieval Parisian timber-framed house given an 18th century stone and plaster front, it had ten rooms all with character: exposed beams, antique furniture and walls painted with indiscreet pastoral scenes. It is owned and run with friendly eccentricity by Monsieur Tahir, a French Algerian. I have been staying there on and off from many years, and it is always a matter of pot-luck which room you end up in. This time I had one of the best, complete with period desk and chair, and a bathroom separated from the sleeping area by a glazed screen.

Unpacked and sorted, I now had the whole of Paris at my disposal, but, as it happened, everything I required could be found in the *arrondissements* adjacent to the hotel. That was the case with my long-suffering Meindl boots: it was time for someone to take a look at them and give them wayleave for the last 450-odd kilometres. In Rue Frédéric Sauton I found the *Cordonnier du Bonheur* and its proprietor from the Côte d'Ivoire, Monsieur Amidou. Looking up at me over his black rimmed spectacles, he broke into a broad grin and pointed to the heels.

"I don't know how you managed to walk on these. Your legs must have bent out like a bow."

He pointed out how the new heels had both been fixed to a worn base. Once again, one cobbler was getting it over another; and this time not just over one, but over all three who had repaired my boots in Ivrea, Arbois and Joigny.

"I'll do a proper job, see. This is Paris, after all, and we don't make rubbish repairs here."

Close by I found a launderette for my dusty clothes. Then, at the local PTT, I sent home my package of used French maps and the canal towpath guide. To replace them with the ones I needed to reach Calais, I sauntered up the Boulevard St Germain to the Librairie Leyrolles. It was time for a *panino* and then a massage; still in the Latin Quarter, I found a skilled lady from Ethiopia who pummelled my tired muscles to the beat of music from the Horn of Africa until I floated away across a thousand miles of hill and dale.

At dinner, too, I stayed local, just crossing the square from Les Degrés to the Beaurepaire restaurant opposite; and I told myself on returning to my room that the following day I would stick as far as possible to within the bounds of the Latin Quarter. For my morning homework, I spread out all my new maps across desk, bed and floor, and made fervent phone calls to tourist offices, hotels and *chambres d'hôtes*. I realised I had set myself a real task: to cover 300 kilometres in seven days, with each stage spaced out over long distances to reach the next available or suitable accommodation, and so my rest day would be just that, with walking kept to a minimum.

There was no better place to start than the Musée de Cluny. The National Museum of the Middle Ages, just off the Boulevard St Michel and housed appropriately in Burgundian stone, is a former Cluniac Gothic mansion. It happens to be built over the one Gallo-Roman monument left in Paris, a thermal bathing establishment which gave me my first direct tie back to Rome since leaving Italy, but my goal – and I was lucky with her so early in the day – was the greatest treasure of the museum, and perhaps one of the greatest art works of the Middle Ages, the *Lady and the Unicorn*: six tapestries woven in Flanders in the late 15th century from wool and silk depicting a lady of singular beauty flanked by a lion and unicorn. Despite having her, for the first time in many visits, to myself, I came no nearer to understanding the real meaning of the motto inscribed above the largest and most alluring of the tapestries and which, presumably, was the key to its understanding by its first viewers, whether household or guests. "*À Mon Seul Désir*", easily translated as "to my only desire", is as elusive in context as a line of Mallarmé. The lady is secreting a necklace in a chest, its lid held open by her maidservants. To her left is a bench with bags of coins on it; what is this all about for our age – love and passion, renunciation and sacrifice? You cannot tell, and yet still you leave the Cluny Museum derailed by the immediacy of such beauty.

Next, fulfilling a promise made to Tom Netter, was an assignation with Voltaire in his resting place at the Panthéon. I turned up Rue St Jacques, the road that pilgrims take setting off from Paris to Santiago de Compostela, passing the Lycée St Louis and faculties of the Sorbonne. The accounts of how much of Voltaire is contained within the marble sarcophagus vary from just his heart to all of his limbs, the verdict of those who were granted a facility in 1897 to lift the lid and ascertain whether he was all present and correct; not that it really matters.

The Panthéon started off as a church, commissioned from an adventurous architect by King Louis XV for the *contrescarpe* behind the Luxembourg gardens. Jacques Soufflot must have had some knowledge of Wren's St Paul's, but the secularist French Revolution blocked in all the side windows and made it the burial place of the new nation's heroes – including some it would claim as pathfinders, such as Voltaire.

As a national mausoleum, it is not a cosy place, and the vaults of its undercroft are cold and chilling until you start reading the inscriptions. On one side, Voltaire's reads "Poet, historian and philosopher, he enlarged the spirit of mankind and taught that man should be free." The other side commemorates his support for tolerance and human rights and his opposition to all religious fanatics. I had journeyed from the philosopher's home near Geneva to his final perch in Paris, and now that I was here I asked myself what he would make of today's extremists in the Middle East and Africa, of the bible-bashing bigots in the United States, and of the illegal settlers on the West Bank who believe that God gave them the right to live on Palestinian land, all of them claiming descent from Father Abraham?

Back in the here and now, it was time to collect my boots from Monsieur Amidou. He had not just repaired them; he had produced a work of art. He was grinning from ear to ear as he held the pair up for me to inspect the multiple layers that he had moulded onto the heel. There were no more gaps; and no nails. They were as good as new.

"They will take you to London, and then back to Rome," he said.

"Oh my God," I sighed, "not another return journey!"

I paid him over the odds, and he handed me his receipt with a motto that I was confident I could trust. It read "Repairs that last".

It was noon, and mass beckoned in Notre-Dame. Afterwards I revisited a favourite haunt from my student days, the island below Pont Neuf, where I lazed away a few hours of the afternoon watching my fellow tourists and resting my limbs in the warm sun. When evening came, a good steak at the Beaurepaire set me up for the start of the long haul to Calais; and back at the terrace of Les Degrés my world would have been almost perfectly formed if Monsieur Tahir hadn't charged me what he did for a nightcap of Armagnac.

The Seine flows through northern Paris in a reverse S shape – at least that's the way the French capital grew out from its medieval core – and I was to cross it three times as I made my way downstream on 8th September. It was seven on a Saturday morning, a bit early for most Parisians. Two bridges took me over the Île de la Cité passing Notre-Dame – too early for that, too, so I made do with the freshly restored Tour Saint-Jacques. This freestanding late Gothic tower is all that remains of the church of Saint-Jacques-de-la-Boucherie which the secularist First Republic tore down in 1793. The church had for ever been the starting point for pilgrims leaving Paris for Tours and Santiago de

Compostela; so here, briefly and symbolically, I interwove my own Via Francigena with the Camino Francés, as the way to Santiago is known.

Secular Paris now enfolded me. I walked the length of the Rue de Rivoli, with its fashionable arcaded shops, including the Librairie Galignani with its claim to be the oldest English bookstore on the Continent. At the steps of the Hôtel Meurice, early-bird briefcased businessmen were being seen off by flunkies into taxis and limousines. At any moment a head of state or film star might emerge, making me look and feel even more of a down-and-out, or perhaps a famous artist. Picasso had hung out here, and Salvador Dalí, who had once demanded that a herd of sheep be brought to his room so that he could shoot them; another time he asked staff to bring up a horse and he even offered them tips to capture flies for him in the Tuileries Gardens. It was pleasant, though, to reflect that all the Meurice grandeur has its humble beginnings in Calais where this tramp was headed.

Paris's largest public square, the Place de la Concorde, is usually like a Formula 1 racing track, but emptied of traffic it now tempted me across to seek out exactly where the guillotine stood with which King Louis XVI and Marie Antoinette, and several thousand others, were executed in the revolutionary bloodbath of the early 1790s. In keeping with its turbulent history, this square has had three principal names: originally Place Louis XV, when it had a hefty equestrian statue of the king at its centre, from 1789 the Place de la Révolution with the statue replaced by the guillotine as the terror intensified, and only comparatively recently, no doubt in an attempt to heal old wounds, its present name. But where exactly was the infamous guillotine?

I eventually found the spot by a red granite Egyptian obelisk from Luxor, placed there in 1836 by King Louis-Philippe during one of several unsuccessful attempts to re-establish monarchy in newly democratised France. A circular bronze plaque on the ground commemorates the victims. What is surprising, however, is that the tablet was only put there in 1989; it took two hundred years before the French nation could openly mark such terrible ground.

I walked up the Rue Royale, another name that must have been changed, to the temple-like Madeleine church, where poor Louis XVI was laid to rest in a bed of quicklime, his severed head at his feet, and where a century later Gabriel Fauré was the organist. It's curious how history, especially bloody events, can make you hungry. It was time for a breakfast of croissant and coffee; and to shake off the dust of the French Revolution, I now turned my newly heeled feet northwest onto one of the Second Empire urbanist Baron Haussmann's finest creations, the Boulevard Malesherbes. But, before marching briskly down it, I stopped by the entrance to Number 9, at the corner with Rue de Surène, to salute Marcel Proust, whose bourgeois Jewish family had moved into a large apartment here in 1873, just ten years after the street was finished. They must have liked it, because they stayed for 27 years, colouring the pages of Proust's great ruminative autobiographical novel, *À La Recherche du Temps Perdu*.

As you follow the Boulevard Malesherbes, the apartment blocks become grander and more ornate. This is the fashionable 17th *arrondissement*, but inner Paris is not a big city, and I was soon across the *Boulevard Périphérique* and into the suburbs, entering a world of 19th century artists, a sort of fault line of Impressionist and Post-Impressionist painters. Walking through the streets of Clichy towards the river bridge to Asnières and Gennevilliers, it was difficult to picture this urban sprawl as a rural landscape, a riverside retreat and playground for these artists. To be sure – and Monet and Sisley recorded them – there were the bold signs of France's industrialisation: smoking factory chimneys along the banks of the river and trains steaming across iron bridges, which the young painters seized on for the pleasure of their topicality.

Here, in the Impressionist heartland, I now crossed the River Seine by the Pont d'Asnières. Turning back, I saw the skyscrapers of La Défense already distant; scanning the river from the downstream parapet, I ran my eyes along the eastern end of the Île de la Grande Jatte, which figures in the right hand margin of Georges Seurat's entrancing *Bathers at Asnières*, to see if I could pick out on the bank the little dog or the long-haired boy with slouched shoulders, or the two bathers in the river. It was curious to think that what is timeless in Seurat's mighty canvas, now in the National Gallery in London – boats, trees, water, sunbathers – could still be re-enacted on any warm summer's day, while the consciously modernist touches of 1884, the belching chimneys of the new factories in Clichy and the steam engine, have all been superseded.

A monument on the bridge commemorates the many artists who painted by the river here – among them Edouard Manet, Claude Monet, Berthe Morisot, Pierre-Auguste Renoir and the man whose boatyard, and friendship and patronage, drew them all down here, Gustave Caillebotte. They left sun-dappled images of fields and orchards, sailing boats and canoes, bathers and river banks, an Arcadian world of lazy summer afternoons by the Seine that has largely vanished, and yet lives on in the popular imagination in the most frequented rooms of the world's art museums.

Today, Asnières-sur-Seine houses what purports to be the world's oldest dog cemetery, and is also home to many immigrants from the former colonies of Tunisia, Algeria and Morocco; and recalling the donkey driver Edouard's warning back at La Locanda Monticelli that I might easily be mugged in the poorer suburbs of Paris, I stuck to the D909, the main road, and stepped through it as hastily as possible.

Still within Impressionist terrain, I crossed the Seine for the third and final time by the Pont d'Argenteuil and, with wooded hills ahead, exchanged one river valley for another to enter the Département of the Val d'Oise. Argenteuil has a similar blend of immigrants, but the only damage I sustained was the loss of a shirt button: it flew off from my sleeve as I squeezed past a crowded bus stop. I spent several minutes groping for it, but the impersonal remit of the capital stretched to this outer suburb: nobody bothered about what I might be up to.

Once across the A15 *autoroute*, where I spotted my first motorway sign for Calais, the suburbs progressively surrendered to the countryside, and by the time I reached the town of Franconville I was back in rural

France. I picked up the old Roman road to Rouen, la *Chaussée Jules César*, and followed its straight course before bearing right into woods to walk back under the outer orbital highway, *La Francilienne*, and cross the River Oise. This navigable tributary of the Seine has its springs in the Belgian uplands; here, though, it appears to be little more than a quiet backwater, both its banks lined with poplars and willows and just a scattering of rowing skiffs tied up at the jetties. I was in the one-time village of Auvers-sur-Oise, 32 kilometres from Notre-Dame, and gratifyingly I had got all the way on pavements or cycle tracks.

Nothing quite prepared me for the industrial scale of the village, which is set among narrow lanes on the lower slopes of the steep valley above the river. It has a 12th century church, a 17th century château, and a famous inn and a *Mairie*, and a still more famous cemetery. Auvers is where in the summer of 1890 Vincent van Gogh spent his last 70 days. In an astonishing burst of energy, he completed 70 canvases during those ten weeks, having come here to be under the guardianship of his patron, Dr Paul Gachet, and to be close to his art dealer brother, Theo, who was then based in Paris. Ironically, it was Theo in the end who came to join Vincent. The canvasses that the Dutch painter left behind include two portraits of Gachet, but are otherwise blazingly dynamic pictures of the village buildings and surrounding landscape; and as a consequence Auvers-sur-Oise draws tourists from the world over. They come not only to see the places he painted but also to stand at the twin tombstones in the church cemetery where Vincent, dead by his own hand, lies side by side with his brother, who followed him to the grave six months later. And if that is not enough, Auvers-sur-Oise holds an annual music festival and was also frequented by other 19th century *plein-airistes*, Charles-François Daubigny, who lived here, and Camille Pissarro and his stumbling protégé, Paul Cézanne.

Small wonder I had difficulty in finding a place to stay; the only hotel was fully booked and none of the town's central *chambres d'hôtes* had rooms. The people at the tourist office couldn't help, and were a bit disdainful about stamping my passport: how come a pilgrim was blown so far off course, and backwards, too? But Madame Hélène Galli came to my rescue. She and her husband have done up the granary of their limestone farmhouse which sits in the shade of a handsome silver birch in its own walled courtyard facing south to the Oise. The guest accommodation of their *chambres d'hôtes* is a well appointed duplex apartment with its own terrace, but the only drawback is that it is located about a kilometre from the town centre and it offered no evening meal. Staying there would therefore entail a lot of extra walking: not a welcome prospect given the enormous distances that lay ahead to Calais. But it was a bed for the night in a charming spot.

Though on grandchild duty when I arrived, Madame Galli took pity on my feet and, as soon as she had taken the young boy back to his mum, she drove me to the end of the village and dropped me at the gates of the cemetery. The two headstones simply state the names of Vincent and Theo van Gogh, with their dates of birth and death. The graves themselves are covered, as if under a duvet, by a swathe of ground ivy. Madame Galli's kindness meant that I could follow the van Gogh village trail, taking my time to see the sights which the Dutchman had painted, each staked out with a copy of the actual work – among them a red and blue landscape view of the valley, the apse and tower of the church, its lines curved and distended, a village alley with squiggly steps, the town hall, the Auberge Ravoux, where the artist was living up to the day he shot himself, Dr Gachet's house and garden with its flaming yucca trees, and finally Daubigny's garden – possibly the artist's very last painting.

Madame Galli's kindness didn't stop with van Gogh. That evening I found myself rattling along in a car with an attractive French lady for the second time in the day as she drove me to a nearby Italian restaurant, leaving me with just the stroll back after dinner. By my bedside on my return, I found *La Voix de la Sagesse*, a book produced and illustrated by artists who paint with feet or mouth because they cannot use or do not have hands. Before sleeping, I turned the pages and lit on an observation of the Dalai Lama, that most people live as though they will never die and then die as though they have never lived, and on another reflection that while many people plan to live a long time, very few plan to live well. I silently thanked my hostess for sharing this wisdom.

For my early Monday start I had no need of my customary BlackBerry alarm – the growl of the first arrivals at Charles de Gaulle airport stirred me. It was a welcome sound: it measured my progress north. I made myself breakfast in the unaccustomed luxury of my own kitchen, and with the fresh scent of Madame Galli's roses outside the window I stepped into another bright, sunny dawn, but now with a perceptible tinge to the sky warning that the long summer was drawing to a close.

From the Galli's farmyard, a narrow lane cut steeply uphill to the D928, and I was suddenly in open, empty country. For the first time in days there was nothing to see but rolling arable fields and clumps of woodland fading into the horizon, broken only by the lip of a valley, a gentle knoll, or the spire announcing a village or hamlet. At Hérouville, I swapped to the D927, but I didn't mind the monotony of French tarmac: I was back on quiet roads, in a seemingly vast arena where at times I could turn through 360 degrees without seeing a single building. As if to confer an official seal on this unfilled landscape, outside the village of Arronville a road sign announced that I was entering Picardy.

The A16, an *autoroute,* sliced between the two villages of Amblainville and Méru, but after that intrusion the road became even quieter, the country more deserted. My water was nearly exhausted, so I diverted into the village of Corbeil-Cerf. There was no sign of a village shop, so I asked a man working in his garden if he would fill my bottle. Was there by any chance a bar or café in the village, I asked him as he handed it back to me.

"Yes. It's just up the road, and it's run by my daughter."

The bar had the welcoming name, *Au Rendez Vous Campagnard*, and there was a jolly atmosphere inside, its three tables occupied by local duck shooters and their dogs – the hunting season had just begun. I sat up at the bar eating a fresh cheese baguette prepared by the pretty daughter. I asked her what was happening in the framed photo on the wall of herself and a Chinese-looking man, rather prepossessing, standing outside a château. Ah, she explained, he was Jackie Chan, the Kung Fu film star and action man, and the nearby château had been used as a location for his latest blockbuster, *Chinese Zodiac*.

"Shooting that film was the biggest thing to happen here in years," she said. I nodded, not daring to admit that I had never heard of him.

I walked all afternoon through this vacant land towards Beauvais, a long haul of 46 kilometres. The strange humped shape of the cathedral finally came into view above the ridge by the town of Allonne, the scene of an air disaster 82 years before which sent shock waves through the British nation, comparable almost to the sinking of the *Titanic* in 1912, and effectively putting paid to Britain's airship development. Here crashed on a stormy night on 5th October 1930 the R101, killing 48 of the 54 on board. The Barnes Wallis dirigible was on its maiden flight to Karachi; as an official government project, it had been rushed into service to coincide with an Imperial conference in London and fly a lot of bigwigs to the far reaches of the Empire, among them Sir Sefton Brancker, Director of Civil Aviation, and Lord Thomson, Secretary of State for Air. The granite memorial at the crash site underscores how complex this 731-foot rigid frame craft must have been to operate and to fly. The roll of dead crew-members includes the captain, the flying and first officers, the flight sergeant, navigator, meteorological officer, wireless operator, the engineers and riggers, the chief coxswain, cook, stewards, the passengers' valet and the lowly galley boy.

The city of Beauvais is no stranger to death and destruction: it was all but reduced to ashes by German incendiary bombs in June 1940, and so there is no old quarter; the towering Cathedral of Saint-Pierre alone survives, and that is only a fragment of what was originally proposed. The cathedral is in effect merely one very tall transept, a choir and an apse; the nave was never built, and had it been completed as intended Saint-Pierre would have been the largest cathedral of the Middle Ages. As it is, the choir is the tallest and most audacious of medieval gothic structures. Dismissed in one guidebook as a stranded whale, the unfinished cathedral stands over Beauvais out of all proportion to its surroundings. Its stonework was in the process of being cleaned, and the south transept, with its richly decorative corner turrets, rose gleaming white into the sky above the portal through which I entered.

The information booth in the transept aisle seemed almost dwarfed beneath the soaring vaults. The friendly male assistant evidently didn't suffer from agoraphobia, nor was he flustered by my pilgrim passport, even though Beauvais was well off the major pilgrim routes. For good measure he stamped me twice with St Peter's keys and cross, apologising for under-inking the first impression. The Apostle himself was watching our transaction from his throne across the other side of the transept – a figure familiar to me because he is a cast from St Peter's in Rome. As with the original, the big toe of his right foot has been worn smooth by the brush of pilgrim hands, and I gladly added my own touch.

The Hôtel Chenal put me in a room overlooking the station, and I dined at a restaurant close by with a name appropriate for what was already becoming northern France, Les Relais d'Alsace: perhaps I was feeling also the tug of the Channel as I tucked into a plate of *moules marinières*.

Monday 10th September turned out to be the last day of my return journey that would be fine and full of summer heat; it would also be one of the longest on the road, 50 kilometres. Once off the busy D149 outside Beauvais, I walked for more than ten hours within inter-locking valleys where the only sound was the trees rustling in the light breeze blowing from the south. I advanced along lanes with a central plume of green, passing through harvested fields with ochre stubble and shady spinneys, free to command the whole space and scarcely having to step aside for a single car. The villages along my way – Pisseleu, Blicourt, Hétomesnil, Beaudéduit, Sentelie, Berigicourt and Blagny-sous-Poix, none with more than a few hundred inhabitants – fell to my newly heeled boots like symbolic trophies, oases of brick and timber farm buildings huddled around modest churches with the slated spires of northern France.

It was around the hamlet of Sentelie that I noticed the transition of the soil to chalk. Descending into the valley of the River Évoisson, I was re-entering the Département of the Somme, though well to the south of my route of 2010. My lane took me up through the woods above Berigicourt to a high spur and then steeply down into the valley carved out by the River Poix, little more than a stream. I followed the lane beside its banks for a while before crossing an old wooden bridge and walking by the meadows towards the prominent Gothic church of Saint Denis on its hill above the old walled town of Poix-de-Picardie. It had been a long, hot day, and I had reached my destination for the night.

Exhausted, I confined myself to my hotel, Le Cardinal, on the corner of Poix's main square, Place de la République. I took my dinner there on the terrace, the last time I sat out in the evening. The hotel was red-brick and modern, and the square itself had a 1950s rebuilt look; I asked my waiter what had happened there in the war.

"Pouf, the damage here was pretty light. If you want to see war destruction then you should visit Abbeville. That city was totally *écrasé*."

"I am going to be there tomorrow."

With the dawn of Tuesday came the first autumn rain. I set off into a mournful sky, feeling the drops on hands and face for most of the morning, once again walking the quietest lanes, the ones that show up on large-scale maps only as thin white streaks. There were now hills ahead, and lights flickered over the elevated horizon like the intermittent flashes of buoys in the sea – the aviation warning lights of giant wind turbines far in the distance, and as I drew closer I could count no less than 15 in a single cluster, unusually all working.

The village of Molliens-Dreuil was just large enough for a shop and a bar, and I stopped there for my elevenses. By the time I joined the D38 to climb the stiff hill out of the valley, the rain had really set in, and the view from the ridge by the hamlet of Montagne-Fayel comprised an eternity of greyness. Negotiating a long curve in the road, I began to think how nice it would be to retreat into a warm car and get this bleak landscape behind me.

At that moment a car stopped, a blue Peugeot, and the passenger window wound down.

"Here, mate, hop in. It's far too wet and miserable to be walking."

He must have registered my astonishment. Did these roads read my mind? Was this another of Harry's angels, or was it, conversely, the Devil tempting me? And could this really be France?

I thanked the young driver from my heart, explaining that I was walking all the way from Rome and that – however tempting a warm dry ride with him might be – it would be regrettable to break the walk at this stage. He shrugged his shoulders, as only the French can do, and sped off.

In the next half an hour, on that long soggy descent to the town of Airaines, I was stopped twice more by motorists offering a lift. The last invitation came from a tractor, driven – definitely, this time – by the Devil himself.

"I'm turning off just before the town," he said, "so nobody will see."

I thought to myself that it's not what others see, it's what I see, and there was just enough of me left that wanted to see me keep on walking; so once again I declined. To be offered three lifts on the same, admittedly lonely, stretch of road in rural France can only have meant one thing; the weather must have been really bad.

As I descended, I could make out to the northeast the line of the Airaines River, a tributary of the Somme, and to the northwest the hills approaching Abbeville. The town of Airaines, pulverised in 1940, didn't detain me for longer than it took to eat a cheese baguette – by now my lunchtime staple. In this region, rivers and settlements often seem to share names; it is true of Airaines, and of Dreuil, too, and I followed the Dreuil brook beside its meadows to the hamlet of Dreuil.

I was in for a wonderful spectacle: in my days walking through France, the spires of churches had beckoned me forward, a welcome first sight of my next landfall as I came up a hill or looked down into the folds of a valley. Here was a 30-metre high *clocher*, not floating above its church but resting on the ground at its side. It had been carefully hoisted down from its perch, like a top hat from a head. A roofer was, despite the weather, aloft on a cherry-picker slating it as part of a major restoration of the church of Saint-Denis. A notice explained that the work was fostered by the commune and undertaken by public subscription; the plain people of Picardy don't just offer lifts to strangers, they care about their historic buildings, too! A month later, I discovered on-line, the *clocher* was duly put back onto its rightful place on top of the newly restored church.

Beyond the next village, Hallencourt, flinty farm tracks took me up into the hilly country bordering the Somme itself. The sharp climbs took me back to Tuscany, and I could almost feel Gail's presence tugging at my side. The sign at the entrance to Bellifontaine proudly proclaimed that it was part of the Commune of Bailleul, the original home of the Norman Balliol family who had given two kings to Scotland and its name to an Oxford college. Strange, I thought, that such glory could arise from a hamlet in a sequestered valley of dairy farms and with a present day population of not more than 300.

I was about to gain the ridge above the River Somme. By now the rain had stopped, so I unhitched my pack and sat for a while, looking down on the lakes lining the river's course and beyond them to the outline of the city of Abbeville, and trying to count up all the purposeless battles fought in this valley and the millions of lives wasted or ruined. Down at the riverside, the south bank offered a quiet approach to the city, lined with willow and alder, and on the way brought me to the junction of the D3 and the D22; nothing in itself, but, as it happens, the point where my return walk from Rome now intersected with my walk to Santiago de Compostela 12 years previously. As I forked right into Abbeville, I looked back up the road leading to Moyenneville, and saw a much younger man striding south, on his back the same yellow Crossbow rucksack that I was still carrying. It was the year 2000, and he was bursting with energy and hope; with that energy now waning, but the hope undiminished, I passed a roadside chapel, which I had not noticed on my way south, and after another ten hours on the road crossed the railway and Somme to enter the city. I was 48 kilometres closer to Calais than when I had set out that morning in the rain.

I stayed in my old hotel, the Mercure de France, now part of the Best Western Group. As in 2000, there was no alternative in the centre of this much rebuilt city; and I couldn't help wondering what else would be the same. That time, I had found Abbeville a sad place; but my second visit proved rather rewarding. In the intervening years I had become more sensitive to modern architecture and town planning, and could now take in the new Abbeville and the distinctly Francophone idiom of red brick and concrete post-war buildings lining the original circuses and squares and the main street, the Rue Saint-Vulfran, with greater appreciation than the guidebook, which dismisses it as of slight interest. Through my new eyes, Abbeville in the 1950s and 1960s had arisen handsomely from the German carpet bombing of 1940.

My destination was the church of Saint-Vulfran –like Beauvais cathedral never completed, but now restored in its original flamboyant style – in the hope of bagging the name of this rather metallic saint for my pilgrim passport, but the young girl at the information desk told me that St Vulfran didn't rise to a stamp, and if I needed one I would have to report to the parish priest. That wasn't an option, so the tourist office in the arcaded shopping centre of another rebuilt square, Place de l'Amiral Courbet, would do instead. By evening the rain had returned, and so I decided to stay put in the hotel, and practically for the first time since leaving Rome I dined inside. It was a good decision. The sea must again have been calling: I ate a most delicious fish soup, followed by the Mercure's cod casserole.

Wednesday's destination even had the sea in its name, Montreuil-sur-Mer, though its geography has changed since its christening. The retired *Route Nationale* from Abbeville makes a beeline for Montreuil, but the volume of traffic ruled it out. I braved it as far as the Hautvillers-Ouville turn, and then embarked on a longer, more scenic route, even though this entailed another ten-hour trek of 48 kilometres. But at least the rain held off, and a fresh autumn day was warmed by sunshine.

Once off the D1001, I was back in the lost world of rural Picardy. Almost the first thing I passed was a notice by a venerable lime, designating it a "remarkable tree". We have tree listings in England in the form of Tree Preservation Orders, but this was the equivalent of a blue plaque. There were many more almost as remarkable trees ahead as I walked through the great forest of Crécy with its endless reserve of hornbeam, oak and beech, the latter reaching to heights that would challenge Beauvais Cathedral. The stands of timber are relieved by rides and glades, some with haunting names such as *Lieu du silence des vieux chênes* – the dell of the silence of ancient oaks. In fact the forest was far from silent; the busy chatter of birdsong saw to that.

The landscape of the forest culminates at the foot of the hill on which Crécy-en-Ponthieu stands. Outside the town in 1346 was fought the Battle of Crécy. Once, every British schoolchild who could pronounce the name Crécy knew it, along with Agincourt, as a famous English victory over the French. It was also a major landmark in the technology of warfare; the smaller English force prevailed in large measure through having adopted a new battlefield weapon of mass destruction – the longbow. The battle also saw an early use of cannon, but the primitive *Ribauldequins* were more scary than effective and were not decisive. Their turn would come, nearly six centuries later, over fields not far to the north.

I walked up the hill to the centre of town and the *boulangerie* in the market square, the Place Jean de Luxembourg. It is named for one of the losers in the battle, the blind King of Bohemia, an ally of Philip VI of France, whose army also numbered Genoese mercenaries and soldiers from the Kingdom of Majorca. The English force of Edward III and his son, the Black Prince, had additional support from knights of the Holy Roman Empire. So, even though Edward and Philip were the main protagonists, it wasn't entirely an England versus France affair; and the statue in the square indeed commemorates "Jean of Luxembourg and his valiant comrades in arms who died for France". The blind King John, led into battle on his charger, was cut down in a *mêlée*. Legend states that after the battle John's personal crest, a pair of black wings, and his motto *Ich dien*, I Serve, were purloined and adopted by the Black Prince, and since then have been part of the escutcheon of all the succeeding Princes of Wales.

The road from the town led up to the ridge where the battle was fought; a little further on I came to a fine 18th century house, Crécy Grange, which would not have been out of place in Dorset. There I left the battlefield, where the woods behind the Grange had once covered the English rear and right flank. I stayed up high as the almost deserted D12 led me over the plateau of Ponthieu to one last upland village, Ligescourt, where nothing stirred; and then, still over 100 metres above sea level, I took a lane steeply downhill, and almost instantly the landscape transformed itself around me. Deep chalk walls, like the cuttings around Gilbert White's Selborne, and a tree-canopy over the top created the impression of a tunnel down to a secret land. The River Authie, gently flowing seawards through a deep valley floor of marshland and lakes, its banks thick with poplar and willow groves, must be one of the prettiest in northern France, and I was quite unprepared for it. The line it marks is historically important, not just because here Picardy and the Département of the Somme end and the Pas de Calais begins, but because it once divided the Kingdom of France from the Hapsburg-ruled Low Countries.

Sticking to a small road alongside the tranquil river, I walked my last few kilometres on the Picardy side by the south bank. But the enchantment was too perfect to last. After the village of Argoules, I approached an obtrusive car park. It was for visitors to the Abbaye de Valloires, built by the Cistercians in the 12th century and later restyled and gentrified as a château. It would be in such a place, of course: the Cistercians had a knack of finding the most remote and fertile valleys in which to build their abbey churches and monasteries. With the monks and gentry long gone, Valloires has been put to many subsequent uses – orphanage, military hospital and boys' reformatory- and is now open to the public, primarily for the landscaped gardens which include a marsh wilderness by the river.

I hurried on past the abbey's solid limestone curtain walls, peeking over them where I could; and it was while craning to make out the lines of the abbey church's west end that I was suddenly aware of a thick stave held downright in the right hand of someone coming towards me. Then I made out bulges either side of him – a rucksack no doubt – and, now, the bare knees: so rare a species since I left Switzerland that it was like sharing a guilty secret. What kind of escapee could he be?

Frédéric was a large man, no more than 40, with a mop of uncombed dark hair and a roundness of stomach indicating not many miles on the road. He was an ex-sales executive from Belgium.

I asked where he was going; his reply still haunts me.

"I am just wandering," he said, "trying to sort out my head. I lost my job twice and I also lost my wife, but not even to another man."

"Have you got a goal in mind – maybe Santiago de Compostela? Many people find themselves walking there."

"I am not so sure with all this weight," he replied, ruefully.

Thus invited, I looked over his baggage with interest. In addition to the rucksack, I could see a tent, a sleeping mat and cooking utensils.

"How much have you got there?"

"It's about 27 kilos," he replied.

I patted my own veteran pack. "That's more than twice the weight I am carrying. You should throw half of it away."

"I can't. I need the tent, it gives me freedom."

Although Frédéric could have lightened it up by a couple of kilos and still kept the tent, he was quite right, of course: it would have been out of order to share my maxim that a credit card weighs less than a tent. Not everyone can afford hotels, any more than everyone wants to end a day spent under open sky boxed up in one. He walked away, his baton's rubber shoe falling softly on the road, and often on my way to the coast I wondered what became of him.

The sandwich bought at the *boulangerie* by John of Luxembourg's monument had been reserved for just this spot: Grand Préau, the end of my Picardy. The bench moored on the willow-fringed meadow by the bridge over the River Authie was hewn from a tree trunk and ample enough to stretch out on and rest in the midday sun.

North of the river, wetlands and flood plain spread more than a kilometre wide, a network of marsh, lakes, ponds and canals which I traversed to terra firma in Roussent, my first village in the Pas de Calais, and onto a road pointing due north which took me up a dry chalk valley all the way to Montreuil-sur-Mer.

The name deceives: the sea has long retreated from the town's hilltop bastions, but Montreuil has been victualling travellers on their way to and from Calais and Boulogne ever since the Channel became a sea crossing. On my own first solo hitch-hiking trip across Europe in 1965 I slept in the Youth Hostel inside the ramparts of the old fort, but this time I was determined on spending the night at the Hôtel de France, a timbered coaching inn with cobbled courtyard, where Victor Hugo stayed in 1837 as *Les Misérables* was taking shape; for it he drew extensively on characters and scenes from the town. An earlier, and quirkier, guest was Yorkshire clergyman Laurence Sterne, who wrote part of his *Sentimental Journey through France and Italy* while staying here in 1765. The inn also served men of the sword from Napoleon to Douglas Haig, the latter frequenting it when the town was commandeered as a British army HQ during the First World War.

In the event the Hôtel de France could not oblige. There was a room, yes, but check-in time was seven o'clock. After a long day's walking I wasn't prepared to wait around, and so I made do with a cell of a former monastery, now the Hôtel Hermitage, although there was nothing monastic about the dinner of pasta with truffles they served me that night at their Jéroboam restaurant.

Thursday's route was defined by the River Course which I followed upstream to its springs in the town of Desvres, 28 kilometres above Montreuil, walking the narrow valley on the D127 till it was no more than a bubbling brook. This was my first leisurely day since Paris.

But nothing on a long-distance walk remains easy for ever, and just after the village of Recques-sur-Course my rucksack went again. The repair in Arbois still held, but now the frame had ripped the sleeve on the other side. Time for more of Harry's angels, and they were indeed waiting for me by the barns of a small dairy farm with 35 milking cows, just enough to provide a livelihood for its two youthful owners, a husband and wife team. In traditional blue farming overalls, the couple was hosing down the courtyard, ducks and geese fleeing from the gushing water. Could they help fix my broken bag? *Bien Sûr!* With wire and a pair of pliers they managed to set the end of the frame back into its pocket and seal the tear.

"That's amazing," I said as I thanked them.

"Hardly," replied the husband. "When you look after cows you get used to fixing things."

Half a dozen earnest cyclists in Lycra, heads down, bent double over their handlebars, whizzed past and were gone in a flash. Soon there were more, but not quite so well-kitted; nor did they appear to be racing. I began to hear civil "*bonjours*" which couldn't have been French. Continental cyclists simply don't say hello to walkers. These were English, participating in one of a growing number of escorted cycle rides from London to Paris, where the participants set off in groups according to the speed they favour. As these pelotons spread out, I recognised an increase in English eccentricity in both the kit and gear. I could also detect increasingly Anglo-Saxon inflexions in that basic greeting in French, which I now began to return with a solidly English "good morning". The stragglers must have marvelled at this unaccustomed French *politesse*.

The day ended with a steady uphill climb across the ridge to Desvres, an unprepossessing town where I stayed just long enough to lunch on a cheese baguette. The hotel was on the far outskirts, a converted farmhouse on an old windmill site – Le Moulin aux Draps – and I arrived early enough to wash my clothes and hang them out to dry in the still hot afternoon sun on the grass terrace overlooking the lake and river on the edge of Desvres Forest. I pulled up a deck chair beside my freshly laundered clothes and lazed there until the last rays of the sun had left the western sky, content in the knowledge that I was now only a day away from Calais.

The *patron* rose early on Friday morning to prepare my breakfast. I was soon making my way through the forest over a succession of short but stiff climbs and descents. After the N42 *autoroute* and the town of Le Wast came a longer climb up to the heath around the village of Boursin, where I was disappointed to find that despite the dairy farms this wasn't the home of the famous cheese.

A last dip down to Hardinghem left me one final hill to climb to the summit of Mont de Fiennes, with its particularly ugly many-eared radio tower, and there at last I had my first sight of the English Channel. This was not, however, a *Thalassa* moment. Under a grey overcast sky, the sea appeared as a distant smudge, defined, if at all, by the silhouettes of the boxy tankers and container ships plying the narrow straits between France and England. Calais hovered somewhere on the shoreline, the Flemish clock tower of its *Hôtel de Ville* barely discernible on the low, murky horizon.

I hurried down the busy road, crossing the tracks of the TGV railway and exchanging greetings with a party of charity walkers from England making their way to Montreuil. My sights were now set on the prominent clock tower in the town of Guînes, where I slotted back into the Via Francigena; like a schoolboy tiring of a long truancy, I reported to the tourist office there and found Séverine, the same blond blue-eyed girl who had welcomed me two years before.

"I've come back for another one of your lovely stamps, and, of course, to see you," I told her. Guînes takes its place on the Via Francigena very seriously, and the tourist office has a stamp on which the pilgrim from Fidenza would recognise himself. With a wide smile, Séverine posed behind her desk for a photograph and handed me a map to show me how to avoid the road alongside the canal by a shortcut across the meadow dykes to the outskirts of Calais.

Approaching the industrial suburb of Coulogne, I had to call once more on Harry's angels. My rucksack broke again, and this time a motorcycle repair shop re-sealed the faulty sleeve with a staple gun. Now all Calais lay before me – a salute to Rodin's Burghers, a spacious room in the once stately Hôtel Meurice, and the massage couch of Émilie from Senegal, who would administer me one last pulse of French Africa before I departed for perfidious Albion.

TEN
Home Run

In my room in the Hôtel Meurice I awoke to the cry of seagulls; as the ferry didn't leave till midday, there was time for a leisurely morning of sightseeing. This is probably an uncommon experience; largely thanks to the clean sweep made of the city by Axis bombs in 1940, Calais is a place most visitors merely pass through, unless on a day's shopping trip.

But it wasn't always like that. Calais was a resort for English travellers right up to the declaration of World War II, and indeed it has never forgotten that for two centuries, if only from 1347, it was part of the Anglo-Norman and then English pale in France. The Meurice belonged to that more leisurely age when travel itself was slower. It was founded in 1771 by the young regional postmaster, Charles-Augustin Meurice, to welcome wealthy English folk to the Continent and accommodate them in a style they would appreciate before sending them on their way by horse-drawn coach to Paris. The business grew, and he played his cards carefully in the tricky years between 1789 and 1815; and when Europe reopened to travel after Napoleon, the elderly Charles-Augustin opened an offshoot in Paris in 1817. This too flourished, evolving over the decades into the luxury establishment I had walked past on the Rue de Rivoli. The original hotel in Calais, moored in its city street like an imperial ocean liner, was rebuilt after World War II in concrete and brick, but it still retains a stylish ballroom and an elegant stairway with wrought iron and brass balustrades. My fellow guests at breakfast, at a strangely late hour for me, all seemed to be British, and of a discerning Continental type – most of them spoke, or at least attempted to speak, in French.

I made straight for the Musée des Beaux Arts, just round the corner. Virtually every building in Calais is a modern re-build, but this one is refreshingly spacious and light.

I was the first visitor that Saturday morning, and there were two special exhibitions. One was a display of the plaster, bronze and terracotta models that Auguste Rodin made as studies for his magisterial sculptural group, the Burghers of Calais. Rodin's Burghers were six elders and merchants of Calais who made the difficult choice to surrender the keys of the city to King Edward III. Fresh from routing the French army at Crécy, Edward had turned on Calais, cutting off all supplies, so that starvation threatened all within the walls. The casting of these reluctant heroes Rodin made for Calais – there are others – stands in front of the *Hôtel de Ville*.

In the second exhibition, with the Channel waters lapping only a few hundred metres away, two engravings by William Hogarth caught my eye; from a less familiar suite, *The Invasion*, they underscore not just Albion's lingering prejudices against the French but also the London satirist's own embedded loathing of France. Hogarth visited Calais twice, in 1743 and 1748; and on one occasion he was arrested on suspicion of espionage while sketching the English arms emblazoned on one of the city gates. The incident did nothing to improve Hogarth's opinion of France: in his *Autobiographical Notes* he refers to the French kingdom as "a coarse war machine, a parade of religion, a great agitation without much real activity".

The biting ribaldry of his two engravings is his reflection of the Seven Years' War and of the real fears in England of an invasion by France and forcible submission to the Papal yoke. Indeed, Hogarth's images would be used to good effect in an army recruiting poster.

In the first, a French monk sharpens his executioner's axe, supported by implements of torture, a statue of St Anthony and a '*Plan pour un*

Monastere dans Black Friars a Londre', all weapons of wholesale conversion. Behind him, a group of French soldiers represents states of degradation such as starvation and fanaticism, while an officer roasts frogs on his sword and points behind him to a flag inscribed with '*Vengeance et le Bon Bier et Bon Beuf de Angletere*'.

The second engraving, with a similar cast-list of caricatures, showcases a jolly squib by the young David Garrick, one of Hogarth's intimates:

"With lantern jaws, and croaking Gut,
See how the half-starved Frenchmen strut,
And call us English Dogs!
But soon we'll teach these bragging Foes
That Beef & Beer give heavier Blows,
Than Soup & Roasted Frogs.
The Priests inflam'd with righteous hopes,
Prepare their Axes, Wheels & Ropes,
To bend the Stiff neck't Sinner:
But should they sink in coming over,
Old Nick may fish twixt France & Dover
And catch a glorious Dinner."

If anyone was affected by the issues raised in this piece of doggerel, it won't have been my competitor fisherman friend from the banks of the Yonne, the one whose tackle I had so disastrously demolished a fortnight before. In case he or others like him visited the show, the Museum owners of both Hogarths, perhaps so as not to scupper the *Entente Cordiale*, had taken the precaution of not appending a French translation.

For my final parade in Calais, I walked to the shore to see what I could spot 'twixt France & Dover'. This was now my *Thalassa* moment. It was a bright sunny day, and I crossed the swing bridge at the inner port, passing the remnants of the fortress of Risban to join the joggers and dog walkers on the sandy beach beyond the promenade. The tide was far out, the fringe of the calm blue sea lined with the white lighthouse on the harbour mole, and I strolled across the sand to the distant water's edge, content to have established that in France at least I could walk no further.

A couple of hours later found me cooped up in the waiting room of the Ferry Terminal, ready to submit my poor old Crossbow rucksack to security. I had swapped the freedom of the open road for conventional travel, and that meant a return to queues and inspections. Looking at my fellow passengers, I saw a man of about my age clutching two collapsible bicycles in each hand and complaining agitatedly to his wife.

"I am sure we're in the wrong place. We should have cycled straight onto the boat."

I, too, felt I was in the wrong place and, like him, I wished that I could have walked on. After all those hard-won miles on foot, it seemed strangely insulting to be herded onto a bus to cross from one side of a dock to the other.

As the *Spirit of Britain* got underway, I pounced on that staple of most of my English walking, a buttered scone to go with my coffee, and made my way to the stern promenade deck, followed soon afterwards by the agitated Englishman and his wife, now minus their collapsible bicycles but still debating whether they should have ridden on, as cars do. I noticed that the man had a slight limp. He asked politely if they could share my table; instinctively we had all three sought refuge from the *Spirit of Britain's* fast-food outlets, amusement arcades, shops and bars in the crowded malls below decks.

Once we had opened up to one another, I was not at all surprised that these two had found their way to the least crowded upper deck. Richard, trim in corduroys and cashmere, is a corporate lawyer who has spent a lot of his life at the controls of aerobatic aircraft. That's how he ended up limping; part of a wing of his Laser aircraft came away when he was flying in an air display in 1984, and he was lucky to crawl out of the wreckage. He and Cary have a well diversified lifestyle; their sanctuary is their hotel in the hills above Kandy in Sri

Lanka, but the trip this time had been shorter, delivering a vintage car from England to France with the bikes tucked into the boot. They were not typical P&O passengers, and as I left Dover Port I saw Richard on his reassembled bike pedalling for all he was worth beside a convoy of artics and container trucks. He was on his own. Cary and her bike had opted for the safety of the bus.

"We had one of our matrimonials over cycling on and off," she whispered to me. "Richard won, but I am glad I am not with him."

It was with a degree of indifference that, from the *Spirit of Britain's* decks, I had watched the cliffs of Dover come into focus. I wasn't exactly disappointed to be back in England, and I was genuinely thrilled that I had walked all but the watery bits from Rome. But even in early autumn sunlight there is something very ordinary about Dover and its situation, huddled up a valley between the cliffs of Western Heights and its castle. Disembarking in 2010 at Calais had been the start of a great adventure – the continent of Europe lay ahead – while Dover was just the beginning of a coda. What gifts had it to offer the returning pilgrim? Within an hour of arriving there, he had shopped both at Marks & Spencers and Boots, and a motorist had called him a "mother fucker" for crossing a street in front of his car.

But I was determined to make the best of Dover; besides, I had something special to look forward to over the coming days: Jon Harris, my companion over many booted miles, was arriving next morning from Cambridge to walk with me through Canterbury and along the North Downs to the River Thames. He had undertaken to be my Vergil and see me back to Essex.

The waterfront hotel in Dover's finest surviving Regency terrace was by pure chance my third Best Western in a row, though the Czech girl at reception did not quite understand when I asked whether that qualified me for a discount.

I was curious, having had such a good experience in the Musée des Beaux Arts in Calais, as to whether Dover could give as good an account of itself. I walked to the Museum in the Market Square and was immediately drawn to the prize exhibit: the Bronze Age sea-going boat unearthed – literally – in compacted creek mud back from the present foreshore during the 1992 excavations for the town's new sewerage. It's big for a deckless craft, nearly 50 foot, its carvel or close-butted oak planks stitched with yew withies, and I spent a good hour in its company imagining how it might have made its own Channel crossings three thousand years before the Romans came. I felt a sort of empathy with the timbers – my journey had been by means just as ancient.

A sundowner pint of '*bon bier de Angleterre*' at the Cinque Ports Yacht Club, open that night to visitors, and a surprisingly tasty *linguine al mare* at Dover's one Italian restaurant, Il Rustico, readied me for the home run.

There was an air of shared expectation at Dover Priory Station. I had told the ticket clerk I was meeting a friend coming down on the first Sunday arrival from London, and that we were planning to walk to Canterbury. A walker himself, he kindly broke off from his ticketing duties to explain how to get to the start of the North Downs Way.

"It's a fair old climb up the hill out of Dover," he warned.

"Yes, but I've just been over the Alps and Jura," I said. "I think I can manage." And I told him about my journey from Rome.

With the usual weekend engineering work – which entailed a coach from Cambridge to London – the earliest Jon could reach Dover was 10.00 am. In our phone talks, I admit to testiness; this planned late arrival had initially irked me. I hate setting out at a time when, on my own, I would already have walked ten kilometres, if not ten miles. But Jon had given me plenty of warning, and over the approaching days I came to reflect on our delayed start for Canterbury as a special gift – an enforced slowing down, a change of gear to prepare me for the end of the journey.

Jon had taught me to walk with my eyes. He took me in hand and showed me that the heart of long-distance walking was not about arrival at the next destination, but about what we take in along the way. An artist with the training of an architect and a late burgeoning delight in botany, he can parse a building and pick out a wild flower with the knowledge of a scholar and the enthusiasm of a child; and he draws maps as well as he can read them.

Approaching 70, Jon is a pretty decent walker, one of the few who has ever been able to keep up with me, and that is probably because he walks faster. So we have evolved a good system: except on the widest paths, I generally go ahead and set the pace, and he falls in behind; and somehow that seems to work for us both. That was the way we had walked in the summer of 2003, recording the borders of Essex, and a good few rambles later he joined me for most of that day in 2010 when I headed Romewards through the confusing London suburbs into Kent. It seemed fitting that he should be the one to meet me in Dover to see me back home, and he had welcomed with alacrity the arrangements I had made for our three-and-a-bit days ahead.

The London train slid in a minute early and delivered my friend with his familiar toothy smile and seasoned white beard. But there was something amiss. When I spotted his broad chequered shirt and worn corduroy trousers, I knew my long hot summer was ended. Jon was not wearing his trademark shorts; he was dressed for the chill of early autumn. The ticket clerk came out of his booth and turned inspector as we left the platform, curious as to who could be mad or brave enough to join me; he examined Harris closely as if to see if he was North Downs Way material.

"I've been training," said Jon as we negotiated the last road crossing in Dover and started uphill through Connaught Park. "I hope I don't hold you up."

"Quite the contrary, I will be the laggard. I'm running on half-empty."

We both struggled on that first hill. The ticket clerk had been right; Dover is well protected by its northern spurs, and it was a slog to climb above the town to the plateau. In fact, it turned out to be a hard day. Having sailed along the metalled roads of northern France, I now had to grapple with exposed chalk and loose gravel on the rugged footpaths of the North Downs Way. With its surfeit of short, sharp climbs and disheartening descents, Jon renamed it quite early on as the Updowns Way; we also grumbled at the way its original planners had given it the awkward dogleg, sending it north from Dover as far as Ashley and the beginning fringes of the old Kentish coalfield before it takes its natural westward line towards Shepherdswell. With Jon map reading, there weren't going to be any crafty short cuts, and, staying close to the coast, it was two hours before we bade farewell to the sea, with a final glimpse north towards the distant Isle of Thanet and the mouth of the River Stour where Augustine and his fellow monks landed.

Next to the flint church of All Saints at Waldershare, Jon posed for a photograph in front of a yew tree, a good five times his own girth. In a side chapel of Queen Anne brick, we found Sir Henry Furnese with his hands clasping his wife Matilda's. Sir Henry, a merchant and politician from Kent, died in 1712, and the affectionate couple lie together beneath their splendid life-size effigies.

"I see he was an Alderman in the City of London," said Jon, peering at the ornate inscription. "Do you all get marble?"

"Slate or Portland stone will do for me," I replied.

At Shepherdswell, we stopped at the Bell, wondering whether they would have anything for our lunch; a friendly local girl produced freshly made sandwiches in a trice. I told her how much the service had improved since Gail and I stopped here for lunch 12 years earlier in the pouring rain. We were on our way from Canterbury to Dover at the start of my Santiago de Compostela walk. The landlord announced we were too wet to be served lunch in his premises, and that, whether or not I was making a pilgrimage, he didn't care a toss.

"Well, you will never guess what happened to the pub after that," said the girl. "It burnt down."

"So there is a God after all," I said. Or was it one of Harry's angels?

Jon took a renewed interest in the interior, spotting features that had been reincorporated. The large open brick fireplace seemed to be the only authentic remnant of the old pub interior still *in situ*, but its successor did us fine.

After lunch, in the hope of catching an earlier glimpse of Canterbury Cathedral, we followed a ridgeway route over evocatively named downs, Three Barrows, Snow, Womenswold and Barnham, to the village of Patrixbourne, to approach the city from the southeast. We were emerging from an orchard a mile out when Jon spotted the pinnacles of Bell Harry, the great central tower. His excitement was palpable. Jon had been a scholarship boy in the shadows of one of southern Britain's great cathedrals, and over the years had visited many others, but somehow missed out on Canterbury. Arriving there was going to be special for both of us – Jon to make his inaugural visit, myself to round off my pilgrimage.

The city contrived to preserve its prime treasures modestly right up to the moment we entered the Cathedral Close. We had stopped first for a few minutes before the gates of St Augustine's Abbey. More than the cathedral itself, this was ground zero of my pilgrim journey from Rome. It was where King Ethelbert of Kent allowed Augustine to found his monastery in 598, just a few months after stepping ashore at Thanet at the end of a two-year journey from Rome; and he made it the headquarters of his mission to re-Christianise England. The abbey thrived right up to the Dissolution, but the grounds of the former monastery are now a city park, and the ruins are fenced off. St Augustine's Abbey was dismantled on royal orders after Henry VIII broke with Rome in 1534, and the extensive remains are today part of Canterbury's World Heritage site. The northern nave arcade stands to the crowns of its rounded arches; so much of the stone and flint of the abbey's upper works had been robbed that, from where we stood, nothing noble remained.

Within the present inner relief road, Broad Street, the cathedral fared better, losing the splendid shrine of Thomas à Becket – Henry avenging his earlier namesake, you could say – but confirmed in its continuing rôle as the mother church of the worldwide Anglican community, with the official title of Cathedral and Metropolitan Church of Christ. In the architectural eloquence of its balancing towers, the flare of its pinnacled flying buttresses and the magisterial complexity of its eastward elaboration, it bows to none of its medieval English competitors; so acknowledged Harris, clapping his eyes on it for the first time.

I had booked to stay inside the precinct at Canterbury Cathedral Lodge, a church-run hotel owned by the Dean and Chapter and set in a private courtyard garden. The rooms are comfortable with en-suite bathrooms, the best overlooking William of Sens' choir and the cathedral's transept and principal tower. And if we didn't actually have all of these in our direct view, our residence allowed us full access to them, inside and out, for free.

We had made heavier weather than I had expected of our walk from Dover, and from Shepherdswell on I was resigned to missing 3.30 pm Evensong. But the Lodge told us we were just in time for its 5.30 pm supplement, a service for King's School sung by its choir, and so we tidied up and crowded into the chancel.

The following morning after breakfast, we returned to the cathedral to attend early morning mass in the Norman crypt. At the end of the service, I told the presiding Canon that I had just arrived on foot from Rome following in the steps of Augustine. "Oh, how nice," he responded. Was there a pattern emerging? The good lady who stamped my pilgrim passport at the visitor centre in the booth by the Close Gate, as we stood rattling our harnesses ready for our walk to Charing, reacted with similar lack of interest.

"Rome," she said, as if adding: next one, please. "Huh, we get pilgrims arriving here all the time from all over the world."

"Don't be disappointed," Jon said. "I am sure you will get a better reception in Essex."

So we shook the dust off our feet at Canterbury's West Gate and crossed the Great Stour, whose course we would now shadow southwest along a contour of the Downs that define and contain the valley. At the first hop farm beyond the city, two joggers halted to greet us, and they showed considerably more interest in my journey than the clerics at Canterbury.

"Hot foot from Rome, who knows, I might even try that myself one day," said the lead runner.

Our next encounter was beyond the A2 amid the Spanish chestnuts in Howfield Wood. These were planted as a cash crop, but the timber has been cleared from part of the hillside to reveal the Iron Age fort of Bigbury, and, where the chestnuts have been left to grow wild, a band of volunteers was busy clearing debris. The volunteers were working under the watchful eye of Chloe, a blond girl in white tee shirt and trekking trousers and boots, by far the prettiest I have met on a footpath. She had a radiant smile and time to talk, and so I asked her the obvious question. Had she studied forestry? Her reply was memorable.

"Good heavens, no! I did one of those Mickey Mouse degrees at Plymouth on the physics of wind surfing. But it was an outdoors activity, so I got involved in trees."

Chloe was now a full time forest warden, but the men working with her, coppicing saplings and dragging the cuttings to a roaring bonfire, were all volunteers, and I would have happily joined them if Jon had not tugged at my arm.

"Time to move on, I promised Gail I'd get you back to Essex."

Between the chestnut groves and the woods just before the hamlet of Chartham Heath, we passed No Man's Orchard, one of the few traditional apple orchards left in Kent. Such old, overgrown trees have mostly been replaced with smaller dwarf varieties, often in wired rows. Here was an orchard of venerable gnarled oldies, most no longer giving off fruit, but now protected and standing like pieces of natural sculpture amid wild flowers and grassland.

A Polish labourer, one of Kent's new generation of apple and hop pickers, helpfully guided us back to the right track after we had taken a false turn through a railway tunnel down into the packing yard at Nickle Farm. Now, as we climbed to the top of the orchards, with occasional hopfields mixed in, Kent opened up, with good views far over the Stour Valley to the South Downs.

"This isn't Tuscany," I said, "but it will do."

Chilham, where we stopped for lunch at the White Horse, was more enclosed. It's a compact feudal village on its own hill, with a big flint church at one end of its pretty square and at the other the gates to a dramatically symmetrical late Elizabethan brick mansion, Chilham Castle, which is set in a park of the age of Capability Brown. Jon was certain that behind the mansion lurked the shell of the original Norman keep, but, suddenly interrupting himself, he pointed to the sign at the gates.

"The best thing about this castle is the name of its late owner. Look – John Clotworthy Talbot Foster Whyte-Melville-Skeffington, 13th Viscount Massereene and 6th Viscount Ferrard, Baron of Loughneagh and Baron Oriel of Collon; now you couldn't invent that name if you tried, even if you were P.G. Wodehouse." A politician and landowner, he died in 1992.

"I can tell you something else quirky about Chilham," I said. "We've just had lunch on an Ordnance Survey map. Look!"

While Jon had been reading the great man's name and titles, I was working out the afternoon's route and distances from the Explorer map for the Ashford area. Folding it shut, I noticed the handsome village scene photographed on the cover, and then did a double take. It showed Chilham: the tower of St Mary's behind the White Horse, and the very table and bench outside on which we were sitting.

Setting off down the steep lane to the southeast, we skirted the extensive grounds of Chilham Park along Mountain Street and resumed our upland path through King's Wood, an ancient forest of chestnut, beech and pine, whose eastward clearings offered fleeting views of the Great Stour valley and the Weald. The path was an old estate road, a rutted mix of chalk and rammed granite, and it made for slow going. Dropping out of the trees above Wye, we pulled up in Boughton Aluph churchyard. It was proving a very long 18 miles, and we were still six miles short of Charing, our destination for the night. I stretched out round a churchyard tree while Jon marvelled at the Norman church, its tower built like a fortress. The rest did me good, and, besides, we were coming down to Boughton Lees where two routes of the North Downs Way converge.

I tried to share with Jon the magic of this particular turning, where in 2000 on my way to Santiago I had struck north for Canterbury and Dover, and ten years later, heading for Rome, had carried straight on, bypassing Canterbury, to reach Dover via Folkestone. As we exchanged track for metalled lane at the junction, Jon echoed a thought I had been nursing.

"Perhaps the folk in Canterbury didn't treat you so well because they knew you had missed them out on your way to Rome."

The North Downs Way swerves westwards away from Ashford, keeping high, and within earshot of the Eurostar for all but the last mile of our remaining six into Charing. It was late in the afternoon when we arrived – eight hours to cover 18 miles, a slow day. As I had suggested to Jon, I was running on empty.

The Oak at Charing made us welcome. A lot had happened since my last visit in 2010. Then it had been a gastro-pub, flying high, but a new tenant had dissipated the business. Now the owners, shaken out of early retirement in France, were in charge once more.

Rowena was philosophical about the unexpected turn of events.

"We had no choice. No one wants to buy pubs today, so we had to come back and run it ourselves."

Jon tucked into a plate of Kentish sausages and I had one last bowl of pasta, still convinced that it provided my essential walking fuel.

Rowena was curious about my journey.

"Did you say that you had walked here from Rome?" she asked after bringing our dinner.

"There and back," I answered with pride.

"There's something very strange going on," she replied. "We had someone else walking back from Rome staying here not so long ago."

"What? He had walked there and back?" asked Jon.

"That's what he said," replied Rowena.

"Ah, so *that's* why Canterbury had no interest in my friend. Somebody had beaten him to it," said Jon.

Rowena looked him up in the book. Andrew Judd, the retired lawyer from Australia who entered my story back at Danilo's ferry, had stayed at the Oak on his return trip from Rome only a few days before us, and his record put mine in the shade. Having made it in just 66 days from Canterbury to Rome in 2011, this year he had walked from Rome to Santiago de Compostela. Time was running short, so he had walked and bussed to Santander to catch the ferry to Plymouth. Trains took him to Rochester so that he could walk the last three days into Canterbury. Even though he had not trudged all those final miles, he had still covered 3,100 kilometres – about 1,000 more than my total.

Rochester, our destination the following day, was a longer haul, 24 miles, but we made it easier by cutting out the high ground after Detling and walking the flat lanes along the valley floor. These could be more rewarding than the official path, whose high hedges deprived us of most of the good views. On our way up the hill to Burnham Common, we somehow missed the Stone Age burial chamber, known as Kit's Coty House, but when we reached the top we had one final glorious hike over high downs with the gravel lakes of the Medway valley glittering below. By now good and tired, we turned towards the M2 Medway Bridge and walked the river's banks towards the shining Norman castle keep. At the pocket-sized Cathedral, we were just in time for the first canticle of Evensong.

"We can't go on praying like this," said Jon, visibly in trouble with his knees.

"I can't go on walking like this," I replied.

The Gordon House Hotel, a sweetly distressed Georgian building on the High Street, provided an appropriate billet for our last night. It looks over to the cathedral spire, illuminated until midnight, and behind it run the trains to Faversham and Margate. It is named for the Royal Engineer, General Gordon, who with the rank of Colonel was based here and at Gravesend, re-equipping the estuary forts on the Medway and Thames against the French Second Empire. We would walk from one river under his charge to the other the following day.

Wednesday was our last day together. We crossed the Strood without once mentioning Charles Dickens, and climbed across the chalky neck of the Hoo Peninsula. Here, in the Napoleonic years, military engineers had cut a seven-mile canal to supply the Medway garrisons with fresh provisions and ordnance, knocking 39 miles off an awkward and exposed estuary voyage. But the canal never took off. The two-mile tunnel below Higham is now used by the railway; the rest, however, was quickly abandoned. We walked the latter part of the way to Gravesend picking blackberries by the canal's silted bed and spotting faded notices listlessly promoting its restoration. Having enjoyed so many carefree kilometres along living French canals, it was sad to see one in England that had been left to rot.

Crossing Shorne Marshes, we closed in on the high Thames bank and the dark hulls of container ships, passing upriver like multi-storey buildings on invisible casters. Behind them the twin chimneys of Tilbury power station feathered steam into a near cloudless autumn sky. The ruin of one of Gordon's forts, on a Roman scale, watched us across the flats. We stopped at a teahouse in the park by the waterfront in Gravesend, guarded by a gun battery mounted on the old citadel, but we didn't linger. It was time to leave Kent, and we raced down the pier ramp just as they were pulling in the ferry gangplank.

I had been carried across the River Pò, Lac Léman, and the English Channel, and now finally I was to cross the River Thames. Each very different ferry crossing had marked a special moment in my journey. This crossing between Gravesend and Tilbury is – *pace* the M25 – the historical route between Kent and Essex; it was on the old pilgrimage ways, and a ferry has been licensed here since the Middle Ages.

On the warm teak of the Tilbury jetty, Jon and I parted. His mission complete, he caught the bus to the station: to an exhibition in London and to Cambridge by evening. My destination, a good 13 miles on yet, was the new town of Basildon – the Dubai of Essex.

I picked my way over the Tilbury Marshes and turned down a track beyond West Tilbury to emerge at the gravel works by Collingwood farm, where I was greeted by a smiling Afro-Caribbean lady with wild, unkempt hair. Smartly dressed, with red accessories, she was sitting on top of a new red suitcase by an oak tree on the bank of one of the old pits, and reciting aloud from a large book clasped in both hands. It was the Bible, and she was reading from the Letter of St Paul to the Colossians. I was startled, and I stopped to exchange greetings and take a photograph. The image of her perched on her suitcase – visibly going nowhere, but reading from the great travelling apostle – sent me confused signals. Was this one of Harry's angels finally appearing in person? Was it a symbol of my own somewhat mad journey? Or was it a tell-tale reminder that I was back in Essex?

Leaving the young woman to her strange offices, I crossed the busy A13 and braced myself for one last uphill pull over the Langdon Hills, which climb quite smartly behind the aprons of creeks and low islands of the Thames Estuary, descending through the old woodlands to the greenery of Gloucester Park and Basildon, which unfolded its not inconsiderable charms along a series of wide cycle tracks and footways. The Holiday Inn, facing the leisure lake, was as good a place as any to rest after another long day of 23 miles. There was something reassuringly functional and welcoming about both hotel and town. Every building was new; there was nothing to see, and yet, by the same token, much to appreciate – not least a final pilgrim dinner at the local *Pizza Express*.

In contrast to Canterbury and Rochester, there were no church bells to wake me on 20th September, but I was just 25 miles from home, and my only problem was how to get out of Basildon. Now, at the end of an enticing lane beyond the Holiday Inn, a threatening notice was warning pedestrians not to cross the A127, a four-lane highway, announcing that it was an accident black spot, so I ended up walking down it on the sanctuary of a pavement almost as far as Wickford before an intersection let me continue my journey north.

From Wickford it was all open country. I skirted Hanningfield Reservoir to the village of East Hanningfield and there, on farm tracks and in woodlands, the last of Harry's Angels came to share my step, or perhaps it was the Apostle himself: I found myself on St Peter's Way, the long-distance footpath from London to the pre-Saxon church of St Peter-on-the-Wall on the remote eastern edge of Essex at Bradwell on Sea. The confluence of the two routes for these few miles filled me with excitement about the meaning of my journey.

After elevenses of a scone and coffee in the shop at Hyde Farm Nursery, I walked to just short of Maldon and descended past Cut-a-Thwart Lane towards Beeleigh Abbey. Crossing the weir at Beeleigh Falls, where the waters of the Rivers Chelmer and Blackwater converge into the tidal basin, I was overcome with the scent of home country – that distinct estuarine Essex blend of mud, fresh water and brine – and I breathed it in like a tracker scout who has picked up the trail to his village. The River Blackwater was now my way home.

Appendix

Daily stages of author's walk from Rome to Coggeshall – 14th July-20th September 2012:

Date	Leg	Kms	Miles
14 July	Roma – Isola Farnese	18	11.3
15 July	Isola – Campagnano di Roma	24	15
16 July	Campagnano – Capranica	34	21.3
17 July	Capranica – Viterbo	30	18.8
18 July	Viterbo – Bolsena	36	22.5
19 July	Bolsena – Proceno	28	17.5
20 July	Proceno – Gallina	45	28.1
21 July	Gallina – San Fabiano	40	25
22 July	San Fabiano	0	0
23 July	San Fabiano – Siena	20	12.5
24 July	Siena – Colle Val D'Elsa	28	17.5
25 July	Colle – Gambassi Terme	30	18.8
26 July	Gambassi – Fucecchio	35	21.9
27 July	Fucecchio – Lucca	32	20
28 July	Lucca – Marina di Pietrasanta	40	25
29 July	Marina di Pietrasanta	0	0
30 July	Pietrasanta – Ponzano Superiore	40	25
31 July	Ponzano Superiore – Pontremoli	35	21.9
1 Aug	Pontremoli – Berceto	28	17.5
2 Aug	Berceto – Bagni S. Andrea	36	22.5
3 Aug	Bagni S. Andrea – Fidenza	22	13.8

4 Aug	Fidenza – Piacenza	38	23.8
5 Aug	Piacenza – Belgioioso	40	25
6 Aug	Belgioioso – Pavia	14	8.8
7 Aug	Pavia – Mortara	45	28.1
8 Aug	Mortara – Vercelli	34	21.3
9 Aug	Vercelli – Caviglia	30	18.8
10 Aug	Caviglia – Ivrea	23	14.4
11 Aug	Ivrea – Hône	27	16.9
12 Aug	Hône – Châtillon	25	15.6
13 Aug	Châtillon – Cervinia	27	16.9
14 Aug	Cervinia	0	0
15 Aug	Cervinia – Zermatt	15	9.4
16 Aug	Zermatt – Visp	40	25
17 Aug	Visp – Sion	44	27.5
18 Aug	Sion – Martigny	32	20
19 Aug	Martigny – Villeneuve	42	26.3
20 Aug	Villeneuve – Lausanne	4	2.5
21 Aug	Celigny	0	0
22 Aug	Lausanne – L'Isle	26	16.3
23 Aug	L'Isle – Mouthe	32	20
24 Aug	Mouthe – Andelot-en-Montagne	32	20
25 Aug	Andelot-en-Montagne – Chaussin	52	32.5
26 Aug	Chaussin – Brazey-en-Plaine	26	16.3
27 Aug	Brazey-en-Plaine – Dijon	25	15.6
28 Aug	Dijon – Pouilly-en-Auxois	42	26.3
29 Aug	Pouilly-en-Auxois – Pouillenay	34	21.3
30 Aug	Pouillenay – Chassignelles	46	28.8
31 Aug	Chassignelles – Flogny-la-Chapelle	44	27.5
1 Sept	Flogny-la-Chapelle – Migennes	32	20
2 Sept	Migennes – Sens	44	27.5
3 Sept	Sens – Montereau-fault-Yonne	38	23.8
4 Sept	Montereau-fault-Yonne – Le Mée-sur-Seine	36	22.5

5 Sept	Le Mée-sur-Seine – Draveil	36	22.5
6 Sept	Draveil – Paris	25	15.6
7 Sept	Paris	0	0
8 Sept	Paris – Auvers-sur-Oise	32	20
9 Sept	Auvers-sur-Oise – Beauvais	46	28.8
10 Sept	Beauvais – Poix-de-Picardie	50	31.3
11 Sept	Poix-de-Picardie – Abbeville	48	30
12 Sept	Abbeville – Montreuil-sur-Mer	48	30
13 Sept	Montreuil-sur-Mer – Desvres	28	17.5
14 Sept	Desvres – Calais	38	23.8
15 Sept	Calais – Dover	5	3.1
16 Sept	Dover – Canterbury	30	18.9
17 Sept	Canterbury – Charing	27	16.9
18 Sept	Charing – Rochester	38	23.8
19 Sept	Rochester – Basildon	36	22.5
20 Sept	Basildon – Coggeshall	40	25
TOTALS		**2,117**	**1,324**